Nazarene Clergy

RESPONSES TO

Homosexuality

AND INTERACTIONS WITH

LGBT People

REGINALD G. WATSON

SacraSage

SacraSage Press
SacraSagePress.com

Print: 978-1-958670-15-6
Electronic: 978-1-958670-16-3

Printed in the United States of America

Library of Congress Cataloguing-in-Publication Data
Nazarene Clergy Response to Homosexuality and Interactions with LGBT People

DEDICATION

I dedicate this research to those who come to the Church seeking God's love and grace, and leave more wounded than when they arrive. Imperfect people make an imperfect organization. One learns that God and the Church are not synonymous.

Table of Contents

Acknowledgements

My heart overflows with gratitude to God the Father who inspired me to take the first step on a lengthy academic journey. I could not have completed it without Him.

I am indebted to my professors and colleagues at Regent University whose guidance and direction helped move this dissertation from idea to published manuscript.

My sincere appreciation to all the people who believed in me, supported me, and provided Godly counsel along my life's path: family, friends, pastors, professors, colleagues, and parishioners.

I am deeply grateful to Andrea who offered her unconditional support and encouragement and provided the space for me to complete this work. Thank you!

Special recognition and admiration go to my sister Chris (Christina) Watson. She chose to share her story with me when it felt risky to share it with anyone. That moment became the catalyst for this research. It is an honor to be her brother.

Abstract

The Church of the Nazarene asserts that homosexuality is a perversion of human sexuality, and that homosexual acts are sinful and subject to the wrath of God. The denomination also states that all people should be treated with dignity, grace, and holy love—regardless of sexual orientation—while firmly maintaining its position that a "homosexual lifestyle" is sinful and contrary to scripture. Nazarene clergy experience a tension between the denomination's position on homosexuality and ministering to LGBT people. This qualitative study explored the lived experiences of thirteen Nazarene clergy responses to homosexuality and their interactions with LGBT people. The resulting themes offer implications for Nazarene clergy, the Church of the Nazarene, LGBT people, counselor educators, and clinical practitioners.

This book is Reginald Watson's doctoral dissertation presented to the Faculty of the School of Psychology & Counseling Regent University, March 2015. It was approved by the committee members that included Anita Neuer Colburn, Ph.D., Linda Leitch-Alford, Ed.D., Thomas Jay Oord, Ph.D., and Mark Newmeyer, Ed.D. Reg Watson died suddenly in 2022. With the approval of his family, Thomas Jay Oord has guided Watson's important dissertation to be published by SacraSage Press.

CHAPTER I
Introduction and Literature Review

Few topics create as much controversy in the church as does the issue of homosexuality (Cadge & Wildeman, 2008). In 1992, a National Council of Churches official announced that the issue of homosexuality in the church was more divisive than slavery (Wilson, 1995). Since then others have made similar pronouncements. Sheler (2000) declared homosexuality is "the most divisive social issue among American churches since slavery" (p. 50). Research conducted during the 1950s and 1960s indicates that religion and religious involvement correlate with negative attitudes about homosexuality (Allport, 1954; Allport & Ross, 1967). Studies that are more recent produced similar results (Herek, 1994; Herek & Capitanio, 1996; Mak & Tsang, 2008; Rowatt et al., 2006; Tsang & Rowatt, 2007). The corporate Church's disposition toward homosexuality and individual Christian's response to homosexuals range from intolerance and rejection to tolerance and acceptance, and all points in between.

Interest in the study of sexual orientation dates back to the 1940s when Alfred Kinsey (1894–1956) developed the Kinsey Scale, also known as the Heterosexual-Homosexual Rating Scale. Using a Likert Scale, Kinsey attempted to measure degrees of sexual orientation ranging from "0" exclusively heterosexual to "6" exclusively homosexual. His research revealed that most individuals are neither exclusively heterosexual nor homosexual but rather span a continuum of sexual orientation (Kinsey, 1948).

Interest in and debate about sexual orientation continues today. Social scientists and researchers attempt to provide clarity about how sexual orientation develops. Two primary paradigms explain the development of sexual orientation: essentialism and social constructivism (Engle, McFalls, Gallagher, & Curtis, 2006; Halwani, 1998, 2008; Trail et al., 2008; Wilcox, 2002; Yarhouse & Burkett, 2002; Yarhouse, 2004). Embedded within these paradigms or worldviews are etiological (causal) theories about how a same-sex orientation develops. These theories suggest that precipitating factors, both internal and external, are the antecedents of homosexuality (Drescher, 2002, 2008; Sheldon, Pfeffer, Jayaratne, Feldbaum & Petty, 2007). These etiological theories include genetic/biological factors (Yarhouse, 2004), environmental forces (Hughes, 2006) and personal choice (Marmor, 1998). Research indicates that one's worldview, as well as one's beliefs about the causes of sexual orientation impact one's attitudes about homosexuality (Altemeyer, 2002; Engle et al., 2006; Hewitt & Moore, 2002; Sheldon et al., 2007).

Social, cultural, and demographic factors influence attitudes about homosexuality. Factors such as gender (male/female), heterosexuality, race and ethnicity, geographical location, age, educational level, and political affiliation affect individual's thoughts and feelings about homosexuality (Brown & Henriquiz, 2008; Herek, 2002; Morrison & Morrison, 2003; Schulte & Battle, 2004). Religion and religious factors appear to influence attitudes about homosexuality and responses to homosexuals most dramatically (Adamczyk & Pitt, 2009; Olson, Cadge, & Harrison, 2006; Sherkat & Ellison, 1997). Research dating to the mid-1900s indicates that religion and religious involvement can incite sexual prejudice toward sexual minorities (Allport, 1954; Allport & Ross, 1967; Herek & Capitanio, 1996; Rowatt et al., 2006). Vocabulary has also developed to include words that describe sexual prejudice. Words such as homophobia, heterosexism, and homonegativity have emerged to indicate fear, dislike, disgust, discrimination, hatred, and hostility directed toward same-sex oriented individuals (Herek, 2004; Marsh & Brown, 2011; Schulte & Battle, 2004).

Within the context of religion, adherence to a specific set of religious and political beliefs increase the likelihood of developing negative attitudes about homosexuality. Right-wing authoritarianism, fundamentalism, Christian orthodoxy, and the Protestant Work Ethic are shown to influence attitudes (Burdette, Ellison, & Hill, 2005; Finlay & Walther,

2003; Ford, Brignall, VanValey, & Malcaluso, 2009; Jonathan, 2008; Malcomnson, Christopher, Franzen, & Keyes, 2006; Marsh & Brown, 2011; Olatunji, 2008; Rosik, 2007a; Rowatt & Tsang, 2006; Schwartz & Lindley, 2005; Stoever & Morera, 2007; Tsang & Rowatt, 2007; Whitehead, 2010; Whitley, 2009).

Within traditional Christianity, specifically Protestant Christianity, homosexuality is an emotionally charged and contentious issue (Tate, 2003; Van Geest, 2007b). This is due in part to the belief that homosexuality is in direct conflict with sacred Christian traditions and biblical proscriptions (Duffield, 2004; Rodriguez, 2010; Trevino et al., 2012). Unfortunately, the church has all too often been an unwelcoming and hostile environment for same-sex oriented individuals (Barnes & Meyer, 2012).

Denominational affiliation and theological views also affect attitudes about homosexuality. Denominations that adhere to more liberal theological positions and advocate for social justice tend to be more accepting of same-sex oriented individuals while theologically conservative denominations, emphasizing personal holiness, often demonstrate negative attitudes toward LGBT people (Loftus, 2001; Olson et al., 2006). Evangelical denominations and evangelical Christians tend to demonstrate the most negative and least accepting attitudes about homosexuality describing it as "sinful" and "willful perversity" (Adamczyk & Pitt, 2009; Cadge & Wildeman, 2008; Halwani et al., 2008). Gays and lesbians often feel ostracized and rejected by conservative, evangelical denominations (Subi & Geelan, 2012; Yarhouse, 2011). Jay Bakker (2010) states that, "Just as former generations had to overcome their supposedly 'God-endorsed' racist and sexist attitudes, so we [the Church] have to overcome our narrow-mindedness on this issue in order to experience (and share) the full potential of God's love" (p. 50). With Bakker, there are those who advocate that the Church begin to develop more compassionate responses to same-sex oriented persons (McGinniss, 2010; McMinn, 2005; Merritt, 2009; Tate, 2003; Yarhouse, 2012; Yarhouse & Carr, 2011; Zahniser & Cagle, 2007).

Despite denominational differences and conservative Christian's negative attitudes about homosexuality the Church of the Nazarene, an evangelical denomination, has taken measures to address how its constituency and its clergy respond to the issue of homosexuality in the current cultural climate. While the Church of the Nazarene does not endorse or condone homosexual relationships, it does acknowledge that for some individuals a homosexual orientation develops early in life although there is no conclusive scientific evidence to support this (Diehl et al., n.d.). The Church of the Nazarene makes a distinction between sexual orientation and sexual behavior. Orientation is amoral while behavior is moral; homosexual behavior is immoral and sinful.

Even though the Church of the Nazarene holds fast to its position that homosexual behavior is wrong, it readily acknowledges that the church must not resort to ridicule or condemnation. Denominational leaders maintain that "every person should be treated with dignity, grace, and holy love whatever their sexual orientation" (Diehl et al., n.d., p. 2). The Nazarene church encourages its pastoral leadership to respond to same-sex oriented individuals in Christlikeness, with unconditional love and hospitality (Diehl et al., n.d.; Porter et al., 2011). At the denominational level, the Church of the Nazarene indicates that same-sex individuals may attend and participate in its fellowship as long as long as the person remains celibate. The church acknowledges that if a same-sex oriented person maintains celibacy he or she may enjoy full participation in the life and ministry of the local church (Diehl et al., n.d.). To date there is a lack of research on the church's ministry and outreach efforts to the LGBT population. There is no extant research that answers the question: "What are Nazarene clergy responses to homosexuality and their interactions with LGBT individuals?"

STATEMENT OF THE PROBLEM

An investigation of the literature revealed a wealth of information concerning attitudes about homosexuality and responses toward homosexual persons. While social and cultural factors presented, the bulk of my investigation revealed that the Church and Christians possess the most negative attitudes. Although typically the Church's foundational tenants are love, grace, and forgiveness, it has often demonstrated negative attitudes and has been decidedly unreceptive—even rejecting—of homosexual individuals (Larsen, Reed, & Hoffman, 1980). For the Church to become a positive influence for Christ with the LGBT population, it will need to let go of its fear, prejudice, and judgment toward LGBT people and begin to demonstrate compassion and love to this often marginalized group (Yarhouse & Carr, 2011; Zahniser & Boyd, 2008).

While the Christian ideal of unconditional love is essential, responding to same-sex oriented persons with compassion and grace may be most effective and meaningful within the context of the local church. Pastors serving in the local church may be more likely to interact with LGBT people than denominational leaders. Consequently, clergy may be the best resource for discovering how they balance the denominational position of the church with their personal convictions and how they minister to people who identify as LGBT.

PURPOSE OF THE STUDY

A thorough review of the literature revealed no in-depth qualitative analysis of the lived experiences of Nazarene pastors and their interactions with the LGBT persons. The purpose of this study was to discover the essential experience and its meaning of Nazarene clergy's responses to homosexuality and interactions with LGBT people. Utilizing the qualitative research tradition, this study proposed an in-depth phenomenological investigation into the lived experiences of ordained Nazarene clergy who serve as senior/lead pastors within the local church context.

REVIEW OF THE LITERATURE

In this literature review, I provide an overview of the various factors that contribute to attitudes about homosexuality and responses to same-sex oriented persons. The information begins broadly with an explanation of the paradigmatic or worldviews of sexual orientation. This is followed by an overview of the etiology of homosexuality. Next, I address the social, cultural, demographic, and religious factors that affect attitudes about same-sex orientation. This is followed by an examination of sexual prejudice. Narrowing the focus, I investigate Christian denominational positions about homosexuality. The information becomes more specific with a description of the Church of the Nazarene's disposition toward homosexuality and its response to LGBT people. The literature review concludes with a rationale for discovering the lived experiences of Nazarene clergy as they interact with same-sex oriented individuals.

PARADIGMS OF THE ETIOLOGY OF HOMOSEXUALITY

Etiological factors underlying same-sex orientation may inform beliefs about how a homosexual orientation develops, and thereby, can influence attitudes about gay men and lesbian women (Altemeyer, 2002; Engle et al., 2006; Hewitt & Moore, 2002; Sheldon et al., 2007).

Antecedents of homosexuality are viewed through two primary paradigms: the essentialist model and the social constructionist model (Engle et al., 2006; Halwani, 1998, 2008; Trail et al., 2008; Wilcox, 2002; Yarhouse, 2004; Yarhouse & Burkett, 2002). These two paradigms differ in their hypotheses regarding the origins of homosexuality (Stein, 1998).

Essentialism

Essentialism presents homosexuality as an essential feature of humankind, and claims that homosexuality is evident, at least theoretically, in all cultures and at all times throughout human history (Halwani, 1998; Stein, 1998; Trail et al., 2008; Yarhouse, 2004). Essentialists maintain that homosexuality is neither time, nor culturally dependent; rather, it is "objective, intrinsic and culturally independent" (Halwani, 1998, p. 6). In other words, regardless of time or culture, homosexuality has existed throughout history and within all cultures. Moreover, the essentialist model posits that individuals have a "true core sexual self" or true sexual essence that does not change (Duncan & Kemmelmeier, 2012). This core sexual self is rooted in a biological predisposition and/or results from familial childhood experiences (Engle et al., 2006). The essentialist paradigm argues that sexual orientation is a naturally occurring and fixed state (Stein, 1998). Individual's attitudes about same-sex orientation are more positive when they believe that sexual orientation is not a matter of choice (Sheldon et al., 2007). Recent research has demonstrated that essentialist views of sexual orientation affect attitudes about homosexuality (Duncan & Kemmelmeier, 2012; Haider-Markel & Joslyn, 2008; Haslam & Levy, 2006).

The essentialist model rests on three assumptions: (a) homosexuality and heterosexuality each have underlying "true essences," (b) both homosexuality and heterosexuality are separate and distinct from one another and not simply points along a continuum, (c) these true essences are consistent across time and culture (Stein, 1998; Engle et al., 2006).

Embedded within the essentialist paradigm are "biogenetic theories and environmental and psychodynamic theories" as determinants of sexual orientation (Engle et al., 2006, p. 69). Essentialists believe that a biological predisposition and/or childhood experiences occur during the developmental process that produces a sexual self, resulting in a core sexual orientation and/or identity (Engle et al., 2006). Essentialist research during the past 20 years has focused on the biological/genetic predisposition of homosexuality (Engle et al., 2006; Stein, 1998). Later, I will present a more thorough analysis of how the biological/genetic theory of homosexuality may influence attitudes toward the LGBT population. For now, I continue by comparing the social constructionist theory with the essentialist theory.

Social Constructionism

Whereas the essentialist model adheres to biology and environment as antecedents to a same-sex orientation, the social constructionist model argues that homosexuality is a personal choice and a social role (Engle et al., 2006; Stein, 1998). When individuals believe that sexual orientation is self-selected, they tend to demonstrate more homonegative attitudes (Sheldon et al., 2007).

The social construction paradigm does not support the notion of a "true essence" to sexuality; rather, homosexuality is a phenomenon that is socially constructed within a specific culture, at a particular time, using that culture's language and informed by its institutions (Engle et al., 2006). Social Constructionism asserts that homosexuality exists only within certain cultures and at certain times in history (Halwani, 1998). In other words, homosexuality is both culture-specific and time-bound. Social constructivism posits that sexuality changes as the culture and society evolve; that is to say, the concept of homosexual orientation found in our current culture did not exist prior to the nineteenth century (Halwani et al., 2008).

Social constructionists argue that words like heterosexuality, homo-sexuality, and bisexuality are "linguistic constructs that capture certain meanings about sexual behavior" (Yarhouse, 2004, p. 243). The word "homosexual" is a term devised during the nineteenth century to describe a form of sexual behavior; according to Halwani (1998), prior to this no such word existed. Constructionists argue that before the nineteenth century individuals did not have any knowledge of homosexuality; before that time people could not conceive of a person whose primary sexual orientation was directed toward someone of the same gender/sex (Halwani, 1998). Moreover, social constructionist's also argue that prior to a certain point in history there were no homosexuals. Homosexuality became evident at a certain period in history, and this is both time-specific and culture-bound (Halwani, 1998).

Researchers have not agreed on which theory—essentialism or social construction—is more accurate. However, Halwani (1998) points out that many scholars tend to subscribe to the social constructionist view, although he is an advocate of the essentialist model. He argues that given historical evidence, both positions are plausible. This suggests that neither essentialism nor social constructionism thoroughly accounts for a same-sex orientation (Sayer, 1997; Yarhouse, 2004). Recently, a "hybrid" model has emerged that integrates both theories to better understand and describe the development of sexual orientation (Engle et al., 2006). This hybrid model provides a more complete picture of the development a same-sex identity.

Couched within the essentialist and social constructionist paradigms are causal theories about how sexual orientation develops. These theories include biology/genetics, environmental/childhood influences and personal choice. Some research suggests that the theory to which one subscribes influences one's attitudes toward same-sex oriented individuals (Sheldon et al., 2007).

Etiology of Homosexuality

Although researchers have attempted to identify the roots of homosexuality, empirical evidence isolating a specific cause for homosexuality remains unidentified (Ashley, 2013; Childs, 2009; Drescher, 2002; Jones & Kwee,

2005). Of the various causal explanations suggested, no single theory has "won the favor of the scientific community" (Sheldon et al., 2007, p. 114). Moreover, many researchers and mental health professionals believe that a variety of factors, rather than a single etiological theory, account for developing a same-sex orientation (Childs, 2009; Hewitt & Moore, 2002).

The origins of the development of a same-sex identity seem to divide into three basic categories: biology, environment, and personal choice (Drescher, 2006, 2008; Sheldon et al., 2007). Although these categories appear discrete, literature suggests that some combination of these factors—biological (genetics), psychosocial (environment), and personal choice—may influence the development of same-sex oriented persons (Hughes, 2006).

Biology/genetics/nature. The biological or genetic theory is one of the more recent theories associated with the etiology of homosexuality (Yarhouse, 2004). Among the scientific studies addressing the etiological causes of homosexuality of late, genetic influence theories have received the most attention (Sheldon et al., 2007). Some researchers divide biological theories of homosexuality into three or more subcategories: (a) genetic inheritance, (b) prenatal hormone development and, (c) hypothalamic structure and brain organization (Engle et al., 2006). The idea behind these theories is that due to direct genetic influence and/or prenatal influences during pregnancy (e.g., excessive hormone secretions) a fetus may develop a predisposition toward homosexuality (Yarhouse, 2004).

Some researchers have demonstrated that positive attitudes toward people who identify as homosexual result from a belief that same-sex orientation is genetically derived (Kahn & Fingerhut, 2011; PEW Research Center, 2003; Sheldon et al., 2007; Wood & Bartkowski, 2004). Individuals who believe that homosexuality is genetic are less negative toward LGB T people than are individuals who believe that homosexuality is a learned or acquired behavior or a personal choice (Hewitt & Moore, 2002). When individuals believe that homosexuality is a genetic predisposition, a same-sex orientation seems more natural and immutable. Consequently, proponents of this view demonstrate positive attitudes toward homosexual people (Mitchell & Dezarn, 2014; Sheldon et al., 2007; Whitehead & Baker, 2012).

The implications of this are important for both LGBT people and conservative religious groups. Since most conservative Protestants believe homosexuality is "sinful" and "unnatural," the possibility of linking homosexuality to a genetic origin may counter the fundamentalist view that homosexuality is a "sinful" condition. This in turn may help to promote more positive attitudes toward gay and lesbian people. Nevertheless, skepticism remains that proving a genetic link to same-sex orientation will improve attitudes toward gays and lesbians (Sheldon et al., 2007).

Environment/childhood experiences/nurture. Some etiological theories of homosexuality suggest that external forces impinge on the individual to create a same-sex orientation. Such external forces may include environmental agents, childhood experience(s), and nurture (including parental involvement). Environmental theories of homosexuality posit that outside influences, e.g., a close-binding mother, distant father, trauma, and/or childhood sexual abuse acts upon the individual to cause him or her to adopt a homosexual orientation (Bieber, 1965; Drescher, 2002; Hughes, 2006; Marmor, 1998).

Psychoanalytic theories of homosexuality—Freudian and neo-Freudian—typically account for a homosexual orientation by citing one or more of these external causes (Drescher, 2002; Yarhouse, 2004). Moreover, the psychoanalytic community typically describes homosexuality occurring in one of three ways: (a) a normal variant of human sexuality, (b) pathological or (c) a demonstration of immaturity (Drescher, 2008). The normal variant theory posits that homosexuality is naturally occurring like left-handedness, meaning that same-sex oriented persons are "born" gay or lesbian. The pathological theory argues that homosexuality is a disease; it is a deviation from normal heterosexuality. External (pathogenic) agents or forces—e.g., familial relationships, abuse, trauma, etc.—impinge upon the individual to create a pathological response which results in a homosexual orientation (Trail et al., 2008). The immaturity theory, drawn from Freudian psychosexual stages, maintains that homosexuality can be a "normal developmental step toward heterosexuality" (Drescher, 2002). However, this theory also argues that if an individual continues with one's same-sex attraction that individual has experienced a developmental arrest or "fixation" at an earlier psychosexual stage (oral/anal) of sexuality and has not progressed to the more mature, genital stage of normal adult heterosexuality (Drescher, 2002; 2008).

Family of origin theories (e.g., close-binding, overly protective, seductive mother and distant, unloving father) were prevalent during the 1960s; however, they are now generally refuted on the basis that just as many heterosexual individuals come from families that exhibit similar parent-child relationships (Marmor, 1998). Studies dating back to the mid-1970s (Siegelman, 1974) indicate that there is "no consistent relationship between the nature of the family constellation and subsequent sexual orientation" (Marmor, 1998, p. 22).

Before 1973, homosexuality was classified as a disorder in the *Diagnostic and Statistical Manual of Mental Disorders*. In 1973 the American Psychological Association (APA) made a decision to remove homosexuality from the *DSM II* as a sexual disorder. As a result, homosexuality is now more widely recognized as a "normal variant of human sexuality" (Drescher, 2008, p. 443). Despite the APA's decision to remove homosexuality as a disorder from the *DSM*, people who believe homosexuality is chosen way of life demonstrate more homonegative attitudes toward gay and lesbian people than do individuals who believe people are "born gay" (Drescher, 2008; Hewitt & Moore, 2009; Trail et al., 2008).

Personal choice. Some individuals adhere to the notion that homosexuality is a matter of personal choice, i.e., people choose homosexuality rather than heterosexuality. Proponents of choice theory believe that since one chooses a sexual orientation, one can also un-choose it (Marmor, 1998). Heterosexuals who believe that sexual orientation is a choice demonstrate less tolerance toward homosexuals than do proponents of inborn or genetic trait theory (Hewitt & Moore, 2009; Sheldon et al., 2007; Whitehead & Baker, 2012). In their study of lay theories of homosexuality, Hewitt and Moore (2009) found that negative attitudes toward homosexuals were associated with the belief that people choose their sexuality. Further, Stoever and Morera (2007) found an increase in homonegative attitudes when it is believed that LGBT persons choose a same-sex identity.

Although each of the aforementioned areas have been discussed as separate categories, recent research suggests a hybrid or combination model to best describe the development of a homosexual orientation; this model is gaining popularity as well as endorsement from scientists and scholars alike (Engle et al., 2006).

CULTURAL AND DEMOGRAPHIC INFLUENCES THAT SHAPE ATTITUDES ABOUT HOMOSEXUALITY

Cultural influences shape attitudes about sexual orientation (Adolfsen, Iedema, & Keuzenkamp, 2010; Barringer, Gay, & Lynxwiler, 2013; Brown & Henriquiz, 2008; Butler, 2005; Gentry, 1987; Glick & Golden, 2010; Herek, 2000a, 2000b, 2002; Kite, 1984; LaMar & Kite, 1998; Lewis, 2003; Meaney & Rye, 2010; Schope & Eliason, 2000; Schulte & Battle, 2004; Steffens, 2005; Steffens & Wagner, 2004; Stoever & Morera, 2007; Sullivan, 2003; Wilcox & Jelen, 1990; Whitley, 1988). These influences issue from several factors including gender and heterosexuality, race and ethnicity, and geographical location. Socio-demographic factors also influence attitudes about homosexuality (Brown & Henriquiz, 2008; Glick & Golden, 2010; Herek, 2002; Hewitt & Moore, 2002; Lewis, 2003; Mitchell & Dezarn, 2014; Morrison & Morrison, 2003; Schope & Eliason, 2000; Schulte & Battle, 2004; Shackleford & Besser 2007; Stoever & Morera, 2007; Sullivan, 2003; Walch, Orlosky, Sinkkanen, & Stevens, 2010). Socio-demographic factors include age, education level, personal contact, and political affiliation. In this section, I will detail the manner in which these cultural and demographic factors may affect attitudes toward people who identify as homosexual. I discuss religion as a cultural influence in a later section.

Gender correlates with negative attitudes toward same-sex oriented individuals (Barringer et al., 2013; Herek, 2002; LaMar & Kite, 1998; Schope & Eliason, 2000; Steffens, 2005). Males are more likely to hold negative attitudes toward all homosexuals than are females, while both males and females are more likely to possess negative attitudes toward homosexual persons of the same-sex (Herek, 2000a, 2000b, 2002; LaFave, Helm, & Gomez, 2014; LaMar & Kite, 1998; Meaney, 2010; Stoever & Morera; 2007; Walch et al., 2010). In general, men demonstrate greater intolerance and are less accepting of gay men than they are of lesbians (Steffens, 2005). Women, on the other hand, are more accepting and less condemning of both gay men and lesbians than men (Herek, 2002). Women are also more accepting of same-sex relationships than are men (Barringer et al., 2013).

Studies suggest that both males and females are less tolerant of contact with a homosexual individual of the same-sex while each is more tolerant of a homosexual person of the opposite sex (LaMar & Kite, 1998; Whitely, 1988). Moreover, both male and females experience increased discomfort when in proximity to a homosexual individual of the same gender as the heterosexual person (Gentry, 1987). Gender is also associated with derogatory or prejudicial verbalizations. For example, males are more likely to make derogatory remarks to same-sex identified individuals whereas females are less likely to comment (Schope & Eliason, 2000). These same authors found that men experience tremendous social pressure to express negative attitudes toward homosexual individuals (p. 74).

Males also show greater anxiety around gay men than around lesbian women (Schope & Eliason, 2000). One of the reasons for this anxiety may be the fear of becoming a target of unwanted advances by a person of the same-sex (Whitely, 1988). Moreover, in an attempt to prove their masculinity and avoid a "gay" label, heterosexual males may also express aggression toward homosexual males (Herek, 2000a, 2000b). Some researchers suggest that negative attitudes and feelings such as intolerance, anxiety, and aggression toward same-sex oriented individuals issue from one's own repressed/latent homosexual desires and/or urges (Herek, 2000a, 2000b; LaMar & Kite, 1998; Mitchell, 2002).

In addition to gender's effect on attitudes, research has investigated the influence of heterosexuality on attitudes about homosexuality (Herek, 2002; Kite, 1984; Schulte & Battle, 2004; Whitley, 1988). Heterosexuals demonstrate more negative attitudes toward homosexuals of the same gender than they do toward homosexuals of the opposite gender (Kite, 1984; Whitley, 1988). Herek (2002) found that heterosexual men "consistently" demonstrate more negative attitudes toward same-sex individuals than do heterosexual women. Moreover, heterosexual males express stronger negative attitudes toward gay males than they do lesbian women (Steffens, 2005). Heterosexual females on the other hand, express fewer negative attitudes toward both lesbian women and gay men than do heterosexual males (Herek, 2002; Kite, 1984; Steffens, 2005; Whitley, 1988).

Both heterosexual males and heterosexual females appear to have negative feelings and attitudes about advances from same-sex identified individuals; which may in part be due to a fear of being approached by a homosexual person (Whitley, 1988). Interestingly however, both heterosexual males and females demonstrate fewer concerns about contact with a homosexual person of the opposite sex (Whitley, 1988, p. 290). Herek (2000) discovered that not only are heterosexual men less likely to harbor negative attitudes toward lesbians, but their attitudes are also as favorable toward homosexual women as they are toward heterosexual females (p. 58–59).

Research focused on the effect of race on attitudes toward same-sex oriented individuals has produced mixed results (Glick & Golden, 2010; Lewis, 2003; Mitchell, & Dezarn, 2014; Schulte & Battle, 2004; Walch et al., 2010). A survey study conducted by Lewis (2003) found that blacks tend to have more disapproving attitudes about homosexuality than do their white counterparts. Glick and Golden (2010) conducted a study of attitudes about homosexuality using data collected from the 2008 General Social Survey (GSS), reporting "race-specific trends" in the United States toward homosexuality. Their findings revealed that 72% of African Americans believe that homosexuality was "always wrong" whereas only 52% of Caucasian Americans felt it was wrong. They concluded, "U.S. attitudes toward homosexuality are characterized by persistent racial differences" (Glick & Golden, 2010, p. 516). Brown and Henriquez (2008) suggested that race is a significant predictor of attitudes toward gay and lesbian individuals; however, their work did not indicate a specific race or ethnicity as results were coded "White" and "non-White." Their results did suggest, however, that white respondents demonstrate fewer negative attitudes toward homosexuals than did non-white participants (Brown & Henriquez, 2008).

Although these studies revealed that blacks are generally more disapproving of homosexuality than whites, religious involvement may be a significant mediating variable. A data analysis conducted by Lewis (2003) shows that African Americans are more likely to attend religious services than are whites. Moreover, many African Americans attend churches that promote conservative attitudes about sexuality. These factors may account for perceived racial differences in negative attitudes regarding homosexuality. Schulte and Battle (2004) found that when controlling for the effects of religious values, the effect of race on attitudes toward gays and lesbians disappears. Therefore, they conclude that religiosity, rather than race, better accounts for negative attitudes toward same-sex identified individuals (Schulte & Battle, 2004). In fact, Lewis (2003) commented, "Evidence that blacks are more homophobic than whites is quite limited" (p. 60) and "once demographic factors are controlled, black-white differences in attitudes are statistically insignificant" (p. 67).

A study of demographic and social factors affecting attitudes by Walch et al. (2010) produced similar results: race and/or ethnicity indicated no significant effect on attitudes about homosexuality. Conversely, data analysis research by Glick & Golden (2010) suggests a significant difference between current Black (72%) and White (52%) disapproving attitudes about same-sex individuals. The obvious differences in results of these studies suggest that isolating race and/or ethnicity as a significant indicator of negative attitudes toward gays and lesbians remains elusive.

Geographical location can affect attitudes about sexual orientation (Barringer et al., 2013; Butler, 2005; Herek, 2002; Glick & Golden, 2010). In some geographic regions, homosexuality is unacceptable, while in other geographic regions, a same-sex orientation is more accepted (Adolfsen et al., 2010; Steffens, 2005; Sullivan, 2003). For example, a study of German college students found that students possess a generally favorable attitude toward gay men and lesbian women (Steffens, 2005). Likewise, opinion poll research conducted in the Netherlands suggests positive attitudes toward same-sex identified individuals (Adolfsen et al., 2010). In a study of 1,607 Dutch Defense Personnel, respondents demonstrated largely positive attitudes toward gays and lesbians (Adolfsen et al., 2010). These attitudes were further broken down into explicit and implicit attitudes as defined by Herek's (1994) *Attitudes Toward Gay Men and Lesbians* (ATLG) scale. The results indicated that explicit attitudes are somewhat positive while implicit attitudes tend to be more negative (Steffens, 2005). Although opinion polls suggest that attitudes toward homosexuals are slowly becoming more positive (Steffens & Wagner, 2004) there are numerous factors demonstrating that homonegative attitudes are still prevalent.

In some parts of the United States, attitudes about homosexuality do not appear so favorable (Barringer et al., 2013; Butler, 2005; Schulte &

Battle, 2004). Negative attitudes about same-sex relationships are most notable in the southern, southwestern, south central, and Midwest regions (Barringer et al., 2013; Sullivan, 2003). On the other hand, studies indicate that attitudes about homosexuality are predominately more favorable in the Northeast regions of the United States (Butler, 2005; Glick & Golden, 2010; Herek, 2002; Schulte & Battle, 2004; Sullivan, 2003) with the Atlantic and Pacific coasts being the most tolerant of LGBT people (Sullivan, 2003). Negative attitudes have shown minor to significant decreases in all regions of the United States from 1987 through 2002 (Butler, 2005). Fortunately, attitudes about homosexuality are slowly improving; it is reasonable to hope this trend continues.

Age has as a moderate influence on attitudes regarding same-sex relationships (Walch et al., 2010). Herek (2002) found that older adults generally possess more negative attitudes about homosexuality than younger adults do. Likewise, Glick and Golden (2010) found a significant association between age and disapproving attitudes of same-sex relationships. It is purported that that older adult's attitudes toward same-sex relationships may be due to the cultural norms and traditional family values of the era of their upbringing rather than their actual chronological age (Lewis, 2003).

Education level appears to have an influence on heterosexual's attitudes about homosexuality. Hewitt and Moore's (2002) research reveals that individuals with a higher degree of educational attainment demonstrate fewer negative attitudes about same-sex relationships than do those with less education (e.g., high school or less). Other researchers have drawn the similar conclusions: higher education (e.g., college and graduate level schooling) correlates with a greater degree of acceptance of LGBT individuals (Hewitt & Moore, 2002; Lewis; 2003; Schulte & Battle, 2004; Walch et al., 2010). Lewis (2003) observes, "Education appears to lead to greater acceptance of differences in others, more liberal sexual attitudes, [and] greater interaction with gay men and lesbians" (p. 66).

Personal knowledge, whether the result of formal education or by knowing a same-sex oriented person, appears to reduce negative attitudes toward LGBT people. Studies have found that positive personal contact with a gay or lesbian individual(s) has a mitigating effect on negative attitudes about homosexuality (Schope & Eliason, 2000; Schulte and Battle, 2004; Walch et al., 2010). Hewitt and Moore (2002) discovered that the level of contact one has with gay or lesbian individuals has an influence on that person's attitudes and beliefs about same-sex relationships. Herek (2002), a pioneer in the field of attitudes about homosexuality research, concluded that knowing a gay or lesbian, or having a relative who is gay or lesbian, produces significantly more positive attitudes toward gays and lesbians overall. Recent research has produced similar findings (Glick & Golden, 2010).

Political affiliation is also associated with attitudes about homosexuality (Brown & Henriquez; 2008; Morrison & Morrison, 2003; Schulte & Battle, 2004; Shackelford & Besser; 2007; Stoever & Morera; 2007; Sullivan, 2003; Walch et al., 2010). While conservative political views are correlated with increased negative attitudes, liberal political views are correlated with reduced negative attitudes. Schulte and Battle (2004) discovered that a liberal political orientation correlates with positive attitudes toward same-sex oriented individuals. Conversely, Morrison and Morrison (2003) discovered that conservative political affiliations correlated positively with negative, prejudicial views about same-sex orientation. Several other studies (Brown & Henriquez, 2008; Shackelford & Besser, 2007; Stoever & Morera, 2007; Sullivan, 2003) corroborate these results indicating that conservative political views are associated with negative attitudes and sexual prejudice directed at gays and lesbians.

SEXUAL PREJUDICE

Literature suggests that in addition to beliefs about etiology and cultural/demographic factors, religious involvement also correlates with negative attitudes toward homosexuals (Herek & Capitanio, 1996; Whitley, 2009). Research dating back to the 1950s and 1960s indicate that religion and religious involvement play a role in prejudicial attitudes toward sexual minorities (Allport, 1954; Allport & Ross, 1967). Studies that are more recent have produced similar findings: religious involvement increases negative and prejudicial attitudes toward gay men and lesbian women (Herek, 1994; Herek & Capitanio, 1996; Mak & Tsang, 2008; Rowatt et al., 2006; Tsang & Rowatt, 2007).

Herek (2000a, 2000b) describes sexual prejudice as demonstrating negative attitudes toward another person or group based on sexual orientation. According to Herek (2000a), sexual prejudice has three principle features: (a) it is an attitude based on "evaluation or judgment," (b) it targets a "social group and its members," e.g., homosexuals as a minority group and gay, lesbian, and bisexual individuals and, (c) "it is negative, involving hostility or dislike" (Herek, 2000a, p. 20.)

Often heterosexuals' attitudes toward gay and lesbian individuals are similar to the attitudes displayed toward other minority groups, e.g., race and ethnic groups (Herek, 2000a, 2000b). As with other forms of prejudice, sexual prejudice targets an individual or group of individuals who do not adhere to the normative values of the majority group. In the case of the homosexuality, heterosexuals can express prejudicial attitudes and behaviors toward those who engage in sexual behavior or who identify as having a sexual orientation other than heterosexual. This includes individuals who are gay, lesbian, and bisexual (Herek, 2000a, 2000b). Negative attitudes of sexual prejudice include disgust, aversion, revulsion, and discrimination (Herek, 2004). Research has found that disgust correlated positively with negative attitudes toward homosexuals and "references to gay sexual activity" (Olatunji, 2008).

Sexual prejudice appears to have several motivating factors including fear (Olantujni, 2008). Fear is often associated with homophobia i.e., an irrational, negative response to homosexual individuals (Herek, 2004; Sullivan; 2003). Homophobia is linked to heterosexual male's fears of being labeled "gay" by their peers (Herek, 2000b). Other factors also generate fear of same-sex identified individuals. For example, one's fears of his or her own homosexual proclivities and/or a general lack of understanding about homosexuals (Herek, 2000b). Still others may fear that homosexuality is contagious or contaminating (Olatunji, 2008). A disagreeable encounter with a same-sex identified person is another motivating factor of sexual prejudice. The heterosexual individual may then generalize the encounter to a person or group of same-sex identified persons (Herek, 2000b). Heterosexuals may also demonstrate sexual prejudice because of their own "in-group" expectations (Vicario, Liddle, & Luzzzo, 2005). This may be especially true if the individual is attempting to conform to the group of which one is apart. For example, conforming to the expectations of a religious group that opposes homosexuality may result in sexual prejudice behaviors.

Alternatively, one who is attempting to prove oneself as a heterosexual may behave with sexual prejudice. Herek (2000b) argues that sexual prejudice may function principally to prove that one is part of the larger heterosexual group and thereby demonstrate conclusively that one is not a homosexual. Sexual prejudice also targets gay, lesbian, and bisexual individuals because of concerns that homosexuality violates traditional heterosexual personal and societal values (Herek, 2000b).

As with other forms of prejudice, sexual prejudice targets same-sex oriented individuals and groups (Herek, 2004). Homophobia, heterosexism, and homonegativity are all expressions of sexual prejudice (Adolfson et al., 2010; Herek, 2000a, 2000b; Herek, 2004; Malcomnson et al., 2006; Marsh & Brown, 2011; Rosik, 2003; 2007a; Schulte & Battle, 2004). To define further sexual prejudice, it is important to understand the terminology embedded within it. Therefore, in the following paragraphs, I provide a brief description of each of these terms.

Homophobia literally means fear of the same or something similar (Herek, 2004). For the purposes of this study, homophobia refers to fear of homosexuals. However, this is not a new term. It was during the late 1960s when George Weinberg, a psychoanalytic psychologist, coined the term *homophobia*. Formulating a description of homophobia Weinberg stated:

> I coined the word homophobia to mean it was a phobia about homosexuals....It was a fear about homosexuals, which seemed to be associated with a fear of contagion, a fear of reducing the things one fought for—home and family. It was a religious fear and it had led to great brutality as fear always does (Herek, 2004, p. 7).

While there is no universally accepted definition for homophobia (Rosik, 2007a), the term itself denotes negative beliefs, attitudes, or behaviors toward gay and lesbian individuals (Rosik 2003). These negative beliefs, attitudes, and behaviors can include aversion, dislike, disgust, hatred, and hostility directed at same-sex identified person (Adolfsen et al., 2010; Herek, 2000a, 2000b; Herek, 2004; Sullivan, 2003). Homophobia generally refers to an individual's response to gay and lesbian people

(Herek, 2004). However, institutions, organizations, and the broader society may also endorse antigay sentiment; this defines heterosexism (Herek, 2004; Schulte & Battle, 2004; Sullivan &Wodarski, 2002).

First coined in the early 1970s, heterosexism is analogous to sexism and racism (Herek, 1992; Herek, 2000a). It endorses a hierarchical value system that elevates heterosexuality as superior to homosexuality (Herek, 2004). Neisen (1993) describes heterosexism as a form of "cultural victimization" that oppresses homosexuals. Herek (2000a) agrees, describing heterosexism as cultural ideologies and "patterns of institutionalized oppression" that stigmatize same-sex oriented persons. Within these institutional and cultural systems are the beliefs and rationale that endorse and promote antigay attitudes. These cultural and institutional ideologies include value-laden beliefs about gender, sexual expression, and morality (Herek, 2004; Neisen, 1990; Neisen, 1993). Behavior, e.g., homosexuality, that does not align with these beliefs is labeled immoral, deviant and a threat to the very culture/institution/system itself (Herek, 2004). When the culture, institution, or system is threatened, it can respond in a variety of negative ways. One author has observed:

> Hostility, discrimination, and violence are thereby justified as appropriate and even necessary. Heterosexism prescribes that sexual stigma be enacted in a variety of ways, most notably through enforced invisibility of sexual minorities and, when they become visible, through overt hostility (Herek, 2004, p 15.)

Schulte and Battle (2004) concur with Herek when they comment, "heterosexism creates a hostile environment for gay men and lesbians" (p. 138).

Another term used to describe fear and/or dislike of homosexual individuals is homonegativity. Homonegativism and homophobia are often used synonymously and refer to the broad spectrum of negative attitudes and prejudicial behaviors directed at gay men and lesbian women (Marsh & Brown, 2011; White & Frazini, 1999). These negative attitudes include discrimination, bias, prejudice, disgust, and hostility (Malcomnson et al., 2006; Marsh & Brown, 2011). Homonegative attitudes are prevalent in the United States with about 14% of hate crimes in the United States targeting sexual minorities (Meaney & Rye, 2010). Several studies have demonstrated that homonegative attitudes are associated with conservative religious beliefs and political affiliation (Malcomnson et al., 2006; Marsh & Brown, 2011; Morrison & Morrison, 2003).

There are multiple reasons heterosexuals exhibit sexual prejudice in the form of homophobia, heterosexism, and homonegativity. These include beliefs about how a same-sex orientation develops (Sheldon et al., 2007); the degree and kind of religious involvement (Stoever & Morera, 2007); fear of one's own latent homosexual tendencies or being labeled a homosexual (Herek, 2000b); fear that homosexuality is contagious (Olatunji, 2008); efforts to conform to one's own religious group (Vicario et al., 2007) and perceived violations of traditional personal and social roles (Herek, 2000a).

RELIGIOUS INFLUENCES ON ATTITUDES ABOUT HOMOSEXUALITY

Although many religions subscribe to the principles of unconditional love and acceptance, some religious individuals demonstrate prejudice and discriminatory behaviors contrary to these teachings (Jonathan, 2008; Zahniser & Boyd, 2008). One example of such prejudicial and discriminatory behavior manifests in the influence of religion and religious beliefs on attitudes about homosexuality (Finlay & Walther, 2003; Tsang & Rowatt, 2007; Wilkinson, 2004). Research demonstrates a correlation between religion and prejudice, i.e., antigay attitudes (Ford et al., 2009; Laythe, Finkel, Bringle, & Kirkpatrick, 2002; Malcomnson et al., 2006). Gordon Allport (1954), a psychologist and one of the first researchers to study the influence of religion on attitudes about homosexuality, wrote of religion:

> The role of religion is paradoxical. It makes and unmakes prejudice. While the creeds of the great religions are universalistic, all stressing brotherhood; the practices of these creeds are frequently divisive and brutal (p. 444).

Current literature suggests that while religion typically condemns various forms of prejudice including racial and ethnic prejudice, religion and religious beliefs correspond with intolerance and prejudice toward certain groups and individuals, including gays and lesbians (Adamczyk & Pitt, 2009; Malcomnson et al., 2006; Rowatt et al., 2006; Whitley, 2009).

There are factors embedded within religion and religious beliefs that influence attitudes about homosexuality and responses to LGBT people. These include religious views and beliefs, intrinsic/extrinsic orientation to one's religious beliefs, right-wing authoritarianism, fundamentalism, Christian orthodoxy, and a Protestant Work Ethic (Adamczyk & Pitt, 2009; Allport & Ross, 1967; Burdette et al., 2005; Finlay & Walther, 2003; Ford et al., 2009; Jonathan, 2008; Laythe, Finkel, & Kirkpatrick, 2001; Mak & Tsang, 2008; Malcomnson et al., 2006; Marsh & Brown, 2011; Morrison & Morrison, 2002; Newman, 2002; Olatunji, 2008; Rosik, 2007a, 2007b; Rowatt et al., 2006; Schulte & Battle, 2004; Schwartz & Lindley, 2005; Stoever & Morera, 2007; Tsang & Rowatt, 2007; Whitehead, 2010; Whitley, 2009). Schwartz and Lindley (2005) suggested that homonegative attitudes may increase when one or more of these factors are combined. In this section, I will demonstrate how these religious factors influence attitudes toward people who identify as homosexual.

Religious views and beliefs affect attitudes about homosexuality and the expression of these attitudes toward same-sex identified persons (Burdette et al., 2005; Ford et al., 2009; Herek, 2000a, 2000b; Olatunji, 2008). For example, research reveals that conservative religious views and ideologies correlate with and predict homonegative, antigay attitudes (Olatunji, 2008; Rosik, Griffith, & Cruz, 2007). Haidt and Hersh (2001) observed that conservatively religious persons were more likely to disapprove of same-sex oriented behavior than were their religiously liberal counter parts. A few studies have indicated minor increases in tolerance of homosexuality among some Christian groups (Petersen & Donnewerth, 1998; Reimer & Park, 2001). Likewise, Burdette et al. (2005) observed that the current generation of young conservative religious individuals is more committed to social tolerance—including LGBT people—than earlier generations. While these studies may suggest a subtle shift of attitudes among some Christians, the vast body of research continues to demonstrate that religion and religious beliefs correlate with negative attitudes about homosexuality.

Allport and Ross (1967) were two of the first researchers to study intrinsic and extrinsic orientations of religious views and beliefs. They describe intrinsic and extrinsic orientation as the way each individual operationalizes his/her religious views and beliefs. For example, an intrinsic orientation is the degree to which religion serves as the primary, internally motivating, and central organizing principle of one's life (Allport & Ross, 1967). An intrinsically oriented person aligns oneself with one's religious teachings and endeavors to live one's life according to those teachings for personal, spiritual growth, and enlightenment (Whitley, 2009). Individuals with an intrinsic orientation attempt to *live* out one's religious beliefs in one's daily life (Ford et al., 2009). Conversely, an extrinsic orientation is one in which the individual *uses* his/her religion as a means to an end or as a way to achieve "nonreligious, extrinsic goals" (Allport & Ross, 1967; Whitley, 2009). Individuals with an extrinsic orientation are "disposed to use religion for their own ends" (Allport & Ross, 1967, p. 434). Extrinsically oriented individuals are often selective of their religious beliefs and then shape those beliefs to match their own personal needs and/ or desires (Ford et al., 2009).

From their study, Allport and Ross (1967) determined that intrinsically oriented individuals were less prejudice than those with an extrinsic orientation. However, later studies indicate that intrinsically oriented individuals also demonstrate homonegative attitudes (Herek, 1987; Herek, 1994; Wilkinson, 2004). Several subsequent studies corroborate these findings suggesting that an intrinsic religious orientation also correlates with homonegative attitudes (Marsh & Brown, 2011; Schulte & Battle, 2004; Tsang & Rowatt, 2007). To clarify, Rosik (2007b) made the following observation:

> Intrinsically oriented individuals tended to limit their homonegativity to the moral dimension of their evaluation and did not necessarily restrict their social contact with gay men and lesbians to any greater degree than they would with other disapproved groups (e.g., liars, overeaters, alcohol abusers). These persons apparently were comfortable being "in the world but not of it," while the extrinsically religious participants were less concerned about ideological consistency than about maintaining effective

social boundaries. Their homonegativity was more broadly based and they tended to seek greater social distance from gay men and lesbians than from other disapproved groups (p. 146).

Other studies confirmed Rosik's observation, finding that religious individuals with an extrinsic orientation also display prejudicial attitudes toward gays and lesbians (Herek, 1994; McFarland, 1989; Wilkinson, 2004). Literature suggests that regardless of whether a person *lives* one's religious beliefs (intrinsic orientation) or the individual *uses* one's religious beliefs (extrinsic orientation) prejudicial attitudes about homosexuality and toward gay and lesbian individuals persist (Allport & Ross, 1967; Ford et al., 2009).

Right-wing authoritarianism and political conservatism are also associated with homonegative attitudes and homophobia (Ford et al., 2009; Jonathan, 2008; Laythe et al., 2001; Morrison & Morrison, 2002; Whitley & Lee, 2000; Wilkinson, 2004). Right-wing authoritarianism is a conservative social ideology that is supportive of traditional values and an unwavering commitment to authority (Altemeyer & Hunsberger, 1992; Jonathan, 2008). Moreover, right-wing authoritarianism and political conservatism often interact with each other contributing to negative attitudes about homosexuality (Morrison & Morrison, 2002). Numerous studies have shown that right-wing authoritarianism is associated with sexual prejudice, negative attitudes/behaviors toward gay men and lesbian women, and homophobia (Jonathan, 2008; Laythe et al., 2001; Tsang & Rowatt, 2007; Whitley & Lee, 2000; Wilkinson, 2004). Studies also indicate that right-wing authoritarianism and fundamentalism are closely associated with sexual prejudice and homophobic attitudes (Altemeyer, 2003; Altemeyer & Hunsberger, 1992; Laythe et al., 2002; Rowatt et al., 2006; Schwartz & Lindley, 2005).

The literature offers a basic description of fundamentalism as the belief there is one true religion (for this research: Christianity) that contains essential and inerrant truth about God and humankind (Ford et al., 2009; Schwartz & Lindley, 2005; Whitley, 2009). Another definition of fundamentalism is "a subgroup within evangelicalism that accepts biblical authority, salvation through Christ, and a commitment to spreading the faith" (Kelstedt & Smidt, 1991, p. 260). As religious fundamentalism increases, so do negative attitudes toward homosexual persons (Rowatt et al., 2006).

Studies show that the more an individual believes his/her religion contains inerrant, biblical truth, the more powerful is her/his negative evaluation of gays and lesbians (Ford et al., 2009; Rowatt et al., 2006). Fundamentalists are generally "closed-minded" to views that do not correspond to their belief system and fight vigorously against opposing views or ideals, both of which correspond to negative attitudes homosexuality and same-sex oriented individuals (Altemeyer, 2003; Altemeyer & Hunsberger, 1992; Laythe et al., 2001; Schwartz & Lindley, 2005). Religious fundamentalists generally view homosexuality as immoral and a moral abomination explicitly forbidden by scripture (Jonathan, 2008). Fundamentalist Christians tend to view LGBT individuals as sinners, and their sexual behavior as "an abomination before the Lord" (Hendershot, 2001). Research demonstrates that as right-wing authoritarianism and fundamentalism combine prejudicial attitudes toward gays and lesbians increase (Hunsberger, 1996; Jonathan, 2008; LaFave et al., 2014; Laythe et al., 2001).

Although right-wing authoritarianism and fundamentalism are predictive of homonegative attitudes, Christian orthodoxy is not (Laythe et al., 2002). When right-wing authoritarianism and religious fundamentalism are controlled, Christian Orthodoxy emerges as a mediating factor of negative attitudes toward homosexuality leading to increased tolerance and acceptance of gay and lesbian individuals (Ford et al., 2009; Jonathan, 2008). Christian orthodoxy is the extent to which individuals agree with, and internalize the core beliefs of their faith while attempting to live out these beliefs in one's daily life (Whitley, 2009). These beliefs include universal Christian creedal statements, e.g., Nicene Creed and Apostle's Creed, one's denominational Articles of Faith, and beliefs about the Bible's authority (Fullerton & Hunsberger, 1982). The internalization of orthodox Christian beliefs and teachings reduces negative attitudes toward homosexuals and serves as an "internal standard" to reduce prejudicial feelings against gays and lesbians (Ford et al., 2009; Rowatt & Franklin, 2004). Laythe et al. (2002) conclude that "orthodox Christian beliefs...appear to be a factor that 'unmakes' prejudice against gays and lesbians" (p. 630–631).

While not strictly a religious factor, the Protestant Work Ethic (PWE) increases negative attitudes and prejudicial behavior toward LGBT persons (Malcomnson et al., 2006; Newman, 2002). One writer describes the PWE as,

A universal taboo placed on *idleness* and *industriousness* [that] is considered a religious ideal; *waste* is a vice, and *frugality* a virtue; *complacency* and *failure* are outlawed, and *ambition* and *success* are taken as sure signs of God's favor; the universal sign of sin is *poverty*, and the crowning sign of God's favor is *wealth* (Oates, 1971, p. 84).

The implicit message of the PWE appears to value work and disparage play. This rule against play and/or pleasure seeking may affect people's sexual relationships as well (Furnham, 1990). The PWE posits that sexual relations are appropriate for procreative purposes—sex for any other reason is for pleasure; therefore, since same-sex relationships are not procreative they are deemed inappropriate and sinful (Malcomnson et al., 2006). Those who subscribe to a Protestant work ethic often display homonegative attitudes (Morrison & Morrison, 2011).

TRADITIONAL CHRISTIAN AND BIBLICAL VIEWS OF HOMOSEXUALITY

Within the context of Christianity, homosexuality is an emotionally charged and divisive issue (Tate, 2003; Van Geest, 2008). One writer observed that, "homosexuality has become a cultural battleground" for Christians (Tushnet, 2007, p. 18). This is partly due to the belief that homosexuality is in direct conflict with sacred Christian tradition and biblical values (Duffield, 2004; Rodriguez, 2010; Trevino et al., 2012). Several studies address the conflict that can occur between Christianity and homosexuality (McMinn, 2005; Schuck & Liddle, 2001; Subhi & Geelan, 2012; Yarhouse & Tan, 2005; Yarhouse, Tan, & Pawlowski, 2005).

Many Christians believe homosexuality violates traditional religious beliefs and undermines Christian values of sexuality, heterosexual relationships, marriage, and family (Burdette et al., 2005). Consequently, a Christian worldview significantly predicts negative attitudes toward LGBT people (Trevino et al., 2012). Kinnaman and Lyons (2007) conducted a three year study to discover how young adults view the Church. Their research found that,

> [T]he perception that Christians are "against" gays and lesbians… has reached critical mass. The gay issue has become the "big one," the negative image most likely to intertwined with Christianity's reputation. It is also the dimension that most clearly demonstrates an unChristian faith to young people today, surfacing a spate of negative perceptions: judgmental, bigoted, sheltered, right-wingers, hypocritical, insincere, and uncaring. Outsiders say our hostility toward gays—not just opposition to homosexual politics and behaviors but disdain for gay individuals—has become virtually synonymous with the Christian faith (p. 92).

Lee (2012) made the following indictment: "The church's 'antihomosexual' reputation isn't just a reputation for opposing gay sex or gay marriage; it's a reputation for *hostility to gay people*" (p. 3). Individual and corporate Christian responses to LGBT people reveal that intolerance and religious homophobia is apparent in many Christian denominations (Rand, 2004; Rodriguez, 2010).

The position of most Christian institutions is that homosexuality is morally wrong and homosexual behavior is sinful (Barnes & Meyer, 2012; Lease, Horne, & Noffsinger-Frazier, 2005; Subhi & Geelan, 2012). Thus, many Christian churches take a firm stand against homosexuality (Zerilli, 2010), and many religious organizations have developed policies against same-sex relationships (Ford et al., 2009). As a result, Christian churches and religious institutions often present a "hostile social environment" to gays and lesbians (Barnes & Meyer, 2012). Historically, Christianity's condemnation of homosexuality is a "well-known and documented aspect of Christian tradition" (Norris, 2008; Rand, 2004) and, for the most part, Christianity continues to be diametrically to homosexuality (McGinnis, 2010). The Barna Group is a research organization that attempts to create an intersection between faith and culture by providing analysis of current trends in contemporary society and the church. One such study conducted by the Barna Group (2007) revealed that,

91% of young non-Christians and 80% of young churchgoers…
believe that Christians show excessive contempt and unloving attitudes towards gays and lesbians. One of the most frequent crit-
icisms [by] young Christians was that they believe the church has
made homosexuality a "bigger sin" than anything else. Moreover,
they claim that the church has not helped them apply the biblical
teaching on homosexuality to their friendships with gays and lesbians (Barna Group Ltd., 2007).

McGinniss (2010) observed, "The church has communicated fairly
well that the homosexual is the object of God's wrath [and] this has been
communicated not with compassion and sorrow but with loud condemnation" (p. 155). Traditional Christian views of homosexuality suggest
that LGBT people are "bad, diseased, perverse, sinful, and inferior" while
emotionally charged language denounces homosexuality "from the pulpit
and is echoed in the pews" (Barton, 2010; Schuck & Liddle, 2001). Jones
(1996) argued that traditional Christian beliefs "fuel the social climate
that accommodates an increasing incidence of hate crimes against homosexuals" (p. 309). Rand (2004) described same-sex oriented individuals as
being "psychologically brutalized" by Christians' adamant condemnation
of homosexuality. The influence of traditional Christian beliefs on people
is considerable and "nowhere is it more considerable and harmful than in
the official position of most Christian churches on the question of homosexuality" (Zerilli, 2010, p.28).

The anti-homosexual religious climate perpetuated by traditional
Christianity finds its basis in scripture (Cassidy, 2004; Davis, 2008;
Duffield, 2004; Ford et al., 2009; Gagnon, 2005; Marmor, 1998;
Marsh & Brown, 2011; Schuck & Liddle, 2001; Subhi & Geelan, 2012;
Trevino et al., 2012). Christians believe that the Bible is the literal word
of a sovereign God and therefore revere it as both a moral and ethical code
for how to live a Christian life (Hodge, 2005). Christians who oppose
homosexuality base their opposition on select verses from both the Old
Testament and the New Testament (Duffield, 2004; Ford et al., 2009;
Marmor, 1998; Marsh & Brown, 2011; Rodriguez, 2010). The Old
Testament verses commonly referenced as prohibitions against homosexuality include Genesis 19:1–14; Leviticus 18:22 and Leviticus 20:13.

New Testament verses include Romans 1:18–32; 1 Corinthians 6:9–11 and, 1 Timothy 1:8–11 (Duffield, 2004). Many Christians argue that these verses explicitly prohibit homosexual behavior and that same-sex relationships are a violation of God's word (Ford et al., 2009; Gagnon, 2005). Christians often cite these verses as justification to condemn homosexuality, causing same-sex oriented individuals to feel ostracized and alienated from the church (Subhi & Geelan, 2012; Yarhouse, 2011).

Some researchers, however, contend that these verses do not actually address homosexuality as commonly understood or apply to same-sex oriented persons in today's culture (Davis, 2008; Duffield, 2004; Locke, 2005; Norris 2008). Some researchers argue that neither Jesus nor the Gospels directly address the issue of homosexuality (Duffield, 2004; Rogers, 2007). Some authors contend that contemporary Christians choose to enforce some biblical prohibitions (e.g., homosexuality) while disregarding others (e.g., Levitical proscriptions). In so doing they selectively choose which biblical commands to follow and which ones to ignore (Locke 2005; Nissinan, 1998). This in turn fuels the conflict between Christianity and LGBT advocates because each side accuses the other of interpreting select scripture passages to support their own position (Davis, 2008). Zerilli (2010) made the following observation:

> Scriptural reasons have been advanced against every kind of moral progress. Powerful and influential preachers decried universal suffrage in England, for hadn't God put the rich man in his castle and the poor man at his gate? Voices rambled against women having the vote because, after all, aren't women identified with their husbands, and isn't the husband the head of every woman as Christ is the head of the Church? The slave trade, too, had its rich tradition of biblical apologetics. Indeed, the plasticity of biblical interpretations is such that almost any viewpoint can be at once defended or opposed. It strikes a moral conservative intrinsically wrong to sanction the union of two men, or two women, in the bond of marriage. So it struck the nineteenth-century ecclesiastical as wrong to accord women a say in the government of the nation's affairs, or the eighteenth-century parson to accept that landless peasants had some dignity worth preserving by suffrage.

And these arguments were likely as fervent as the feelings expressed now against same-sex unions. Yet life goes on, mentally dissolves, and new scriptural explanations are offered so that scriptural faith may adjust to human needs. Sooner or later those who try to fit people to creeds have to make way for those who would prefer to fit the creeds to people (p. 31).

Current literature reveals important information concerning the lack of clearly defined biblical injunctions against homosexuality (Brownson, 2013; Cassidy, 2008; Davis, 2008; Duffield, 2004; Johnson, 2007; Martin, 2008; Norris, 2008; Zerilli, 2010). Norris (2008) argues that the Bible is not preoccupied with questions or statements about homosexuality—especially not as preoccupied as the current religious climate seems to be—and, in the broader context of scripture, has relatively little to say about it. Nevertheless, Christians often argue that simple reading of scripture reveals definitive prohibitions against homosexuality; however, no reading of the Bible is simple because an accurate understanding of scripture requires complex interpretation and these interpretations may, and often do, conflict with interpretations offered by other Christian scholars (Brownson, 2013; Martin, 2008). In fact, when considering the scriptures delineated as prohibiting homosexuality, compared to the whole of scripture, there are only a few that appear to address the issue and, the precise intent of their meaning is hotly debated (Brownson, 2013; Duffield, 2004).

Despite the relatively few scripture verses used to support an anti-homosexual mindset and the interpretations used to support each side of the controversy, Christians should be careful not to assert a "clear teaching of the Bible" on homosexuality (Duffield, 2004). Norris (2008) recommends that scripture should be studied in the broader context of "tradition, reason, experience and community" in order to obtain the most accurate understanding of the biblical intent. Cassidy (2008) warns against using the Bible as a weapon or using it to oppress gays and lesbians. Instead, the Christian's interpretation of scripture can be guided by the biblical principle of love of God and neighbor (Matthew 22:36–40) (Johnson, 2007; Norris, 2008).

OTHER RELIGIOUS VARIABLES AFFECTING ATTITUDES

Biblical literalism, frequency of church attendance, religiosity, and religious affiliation also affect individual's attitudes toward homosexual persons (Barringer et al., 2013; Brown & Henriquez, 2008; Burdette et al., 2005; Deeb-Sossa & Kane, 2007; Schulte & Battle, 2004; Schwartz & Lindley, 2005; Wilcox & Jelen, 1990; Wilkenson, 2004). Biblical literalism refers to the way one reads and interprets the Bible. A biblical literalist believes the Bible to be the divinely inspired, inerrant word of God and the Bible is the source of absolute, authoritative truth for living the Christian life providing codes of conduct for acceptable personal and social behavior (Burdette et al., 2005; Deeb-Sossa & Kane, 2007). For Christians who subscribe to biblical literalism, homosexuality stands in direct opposition to a Christian sexual ethic (Burdette et al., 2005; Deeb-Sossa & Kane, 2007). Consequently, biblical literalists demonstrate less tolerance for LGBT people (Burdette et al., 2005), and greater negative attitudes about homosexuality (Deeb-Sossa & Kane, 2007). Scriptural injunctions proscribing homosexual behavior are the yardstick by which appropriate sexual conduct and relationships are measured (Burdette et al., 2005). The New Testament provides an example when the Apostle Paul writes to the Corinthian church stating,

> Do you not know that wrongdoers will not inherit the kingdom of God? Do not be deceived: neither the sexually immoral nor idolaters nor adulterers nor men who have sex with men nor thieves nor the greedy nor drunkards nor slanderers nor swindlers will inherit the kingdom of God (1 Corinthians 6:9–10, NIV).

Different translations of the Bible differ in word choice. The New International Version, as cited above, refers to "men who have sex with men," while the New American Standard Bible specifically uses the word "homosexuals,"

> Do you not know that the unrighteous will not inherit the kingdom of God? Do not be deceived; neither fornicators, nor idolaters, nor

adulterers, nor effeminate, nor *homosexuals,* nor thieves, nor the covetous, nor drunkards, nor revilers, nor swindlers, will inherit the kingdom of God (1 Corinthians 6:9–10; NASB, *italics mine*).

Other versions express it differently. For example, the New Revised Standard Version reads as follows:

Do you not know that wrongdoers will not inherit the kingdom of God? Do not be deceived! Fornicators, idolaters, adulterers, male prostitutes, sodomites, thieves, the greedy, drunkards, revilers, robbers—none of these will inherit the kingdom of God (1 Corinthians 6:9–10, NRSV).

The King James Version states:

Know ye not that the unrighteous shall not inherit the kingdom of God? Be not deceived: neither fornicators, nor idolaters, nor adulterers, nor effeminate, nor abusers of themselves with mankind, nor thieves, nor covetous, nor drunkards, nor revilers, nor extortioners, shall inherit the kingdom of God (1 Corinthians 6:9–10, KJV).

Despite the differences between each translation of the Bible, many Christians argue that these verses explicitly forbid same-sex relationships (Burdette et al., 2005; Gagnon, 2005; Locke 2005). Whether the translation utilizes the term "homosexuality" or, "male prostitution" or, "sodomy" or, "effeminate," these are but one among a list of wrongdoings and unrighteousness. Although homosexuality is not singled out as more reprehensible than the others, the biblical writer indicates that any one of these will prohibit one from inheriting the Kingdom of God. The problem of interpretation becomes increasingly complex when one attempts to seek clarity from the original language of the Old Testament (Hebrew) and the New Testament (Greek) meanings, intentions, and cultural norms (Locke 2005). Biblical scholars disagree regarding the Bible's original intent behind these verses (Brownson, 2013; Cassidy; 2004; Duffield; 2004; Gagnon, 2005; Locke 2005; Nissinan, 1998; Norris; 2008).

Church attendance is another contributing factor to homonegative attitudes toward LGBT people (Allport & Ross, 1967; Barringer et al., 2013; Burdette et al., 2005; Morrison & Morrison, 2002; Satcher & Schumacker, 2009; Schulte & Battle, 2008; Stoever & Morera, 2007; Whitley, 2009). An early study conducted by Allport and Ross (1967) reported that individuals who attend church regularly demonstrate more negative attitudes toward homosexuals than do people who do not attend church regularly. Later studies (Morrison & Morrison, 2002; Stoever, & Morera, 2007; Whitley, 2009) found that regular religious involvement was a significant predictor of negative attitudes toward gays and lesbians. As church attendance increases, tolerance toward gay men and lesbian women decreases (Burdette et al., 2005). The more often individuals attend religious services the more they are exposed to messages of morality and to other individuals who adhere to similar views, values, and beliefs (Sherkat & Ellison, 1997). As people internalize messages of sexual morality, they become less tolerant of LGBT persons (Schulte & Battle, 2004; Trevino et al., 2012).

Degree of religiosity also contributes to anti-homosexual attitudes (Brown & Henriquez, 2008; Schulte & Battle, 2004; Schwartz & Lindley, 2005; Wilcox & Jelen, 1990). As religiosity increases so do homonegative attitudes (Rowatt et al., 2006). Religiosity appears to carry a variety of connotations (Brown & Henriquez; 2008; Marsh & Brown, 2011; Schutle & Battle, 2008; Schwartz & Lindley, 2005; Vicario et al., 2005; Whitley, 2009).

Schwartz and Lindley (2005) defined religiosity as "religious fundamentalism," i.e., "the belief that there is one religion which contains inherent truth" (p. 147). Their study revealed an association between religious fundamentalism, homophobia, and negative attitudes toward same-sex oriented individuals. They concluded that "religious fundamentalism and closed-mindedness to other views" was highly predictive of negative attitudes toward homosexuals (Schwartz & Lindley, 2005, p. 153). Religiosity is also described as the degree to which people are involved in their religion (Whitley, 2009). The more involved one is in her or his religion and religious practices, the more one demonstrates intolerant attitudes toward LGBT people (Vicario et al., 2005). Highly religious individuals are more likely to possess more homonegative attitudes (Vicario et al., 2005; Whitley, 2009).

On self-rating scales, people who rate themselves "very religious" demonstrate higher levels of sexual prejudice than those who do not consider themselves very religious (Stoever & Morera, 2007). Marsh and Brown (2011) define religiosity as "the degree of dedication to specific religious beliefs and the extent to which those beliefs are influential in one's life" (p. 576). These same researchers also conducted a review of previous research investigating the relationship between homonegativity and religion (Marsh & Brown, 2011). These earlier studies (Altemeyer & Hunsberger, 1992; Laythe et al., 2001; McFarland, 1989) indicated religiosity positively predicted negative attitudes toward same-sex identified individuals. Regardless of the description used, religiosity correlates positively with negative attitudes toward gay and lesbian individuals (Adamczyk & Pitt, 2009; Brown & Henriquez, 2008; Morrison & Morrison, 2002; Stoever & Morera, 2007; Whitley, 2009).

DENOMINATIONAL AFFILIATION AND ATTITUDES ABOUT HOMOSEXUALITY

Homosexuality is one of most controversial issues in the church today (Cadge & Wildeman, 2008; Olson & Cadge, 2002). While a few Christian denominations may respond to homosexuality graciously, many Christian denominations respond negatively to LGBT people (Barton, 2010; Ford et al., 2009; McGinniss, 2010; Olsen et al., 2006; Rodriguez, 2010). In fact, most mainstream denominations regard homosexuality with disdain, maintaining that it is immoral and contrary to a biblical understanding of male-female relationships (Richards & Bergin, 2000). Consequently, many Christian denominations exhibit homonegative attitudes, homophobic responses, and heterosexist policies (Barnes & Meyer, 2012; Barton, 2010; Reimer & Park, 2001). Numerous studies address denominational attitudes about homosexuality (Adamczyk & Pitt, 2009; Burdette et al., 2005; Cadge, Olson, & Wildeman, 2008; Croy, 2008; Finlay & Walther, 2003; Halwani, 2008; Herek, 2000a; Kailla, 2012; Kapinus, Kraus, & Flowers, 2010; Lewis, 2003; Loftus, 2001; Malcomnson et al., 2006; Newman, 2002; Olatunji, 2008; Olson et al., 2006; Rosik et al., 2007; Schulte & Battle, 2004; Van Geest, 2008; Whitehead, 2010; Yarhouse, 2011).

Research suggests that denominational affiliation has an influence on individuals' beliefs about homosexuality and that religious association provides a moral foundation that influences attitudes about homosexuality (Loftus, 2001; Olson et al., 2006). The literature reveals that Protestant denominations tend to be described as liberal, mainline, evangelical, and conservative; although, liberal/mainline and evangelical/conservative are sometimes merged (Kapinus et al., 2010). To facilitate clarity, in the section that follows, I describe each of these four denominational types (liberal, mainline, evangelical, and conservative). However, these categories are more dynamic than static, so there may be some overlap between denominations regarding attitudes about homosexuality.

Liberal denominations such as Episcopalians, Presbyterians, United Church of Christ, Quakers and the Metropolitan Community Church demonstrate the most open and affirming attitudes about homosexuality and, therefore, are the least likely to demonstrate negative responses toward LGBT people (Burdette et al., 2005; Kapinus et al., 2010; Loftus, 2001; Malcomnson et al., 2006). Liberal Protestants do not generally subscribe to a literal interpretation of the Bible or stress the importance of personal salvation in the same manner as more religiously conservative denominations (Kapinus et al., 2010). Although liberal Protestants are less likely to display homonegative attitudes than conservative Protestants, debates about homosexuality within liberal denominations continue (Burdette et al., 2005; Malcomnson et al., 2006; Newman, 2002).

Compassionate and affirming denominational responses to gays and lesbians characterize mainline Protestant denominations (Van Geest, 2007). In fact, some mainline Protestant denominations welcome LGBT people into their fellowship (Cadge et al., 2008). Like their liberal brothers and sisters, mainline Protestants do not tend to subscribe to a literal interpretation of the Bible; therefore, some mainline Protestants such as Evangelical Lutherans, United Methodists, and American Baptists are more accepting of gays and lesbians than are their conservative counterparts (Kapinus et al., 2010; Olson et al., 2006; Stenschke, 2009).

As with liberal denominations, concerns around issues related to homosexuality continue to cause debate among mainline denomination leaders and laity (Croy, 2008). Some have argued that the issues related to homosexuality are "centrally contentious" and an "intractable, locus of conflict" creating controversy within mainline churches (Cadge et al., 2008; Cadge & Wildeman, 2008; Olson & Cadge, 2002; Kapinus et al., 2010). Part of the conflict rests with mainline Protestant denominations' struggle between the moral, theological, and traditional understanding of sexual behavior and the acknowledgement of the sacred worth and dignity of every individual regardless of sexual orientation (Croy, 2008). Mainline denominations wrestle with how to welcome homosexual individuals while not necessarily approving of same-sex relationships (Cadge et al., 2008; Stenschke, 2009). Although the issue of homosexuality continues to be a divisive issue among mainline denominations, many mainline Protestants recognize that LGBT individuals deserve a more compassion-ate response than they have typically received from the Christian church (Halwani, 2008; Kapinus et al., 2010; McGinniss, 2010; Streensland et al., 2000; Zahniser & Cagle, 2007). Liberal and mainline denomi-nations attempt to transform social structures and institutions through socio-political involvement (Van Geest, 2007). Consequently, mainline Protestants focus on social reform issues such as equality and advocat-ing for gay rights, and less on moralistic preaching, religious conversion, and personal piety than their conservative brothers and sisters (Djupe & Gilbert, 2002; Van Geest, 2007a, 2007b, 2008).

While liberal and mainline Protestants are the most tolerant of LGBT people, evangelicals and conservatives are the most disapproving (Bean & Martinez, 2014; Burdette et al., 2005; Kailla, 2012; Lewis, 2003). Some evangelical denominations include: Southern Baptists, Assemblies of God, and Seventh Day Adventists (Kapinus et al., 2010). Evangelicals demon-strate conservative attitudes that reflect theological beliefs as well as de-nominational and congregational positions on homosexuality (Finlay & Walther, 2003; Olson et al., 2006). Evangelicals tend to be very clear about their objections to, and condemnation of, homosexuality; they ground their position on the theological tenet of the authority of scripture as the inspired word of God which, for evangelicals, expressly prohibits same-sex relationships (Kapinus et al., 2010). Evangelical denominations have labeled homosexuality as a "sin" and consequently homosexuals behave in a sinful manner (Cadge & Wildeman, 2008; Kailla, 2012). Evangelicals posit that same-sex orientation and "homoerotic behavior is evidence of willful perversity" and "a turning away from God's ordained plan for proper fulfillment" of human sexual expression (Halwani, 2008). Moreover, evangelicals believe that any sexual relationship outside the bounds of a traditional marriage between a man and a woman is forbidden by scripture and therefore impure and inappropriate (Kapinus et al., 2010). Additionally, same-sex oriented individuals are frequently denied full membership in the church due to her/his sexual orientation (Rogers, 2007).

Evangelicals are opposed to civil rights for LGBT people and have been a powerful force in anti-gay rights movement in the United States (Olson et al., 2006; Van Geest, 2008). Recent research, however, has demonstrated that evangelical opposition to civil rights for LGBT people may be declining (Bean & Martinez, 2014). Evangelicals' primary focus is on moral reform; therefore, they tend to focus their initiatives on issues such as abortion, pornography, substance abuse, and sexuality (Van Geest, 2007a). With their adherence to traditional/biblical definitions of marriage and attention to morality, evangelicals assert that a myriad of social ills, including the disintegration of the family and church, link directly to homosexuality (Kapinus et al., 2010).

Conservative Protestants, like evangelicals, demonstrate negative attitudes about homosexuality and unfavorable attitudes toward same-sex oriented individuals (Adamczyk & Pitt, 2009). Studies have found that homonegative attitudes and hostility toward gays and lesbians correlate positively with conservatively religious individuals (Herek, 2000a Loftus, 2001; Rosik et al., 2007; Schulte & Battle, 2004). Conservative Protestant churches can include Fundamentalist, Pentecostal, and Charismatic groups; although, evangelicals are sometimes also categorized as denominationally conservative (Burdette et al., 2005). Conservative denominations argue that homosexuality is condemned by both the Old and New Testament scriptures and is therefore considered morally impure and sinful (Malcomnson et al., 2006).

Conservative Protestants' commitment to biblical literalism and scriptural prohibitions consistently link to homonegativism (Burdett et al., 2005). Conservative Protestants also exhibit the most traditional views about sex and relationships and therefore tend to be the most opposed to same-sex relationships (Adamczyk & Pitt, 2009). Conservative Protestants argue that homosexuality is a threat to the nuclear family

structure—even the existence of America—and are one of the most publicly outspoken Christian groups against same-sex relationships (Burdette
et al., 2005). Conservative Protestants strive to preserve the traditional
concept of heterosexual relationships and they view homosexuality as a
threat to the status quo (Haidt & Hersh, 2001; Olatunji, 2008). One
researcher states it like this:

> In the minds of conservative Protestants, morality is more than a
> private decision. It is a public concern. As a result, conservative
> Protestant affiliates may feel an obligation to mobilize politically
> to oppose groups defined by religious leaders and interpreted by
> biblical texts as posing a threat to society. Therefore, restriction of
> gay men from public speaking, teaching in colleges and having
> accessible books is not just a choice made by some conservative
> Protestants, but it is viewed as an obligation to protect society
> from exposure to and perhaps temptation by immoral, unbiblical
> ideas, and lifestyles (Burdette et al., 2005, p. 183)

There is a range of denominational attitudes about homosexuality.
Liberal and mainline denominations tend to be the most accepting, while
evangelicals and conservatives are the least accepting and the most intolerant. As a result, because of their same-sex attraction, LGBT people often
feel isolated and ostracized by many Christian denominations (Subi &
Geelan, 2012; Yarhouse, 2011).

DENOMINATIONAL RESPONSES TO LGBT PEOPLE

Negative responses to LGBT people abound in various Christian denominations and "the preponderance of mainstream Christian denominations"
do not view homosexuality in a positive light (Rodriguez, 2010; Whitehead,
2010). Research suggests that denominational beliefs about homosexuality
influence local congregations' attitudes about homosexuality (Cadge et al.,
2008; Kapinus et al., 2010; Lalich & McLaren, 2010; Super & Jacobson,
2011). Moreover, the demonstration of negative attitudes toward gay and
lesbian individuals is correlated with the strict adherence to religious beliefs
and religious doctrine (Super & Jacobson, 2011; Whitley, 2009).

When negative attitudes and negative denominational responses confront LGBT people it can leave them feeling stigmatized, ostracized, and alienated from the church (Lalich & McLaren, 2010; McMinn, 2005; Super & Jacobson, 2011; Zahniser & Boyd, 2008). This can cause same-sex oriented people to feel distant from and condemned by God (Barton, 2010; Super & Jacobson, 2011; Whitley, 2009). As a result, LGBT individuals may experience an identity crises when attempting to reconcile their religious, spiritual, and sexual identities (Super & Jacobson, 2011; Valera & Taylor, 2011; Weiss, Morehouse, Yeager, & Berry, 2010).

Nevertheless, denominations respond differently to LGBT concerns (McGinniss, 2010). The myriad of Christian denominations represented in the United States creates the possibility for LGBT people to experience a range of responses from the religious community (Halkitis et al., 2009; Super & Jacobson, 2011). Some denominations affirm and welcome gay and lesbian individuals, while other denominations can be unwelcoming and even rejecting of LGBT people (Croy, 2008; Ganzevoort, van der Laan, & Olsman, 2011; Hendershot, 2001; Kapinus et al., 2010; McMinnn, 2005; McQueeney, 2009; Whitehead, 2010; Zahniser & Cagle, 2007). Research indicates that denominational responses run along a continuum of gay-affirming and/or welcoming, to non-affirming and unwelcoming, with some even rejecting same-sex oriented people (Halikitus, 2008; Helminiak, 2008; Super & Jacobson, 2011; Yakushko, 2005).

Liberal denominations generally take an inclusive stance toward homosexuality and LGBT people, openly welcoming them into the faith community (Hendershot, 2001; McQueeney, 2009). These "gay-affirming" churches believe that the Bible supports same-sex relationships and foster the integration of spirituality and sexual identities (Super & Jacobson, 2011; Yarhouse and Carr, 2011). Gay-affirming churches preach and teach positive messages about same-sex orientations and welcome same-sex identified individuals unconditionally and without qualification; they also minister primarily to the LGBT community (Rodriguez, 2009; Yakushko, 2005). One openly gay-affirming denomination is the Metropolitan Community Church (MCC) (Yarhouse & Carr, 2011). The MCC subscribes to a theology of inclusivity and integration of sexual identity and spirituality (www.mcchurch.org).

"Gay-welcoming" churches and denominations, although subscribing to a traditional interpretation of scripture, are typically "hospitable and accepting" of LGBT people and endeavor to make the church a safe place for same-sex individuals to grow and mature spiritually, but by holding to a traditional interpretation of scripture, these churches endorse a traditional sexual ethic (Yarhouse & Carr, 2011). Mainline denominations may also "advocate for legislative action to acknowledge the legal rights" of same-sex partners as well as call upon their ministers to perform "religious ceremonies celebrating non-traditional sexual relationships" (Kapinus et al., 2010). While for some mainline denominations, homosexuality has been a "highly contentious issue," many continue to advocate for "accepting all people regardless of sexual orientation or practice" (Kapinus et al., 2010). Gay-welcoming mainline denominations are typically more accepting of same-sex oriented individuals than are evangelical denominations (Whitehead, 2010).

Affiliation with an evangelical denomination appears to foster negative attitudes toward same-sex relationships (Whitehead, 2010). Conservative evangelical denominations often condemn homosexuality and appear united in their rejection of same-sex relationships calling homosexuality sinful and an abomination to the Lord (Hendershot, 2001; Kapinus et al., 2010). Non-affirming denominations do not agree with an integration of a same-sex identity with religious beliefs. This often leaves the LGBT person feeling alienated by their religious community (Lease et al., 2005; Super & Jacobson, 2011).

Non-welcoming denominations may openly reject or despise gay and lesbian individuals (McMinn, 2005; Yarhouse & Tan, 2005; Zahniser & Boyd, 2008). When rejecting churches and denominations denounce same-sex orientation it can cause spiritual, emotional, and psychological harm to LGBT people (Barton, 2010). In these settings, LGBT persons experience "religious abuse" (Bent-Goodly & Fowler, 2006; Super & Jacobson, 2011). This may cause the same-sex oriented person to question his or her beliefs, undermine her or his confidence in God, and weaken one's desire to participate in a religious community (Whitley, 2009).

As outlined in this section, denominations, local churches, and individual Christians have tended to respond negatively to LGBT people (Lease et al., 2005; McMinnn, 2005; Schuck & Liddle, 2001; Yarhouse,

2011). As a result, same-sex identified individuals may feel unwelcome and alienated by the church, and even begin to doubt God loves them (McMinn, 2005; Robinson, 2000; Yarhouse & Tan, 2005). One author observes, "The church should not be adding to the perception that evangelicals hate homosexuals" (McGinniss, 2010, p. 157). Although love for all people should be the defining characteristic of Christian churches (Tate, 2003), another author observed there is no word that is more used and misused in the church than the word *love* (Robinson, 2000). The literature indicates that the Church may need to consider developing more compassionate, loving responses to the LGBT community.

DEVELOPING A COMPASSIONATE RESPONSE TO SAME-SEX ORIENTED INDIVIDUALS

Given the apparent divide between the church and the gay and lesbian community, the church faces a decision about how to respond to the issue of homosexuality (McMinn, 2005; Montoya, 2008). Research suggests that the church needs a new approach to respond to same-sex oriented individuals (McMinn, 2005; Zahniser & Boyd, 2008). Additionally, the church may need to reconsider how it relates to LGBT persons as it attempts to communicate its position on homosexuality (Tate, 2003; Zahniser & Cagle, 2007). Some scholars recommend this include demonstrations of genuine love to and compassion for the LGBT community in general and to LGBT individuals in particular (McGinniss, 2010; Merritt, 2009; Robinson, 2000; Tate, 2003; Yarhouse & Carr, 2011; Zahniser & Boyd, 2008; Zahniser & Cagle, 2007).

Likewise, for the church to find a voice with the LGBT population, contemporary writers propose that the church become more loving and respectful toward LGBT people rather than ostracizing them or making them feel unacceptable because their sexual orientation (Marin, 2009; Robinson, 2000; Vines, 2014; Zahniser & Cagle, 2007). For this to happen, the church may need to consider how it can respond with genuine acceptance to gays and lesbians, so they feel welcomed and cared for rather than despised or rejected (Marin, 2009; Yarhouse, 2012; Zahniser & Boyd, 2008). To accomplish this task, the church can no longer isolate itself from the real life experiences and sexual orientation concerns of individuals to whom it hopes to minister (Robinson, 2000). Even if the church disagrees with a same-sex orientation, Christlike love recognizes that every person is "uniquely created by God" and of inestimable worth before the Creator (Zahniser & Boyd, 2008). Merritt (2009) encourages the church to respond in this way:

> Now is the time for those who bear the name of Jesus Christ to stop merely talking about love and start showing love to our gay and lesbian neighbors. It must be concrete and tangible. It must move beyond cheap rhetoric. We cannot pick and choose the neighbors we will love. We must love them all (*USA Today*, April 20, 2009).

Given this, the challenge before the church is to identify ways to "minister effectively" to LGBT individuals (Yarhouse & Carr, 2011). This may include the church revisiting its interpretation of scripture, making intentional efforts to reach out to the LGBT community, and demonstrating unconditional love and acceptance to same-sex oriented individuals (Yarhouse & Tan, 2005).

While demonstrating love to others is a foundational tenet of Christian thought, many Christians also believe in acts of compassion (Keefe, 2011). Often the church attempts to demonstrate compassion for marginalized groups; however, this may not always be true of the church's response to the LGBT community (McGinniss, 2010). Unfortunately, "[t]he contrast between 21st century Christianity and the Jesus of the Bible is stark. The biblical Jesus—the compassionate, loving, 'friend of sinners'—is difficult to reconcile with an often disconnected, insular, us-vs.-them Christianity" (Merritt, 2009, p. A11). Some churches posit that LGBT people are "objects of God's wrath" and this message is often communicated with condemnation rather than compassion. McGinniss (2010) argues that "the church needs to tone down its rhetoric concerning homosexuality and turn up its compassion" for gay men and lesbian women (p. 156).

In its attempt to find ways to minister effectively to the LGBT population, the church may choose to look for ways to respond compassionately toward same-sex oriented persons (Beck, 1997; Montoya,

2008). Compassion includes empathy and understanding (Keefe, 2011). Empathy allows one to enter into the feelings of the other (Zahniser & Boyd, 2008). Understanding is obtaining accurate knowledge of another's situation (Keefe, 2011). However, if Christians isolate themselves from the experiences and challenges of LGBT people, believers will not "be exposed to the hurt, the struggle, and the suffering" same-sex oriented individuals endure (Zahniser & Boyd, 2008).

One of the ways to develop a compassionate response toward LGBT people is to look for opportunities to cultivate caring and respectful relationships with them. In so doing, same-sex oriented persons may feel more loved and accepted by the church and Christians alike (Zahniser & Cagle, 2007). Research indicates that some churches do attempt to find effective ways to minister to LGBT people (Yarhouse & Carr, 2011). These churches have been defined as "exemplary" in their ministry to the LGBT community because they consistently demonstrate love and compassion to this population (Yarhouse & Carr, 2011).

The literature clearly reveals a variety of denominational beliefs about homosexuality and a wide spectrum of denominational responses to LGBT people. The literature also recommends the Church consider how it can respond more compassionately to the LGBT population. One's denominational affiliation is likely to influence one's beliefs and attitudes about homosexuality. As has been stated, conservative, evangelical churches tend be the least accepting. Yet, some evangelical denominations may attempt to minister to gay and lesbian individuals. One such denomination is The Church of the Nazarene. In the section that follows, I provide a review of the tenets of the Church of the Nazarene and the extant literature of its denominational beliefs about, and responses to, homosexuality.

THE CHURCH OF THE NAZARENE: AN OVERVIEW

The Church of the Nazarene is a conservative evangelical denomination that traces its roots to revival in the Church of England during the 18th century, led principally by John Wesley. Three theological convictions characterized this revival: regeneration by grace through faith; Christian perfection, i.e., entire sanctification, and the witness of the Spirit to the "assurance of grace" (Blevins, Rodes, Seaman, Sowden, & Wilson, 2013, p. 15). Entire sanctification or Christian perfection was one of the distinctive contributions of John Wesley. As a distinctive of Wesleyan theology, entire sanctification warrants a brief description:

> Entire sanctification may be described as an act of God's grace by which the believer is cleansed from "original sin and brought into a state of entire devotement to God" as one lives his/her life in loving obedience to Christ. The process of entire sanctification is both instant and continuous, accomplished by the infilling presence of the Holy Spirit, empowering the believer for life and service to God, the church, and humanity (Blevins et al., 2013, pp. 32–33).

Following the Wesleyan revival in England, an emphasis on holiness began in the eastern United States spread across the country (Blevins et al., 2013, p. 15). The idea of Christian holiness gained popularity and several Holiness denominations originated including, Church of God, Mennonites, Brethren, and Friend. Each of these adopted the Wesleyan view of entire sanctification (Blevins et al., 2013, p. 16). Independent churches and parachurch organizations also emerged, including churches, urban missions, rescue homes as well as missionary and evangelical organizations. Individuals involved in these organizations began to lobby for a "national holiness church" and from this, the "present day Church of the Nazarene was born" (Blevins et al., 2013, p. 16).

In 1895, Phineas Bresee and others organized the Church of the Nazarene in Los Angeles, California. They believed the Church of the Nazarene to be the first denomination to teach and preach entire sanctification as a work of grace received by faith in Christ (p. 18). Bresee maintained that part of the church's mission was to emulate Christ, preach the good news to the poor, and provide relief to the needy (p. 19).

During 1907 and 1908, the Association of Pentecostal Churches of America and the Holiness Church of Christ merged with the Church of the Nazarene and in 1908 Phineas Bresse organized what was then named the Pentecostal Church of the Nazarene in Peniel, Texas. In 1919 the denomination officially changed its name to the Church of the

Nazarene dropping "Pentecostal" due to developing definitions beginning to be associated with the word (Blevins et al., 2013, p. 20).

Demographics

The Church of the Nazarene is a global denomination. As of 2013, the Church of the Nazarene reported reaching 159 world areas with a global influence of more than 2 million members worshiping in more than twenty-nine thousand churches worldwide (http:www.nazarene.org/files/docs/StatisticsAnnual.pdf). Its global ministries focus on evangelism, compassionate ministries, and education (Blevins et al., 2013, p. 23).

Manual of the Church of the Nazarene

The *Manual* of the Church of the Nazarene (Blevins et al., 2013) is the "official statement of the faith and practice of the church" (p. 5) which finds its authority grounded in scripture. The *Manual* contains a history of the Church of the Nazarene, the Constitution of the church, its Articles of Faith, guidelines of Christian character for living a holy life, statements about Christian conduct that address the "key issues of contemporary society," and the policies and procedures for local, district, and general church government and organizational structure (pp. 5–6). Blevins et al. (2013) make the following the declaration:

> Because it is the official statement of the faith and practice of the church and is consistent with the teachings of the Scriptures, we expect our people everywhere to accept the tenets of doctrine and the guides and helps to holy living contained in it. To fail to do so, after formally taking the membership vows of the Church of the Nazarene, injures the witness of the church, violates her conscience, and dissipates the fellowship of the people called Nazarenes (p. 6).

***Manual* statement: homosexuality.** Within the *Manual* of the Church of the Nazarene (Blevins et al., 2013) is a section titled, "Covenant of Christian Conduct." This section provides a description of the various actions and behaviors that are both consistent and inconsistent with living a holy Christian life guided by the Holy Spirit, Scripture, and the teaching of the church (Blevins et al., 2013. pp. 46–60). Under the larger section of the "Covenant of Christian Conduct" is a subsection titled, "Human Sexuality." It is here that one finds descriptions of appropriate and inappropriate sexual behaviors and relationships—including homosexuality (Blevins et al., 2013, pp. 56–57). The following is the Church of the Nazarene's *Manual* statement regarding homosexuality:

> Homosexuality is one means by which human sexuality is perverted. We recognize the depth of the perversion that leads to homosexual acts but affirm the biblical position that such acts are sinful and subjected to the wrath of God. We believe the grace of God sufficient to overcome the practice of homosexuality (1 Corinthians 6:9–11). We deplore any action or statement that would seem to imply compatibility between Christian morality and the practice of homosexuality. We urge clear preaching and teaching concerning Bible standards of sexual morality. (Genesis 1:27; 19:1–25; Leviticus 20:13; Romans 1:26–27; 1 Corinthians 6:9–11; 1 Timothy 1:8–10) (Blevins et al., 2013, p. 57).

The *Manual* addresses homosexuality in one other section entitled, "Ministry and Christian Service," a section that primarily addresses church leaders. This subsection, "The Restoration of Members of the Clergy to Church Membership and Good Standing," outlines the process of restoring a clergy member who has been removed from leadership due to conduct unbecoming a church leader. The *Manual* states,

> Because some types of misconduct, such as sexual misconduct involving children or a homosexual nature, or repeated marital infidelity, are rarely the result of a one-time moral lapse, individuals who are guilty of sexual misconduct that involves a high probability of repeated misconduct should not be restored to good standing. These individuals also should not be permitted to serve in any position of leadership, trust, or ministry in the local church (Blevins et al., 2013, p. 229).

Supplemental Nazarene documents addressing homosexuality. In addition to the *Manual* statement about homosexuality, another document written by a consortium of Nazarene educators and church leaders and approved by the Board of General Superintendents addresses the issue of homosexuality. It is titled, *Pastoral Perspectives (from your General Superintendents) on Homosexuality* (Diehl et al., n.d.). The intent of this document is to provide clarity of understanding as well as recommendations for how the church should respond to homosexuality and same-sex oriented persons.

Later this document underwent a revision and was redistributed under a similar title, *A Pastoral Perspective on Homosexuality* (Porter et al., 2011). Both *Pastoral Perspectives* (Diehl et al., n.d.; Porter et al., 2011) documents were written to assist pastors struggling to know how to minister to individuals and families dealing with same-sex concerns as well as to affirm the church's position on homosexuality and to provide clarification of scripture. The Board of General Superintendents states that homosexuality is an issue that "challenges social convention," has "eroded the foundation of society's strongest institutions," and "challenged the foundational tenets of biblical understanding" (Porter et al., 2011, p. 1). The question is then posed, "How does [the Church of the Nazarene] come to the position it does on homosexuality?" (Diehl et al., n.d., p. 4). To arrive at its position, two sources of authority are identified: Scripture and Christian tradition (Diehl et al., n.d., p. 4).

Subsequently, two additional sources of authority were added: "the collective experience of our faith community" and "a reasoned perspective informed by our Wesleyan theology" (Porter et al., 2011, p. 1).

The authors acknowledge that the Bible says nothing about homosexuality as understood in our contemporary culture; however, the Bible does address same-sex acts or practices. To substantiate their position they cite seven scripture passages. Old Testament passages include Genesis 19:1–11, Judges 19, and Leviticus 18:22 and 20:13. Passages from the New Testament include, Romans 1:18–32, 1 Corinthians 6:9–11, and 1 Timothy 1:9–10. According to the writers, it is clear that these biblical texts demonstrate the "unqualified disapproval" of same-sex behavior or practice (Porter et al., 2011). Moreover, they argue that the whole of

Scripture resonates with "prohibiting homosexual activity" (Diehl et al., n.d., p. 7).

The church also posits that the "sexual instructions of Scripture are universal" (Porter et al., 2011). This means that the God-ordained design of intimate sexual relationship is scripturally permissible only between one man and one woman within the scared covenant of marriage. The only exception to this is celibacy (Porter et al., 2011). According to the authors, "from a biblical perspective homosexual practice is sin" (Diehl et al., n.d., p. 7).

They also draw on the historical position of the Church regarding homosexuality, arguing that for more than nineteen hundred years, Church tradition has strengthened the prohibitions of same-sex practice as contrary to God's will. Church historians and Christian scholars such as Tertullian, Origen, Augustine, Aquinas, Luther, Calvin, and John Wesley have condemned homosexual behavior as sinful (Diehl et al., n.d.). Moreover, "[a] Wesleyan response to homosexuality is defined by a clear conviction that homosexual behavior is immoral" and "part of the fallen nature" (Porter et al., 2011, p. 5).

The writers continue by addressing whether or not scientific research has provided proof that homosexuality is a natural occurring event or a choice (Diehl et al., n.d.). Although they seem to imply that homosexuality is a pathology (Porter et al., 2011, p. 5), it is acknowledged that homosexuality is real and that it tends to begin early in one's life and is rarely a choice one makes (Diehl et al., n.d., p. 8). Despite the significant research conducted on the etiology of homosexuality, the church states that this research is "inconclusive" and no one theory, e.g., genetic, hormonal, physical, environmental, or experiential has been proven (Diehl et al., n.d., pp. 8–9; Porter et al., 2011, p. 5). Furthermore, scientific research does not override the biblical prohibitions against homosexual activity (Diehl et al., n.d., p. 9).

The authors also address sexual orientation. They argue that sexual orientation is not a choice and is therefore neither a moral nor an immoral issue. Sexual behavior, on the other hand, is a moral decision. While the Bible does not address same-sex orientation, it clearly prohibits homosexual behavior and practice. The reader is reminded that the "*Manual of the Church of the Nazarene* and the Official Statement of the Board of General Superintendents makes a clear distinction between behavior and orientation. "One is sinful, the other is not (Diehl et al., n.d., p. 9). The Official Statement of the Board of General Superintendents reads as follows:

> The Church of the Nazarene believes that every man or woman should be treated with dignity, grace, and holy love, whatever their sexual orientation. However, we continue to firmly hold the position that the homosexual lifestyle is sinful and is contrary to the Scriptures. We further wish to reemphasize our call to Nazarenes around the globe to recommit themselves to a life of holiness, characterized by holy love and expressed through the most rigorous and consistent lifestyle of sexual purity. We stand firmly on the belief that the biblical concept of marriage, always between one man and one woman in a committed, lifelong relationship, is the only relationship within which the gift of sexual intimacy is properly expressed (Diehl et al., n.d., p. 4).

The Church of the Nazarene argues that a person cannot claim to be a practicing homosexual and a follower of Jesus Christ; the two claims are incompatible and contradictory (Porter et al., 2011). The church holds that the Christian homosexual will be an individual who does not engage in same-sex practice, behavior, or relationships and will faithfully practice "a life of disciplined sexual abstinence" (Diehl et al., n.d., p. 11).

Although the church states that homosexual behavior is wrong it also readily acknowledges that the church must not be a place of ridicule or condemnation (Porter et al., 2011). Love, grace, and redemption should be the primary characteristics of the church; however, there is a fine line between condemning and condoning homosexual behavior (Diehl et al., n.d.). Nazarene clergy and the church are encouraged to love homosexual persons "unconditionally" (Diehl et al., n.d.; Porter et al., 2011). Clergy and ministry leaders are not to love someone less because he or she is gay or lesbian; the expression of God's grace comes through the demonstration of unconditional love by God's people. Christian leaders are to walk the often difficult and complex journey alongside the same-sex identified person (Diehl et al., n.d.). The authors state that Wesleyan theology offers a "hopeful grace" that God can deliver the homosexual person from same-sex desire and/or empower the individual to live a celibate life (Porter et al., 2011). The church encourages "consistent, rich hospitality;" however,

> [The church] must not shy away from telling the truth about homosexuality, its roots, and its consequences. From Scripture, Christian tradition, and the doctrines of our church, we compassionately and persistently affirm that homosexual practice is contrary to God's will and cannot be acceptable behavior for followers of Christ. At the same time, we must always point to the hope in the Christ who came to redeem all of us from the power of sin (Porter et al., 2011, p. 9).

Despite its unequivocal position on homosexuality, the Board of General Superintendents state that if a same-sex identified person can attest to celibacy or a sexual reorientation s/he will be "invited to full participation in the life and ministry of the church, leading ministries, serving on boards, and singing in choirs" (Diehl et al., n.d., p. 13).

The *Pastoral Perspectives* documents may have sparked some controversy among Nazarene leaders. Some raised questions about the church's fidelity to scripture as well as whether the church was softening its position on homosexuality. To address these concerns the Board of General Superintendents later released another document titled, "Further Clarification Concerning the Document 'A Pastoral Perspective on Homosexuality'" (no author, n.d.). This document provides a concise restatement of the original *Pastoral Perspectives* documents (Diehl et al., n.d.; Porter et al., 2011) position. However, the "Further Clarification" document's purpose was to respond to questions raised by church leaders about homosexuality and same-sex oriented persons. To answer these questions, the Board of General Superintendents provided four admonitions worth noting. To their earlier statement, "The reoriented or celibate single homosexual will be invited to full participation in the life and the ministry of the church, leading ministries, serving on boards, and singing in choirs," the General Superintendents reiterated the church's position stating,

It is important to recognize the operative terms in this statement: "reoriented," "celibate," and "single." These three terms offer clarification that must not be overlooked. It should not be interpreted that the Church of the Nazarene is relaxing its traditional standard concerning participation in the life, ministry, and governance of the local church. Without clear compliance of these three very important clarifiers, those individuals wanting to express participation in the life of the church would be barred (no author, n.d., p. 5).

Additionally, the Board of Generals Superintendents concluded with three "take-away" points that may be worth noting. They read as follows:

- We urge our clergy to remain faithful to the authority of Scripture. In these challenging times, the message of Christ is subject to enormous pressures from many sources. We must not allow the culture to shape the values of our proclamation or our practice. We remain committed to proclaiming the biblical message faithfully.
- We urge our clergy to preach a message of hope for deliverance and transformation. Without the transformative message of redemption and sanctification, our preaching leaves listeners with little more than a moralistic ideal.
- We urge our clergy to be redemptive without compromise. It should be clear from this document that your Board of General Superintendents has courageously engaged a dialogue that is complex as well as complicated. We anticipate that our readers will extend grace where it is so desperately needed while simultaneously adhering to and proclaiming the ethic of scriptural holiness (no author, n.d., p. 4).

Finally, the Church of the Nazarene admits, "homosexuality is real and sooner or later we [i.e., the denomination] may be asked to respond to the serious questions regarding the attitude of the Church regarding this important topic" (Porter et al., 2011, p. 7).

RATIONALE FOR THE STUDY

To date, no research has investigated the feelings of Nazarene clergy about homosexuality or their interactions with LGBT people. To verify this, I conducted a thorough search of not less than seven academic search engines. Some of my search terms included, "homosexual," "homosexuality," "gay," "lesbian," "bisexual," "GLBT," "LGBT," "attitudes," "Nazarene," "conservative," "evangelical," "Protestant," "clergy," "denomination," "denominational," "Christian," "religious," "religion," "religiosity," "homophobia," "homonegativity," "heterosexism," "sexual prejudice," "sexual orientation," etc. Furthermore, I consulted approximately 180 academic journal articles and publications for this research project. My investigation uncovered only one study analyzing attitudes toward premarital sex and homosexuality (Morgan, 2008). This quantitative study utilized a convenience sample of 379 undergraduate college students attending a Nazarene University in the Midwest. Although the sample utilized students from a Nazarene college campus, the study did not specifically address Nazarene attitudes; other denominational affiliations were represented among the respondents. The study did not address Nazarene clergy responses to homosexuality.

There is a gap in the literature concerning Nazarene clergy attitudes about and responses to homosexuality and their interactions with same-sex oriented persons. From the documents published by the Nazarene church that I reviewed, *Manual of the Church of the Nazarene 2013–2017, Pastoral Perspectives on Homosexuality* and, "Further Clarification Concerning the Document 'Pastoral Perspective on Homosexuality,'" it appears that Nazarene church takes a firm and unequivocal stand against homosexuality and same-sex oriented relationships. However, it also encourages its clergy to love same-sex oriented persons unconditionally.

This research proposes to discover how Nazarene ministers live within the tension of these two seemingly dichotomous propositions. With this in mind, this study will investigate Nazarene clergy beliefs about homosexuality as well as their lived experience when responding to LGBT persons, both inside and outside the church. To this end, this study will attempt to bridge a gap in the literature and help to generate dialog about how Nazarene pastors respond to this ever-pressing and controversial topic.

CHAPTER II
Research Methods

This purpose of this study was to discover the lived experience of Nazarene clergy responses to homosexuality and their interactions with LGBT people. This chapter focuses on the methods and procedures I used to conduct the study, including the research question, rationale for the research design, the researcher's role in the study, definitions of key terms, data collection and analysis, strategies for optimizing trustworthiness, and ethical considerations.

RESEARCH QUESTION

The following research question guided this study: What are the lived experiences of Nazarene clergy responses to homosexuality and interactions with LGBT people?

RATIONALE FOR RESEARCH APPROACH

Qualitative Research Design

According to Creswell (2007), there are four reasons for conducting qualitative research. First, following a thorough review of the literature, the need exists for a detailed, complex understanding of the phenomenon. Second, conducting participant interviews within the context or setting where the phenomenon occurs will provide the greatest insight. Third, the phenomenon under investigation is not well suited for quantitative analysis. Fourth, a qualitative study will provide a comprehensive understanding of the issue. This study proposed to satisfy each of these criteria.

Methodology

The goal of this research was to discover the essential essence or central meaning (Creswell, 2007) of Nazarene clergy responses to homosexuality and their interactions with LGBT people. To achieve this goal I utilized a qualitative research design and phenomenological data analysis (Moustakas, 1994; van Kaam, 1959; 1966). Qualitative inquiry differentiates itself from quantitative analysis in that it focuses on descriptions of experience rather than causal relationships (Creswell, 2007; Hays & Singh, 2012). Accordingly, quantitative research did not fit this study's intent since its purpose was to discover the "lived experiences" of Nazarene clergy and their interactions with LGBT persons (Creswell, 2007). In order to grasp the deep meaning and essential essence of Nazarene clergy's experience, I elected to conduct this study utilizing the phenomenological research tradition.

The purpose of phenomenology is to elicit rich, thick descriptions from participants' statements in order to discover the individual essence of each participant's experience of the phenomenon in question (Creswell, 2012; Moustakas, 1994). From these individual essences, (i.e., participants' textural-structural descriptions) the researcher develops a composite essence describing the collective experience of the phenomenon for all participants (Moustakas, 1994; Hays & Singh, 2012). This study was well suited for qualitative inquiry because it sought to describe the deep meaning of the phenomenon from the participants' experiential perspective (Bloomberg & Volpe, 2012; Ponterotto, 2005).

As indicated, a thorough review of the literature revealed no extant research examining Nazarene clergy responses to homosexuality or the lived experience of Nazarene clergy's interactions with LGBT persons. Denominational policy on homosexuality is available, but no voice has been given to the Nazarene men and women serving as clergy in the day-to-day life and ministry of the church. By utilizing a qualitative research design and phenomenological data analysis, I was able to provide a thorough, multifaceted description of Nazarene clergy feelings about homosexuality and their interactions with LGBT people. I obtained this information by interviewing Nazarene clergy in the context of their local church setting where they interacted with same-sex oriented individuals and/or couples. I analyzed the data from participant interviews noting the relevant themes that emerged. From the participants' narratives, I constructed rich, thick descriptions of the individual essence of the participants' experience of the phenomenon (Bloomberg & Volpe, 2012; Creswell, 2007; Hays & Singh, 2012). Following this, I developed a description of the composite essence of experience representing all the participants (Moustakas, 1994).

This study reveals important information about the practical implications of balancing the Nazarene church's position on homosexuality in the context of day-to-day pastoral ministry. I hope that the results generated by this research will help establish a dialog between the Church of the Nazarene, its clergy, and the LGBT community.

Emergence of Phenomenological Research

The historical development of qualitative research is traceable to the 15th century when early "anthropologists and sociologists" set out to acquire a meaningful understanding of other cultures (Hays & Singh, 2012, p. 15). Although this endeavor provided the genesis of qualitative methodology, the phenomenological research tradition was not widely practiced in academia or by other social scientists until the mid-1900s (Bogdan & Biklen, 2003; Hays & Singh, 2012). During the 17th, 18th, and 19th centuries, positivism and post-positivism guided scientific research with a focus on "truth" (Hays & Singh, 2012). Positivism asserts that objective, universal truths exist but are discoverable only through empirically verifiable, direct observation of the phenomenon under investigation (Hays & Singh, 2012; Patton, 2002). Like positivism, post-positivism also asserts that objective, universal truths exist; however, only a partial understanding of these truths is available because no theory thoroughly describes a particular phenomenon (Hays & Singh, 2012).

During the latter part of the 1700s, Immanuel Kant's seminal work, *Critique of Pure Reason* (1787) paved the way for constructivism (Vidich & Lyman, 2003). Constructivism or, as it is sometimes called, "social constructionism" asserts that reality is socially, culturally, and historically defined, i.e., "constructed" (Lincoln & Guba, 2000). In other words, individuals view reality through a context specific lens (Bloomberg & Volpe, 2012) and define their reality through the perspective of that lens. Hermeneutics (i.e., interpretation) emerged from constructivism. Hermeneutics asserts that human beings and cultures are not fully understandable apart from their historical and literary contexts (Sandage, Cook, Hill, Strawn, & Reimer, 2008). Moreover, hermeneutical phenomenology is oriented toward interpreting the "texts" of life as well as "lived experiences" (Creswell, 2007, p. 235). In this enterprise, the investigator returns "again and again" to the text, each time returning to it with more insight and understanding (Bloomberg & Volpe, 2012).

The early 1900s to the mid-1940s mark the "traditional period" of the emergence of qualitative inquiry (Lincoln & Guba, 1985). Hays and Singh (2012) assert that this period is an important time in the expansion of qualitative research because the "greatest amount of growth in ideas and traditions occurs across a variety of disciplines" (p. 18).

Although "phenomenology as a concept" emerged from Kantian thought (Hays & Singh, 2012, p. 50), it is German mathematician and philosopher, Edmund Husserl (1859–1938) who is "credited as the father of phenomenology" (Hays & Singh, 2012, p. 50). Husserl developed phenomenological inquiry as a form of qualitative investigation within the school of psychology (Jennings, 1986). Husserl argued that positivist and post-positivist modes of scientific inquiry—largely confined to laboratory settings—failed to explain fully the essence of human experience (Groenwald, 2004; Hays & Singh, 2012). Husserl wanted to capture the "essence" of a phenomenon and understand the "nature of things as they are" (Giorgi, 1985). For Husserl this meant investigating the lived experience of individuals in relation to the phenomenon (Hays & Singh, 2012). This is a fundamental tenet of phenomenology according to Husserl, because any phenomenon (the object, thing, event under investigation) is understandable only in relation to the individual's (the subject's) experience of it (Giorgi, 1997).

Although phenomenological research did not begin to achieve a foothold in the social sciences and academic research until the 1970s (Creswell, 2007), Husserl's philosophy influenced other existentialist writers including Martin Heidegger (1889–1976), Jean-Paul Sartre (1905–1980) and

Merleau-Ponty (1908–1961) (Bloomberg & Volpe, 2012; Groenwald, 2004). While considered "abstract" by some, Husserlian thought continues to influence contemporary existentialist philosophers and phenomenological researchers (Creswell, 2007).

Philosophical Assumptions of Qualitative Research

There are several philosophical assumptions embedded within the qualitative research tradition that are foundational to sound research (Hays & Singh, 2012). These assumptions include ontology, epistemology, axiology, rhetoric, and methodology (Creswell, 2007; Hays & Singh, 2012). These assumptions influence the study's design, implementation, data collection, and data analysis; therefore, "good research requires" the qualitative researcher explicitly state his/her position on each of these (Creswell, 2007, p. 15).

Ontology addresses the nature of reality. Qualitative research examines how "real" a phenomenon is by viewing it through the subjective lens of the researcher, the participants, and the reader (Lincoln & Guba, 2005; Hays & Singh, 2012; Ponterotto, 2005). Since individuals construct reality through their subjective experience of a phenomenon, qualitative inquiry allows for multiple realities; moreover, differing perspectives are equally valid and valued (Hays & Singh, 2012).

Epistemology refers to the process of knowing (Hays & Singh, 2012). In qualitative research, epistemology concerns obtaining knowledge about a phenomenon of interest (Lincoln & Guba, 2008). Here the researcher's task is to intersect the participants' experience and context as closely as possible in order to understand it (Creswell, 2007; Moustakas, 1994). In this way, the qualitative inquirer attempts to minimize the separateness between the researcher and the participant in an effort to "know" more fully each participant's experience of the phenomenon (Lincoln & Guba, 2005; Ponterotto, 2005). To decrease separateness, I interviewed each participant in the context of the participant's local church. Conducting interviews in context gave participants greater access to their first-hand experiences of the phenomenon.

Axiology concerns the researcher's values and biases, as well as the impact of these on the study (Bloomberg & Volpe, 2012). Researcher values and assumptions may influence the values of the research participants in the research design; therefore, axiology also involves considering the values of the participants (Ponterotto, 2005). To maintain the integrity of the study, it was vital the researcher openly acknowledged and discussed his values and biases (Creswell, 2007). Later, I address my assumptions and biases in the section, "Researcher Assumption and Biases."

Rhetoric describes the language structure of qualitative inquiry and the manner of the presentation of data (Ponterotto, 2005). A qualitative presentation is typically less formal, more personal, and literary in style (Creswell, 2007). As a phenomenological study, I present the data in a narrative format using the participants' own voices to describe their experiences of the phenomenon (Hays & Singh, 2012).

Methodology refers to the actual practice of qualitative research. This involves decisions about selecting a specific research design, research question(s), as well as data collection, and analysis (Creswell, 2012). I selected a phenomenology as my research paradigm in order to understand the lived experience of Nazarene ministers' response to homosexuality and their interactions with LGBT individuals. I detail this methodological approach in the section titled, "Core Concepts of Phenomenology."

To summarize, the philosophical assumptions of ontology (reality), epistemology (knowledge), axiology (values), rhetoric (participant's voice), and methodology (research tradition) overlap and influence the design of one's research (Hays & Singh, 2012). In the next section, I provide an overview of the philosophical paradigm and lens through which I interpreted data.

Philosophical Worldviews of Qualitative Research

In addition to the aforementioned philosophical assumptions, there are philosophical worldviews or paradigms that influence qualitative research. For the purposes of this study, I highlight three: positivist, post-positivist, and social constructivism (Bloomberg & Volpe, 2012; Creswell, 2007; Hays & Singh, 2012).

Positivists espouse that the attainment of objective, universal truth comes through the direct observation and experience of a phenomenon and as such, only valid, verifiable claims are genuine knowledge (Hays & Singh, 2012). Positivists are interested in empirical verification through hypothesis testing, operationally defined constructs, and replicable methods of analysis that generalize to larger populations (Patton, 2005).

Similar to positivists, post-positivists subscribe to a scientific approach to research; they emphasize empirical data collection, cause-and-effect relationships, and determinism based on a priori theories (Creswell, 2012). Post-positivists adhere to rigorous methods of data collection utilizing multiple levels of analysis to ensure rigor (Creswell, 2007; Moustakas, 1994). Although post-positivists adhere to similar scientific assumptions as positivists, post-positivists argue that no one theory fully describes a phenomenon and therefore a universal reality is not possible (Hays & Singh, 2012). Post-positivists recognize the value of multiple perspectives of meaning espoused by participants (Creswell, 2007).

Although the positivists and the post-positivists make tremendous contributions to scientific inquiry, these paradigms do not address the specific questions of qualitative inquiry (Hays & Singh, 2012). Consequently, other paradigms were developed to better answer questions more suited for qualitative research (Lincoln & Guba, 2005). One of these paradigms is social constructivism.

Social constructivism posits that reality is historically, culturally, and socially constructed (Lincoln & Guba, 2000). The central tent of this paradigm is that individuals construct reality through the subjective experience of a phenomenon; this results in multiple meanings of experience for similar phenomenon (Bloomberg & Volpe, 2012). Moreover, clarification and definition of these multiple subjective meanings occur in contact with other individuals within a social, cultural, and historical context (Lincoln & Guba, 1985). In the qualitative tradition, the researcher's role is to gain understanding of these multiple meanings, using the voice of the participant to describe her/his experience of the phenomenon (Creswell, 2007). Constructivist research also seeks to understand the phenomenon from a context-specific perspective, meaning that the phenomenon is examined within the context or setting where it occurs (Lincoln & Guba, 1998). Social constructivist researchers understand that their own experiences influence their interpretation of the data and therefore recognize the need to acknowledge their own social, cultural, and historical background (Bloomberg & Volpe, 2012).

The current study, a phenomenological research design, utilized the social constructivist paradigm (Moustakas, 1994). Rather than beginning with a theory (as in positivism or post-positivism) I proposed an overarching research question, coupled with in-depth interview questions to extract the essential meaning of the phenomenon from the data I collected in the field (Bloomberg & Volpe, 2012). To determine the essential essence of the phenomenon I employed Moustakas' transcendental phenomenological methodology based on Husserl's phenomenology (Hays & Singh, 2012).

Core Concepts of Phenomenology

Phenomenological data analysis examines the lived experiences of individuals in relation to a particular phenomenon of interest. Padgett (2004) referred to phenomenology as burrowing inward. Moustakas (1994) argues that that the sole purpose of the phenomenological enterprise is to understand the depth and meaning of the participants' experience(s). To gain a meaningful understanding of these lived experiences, phenomenology utilizes four key concepts to examine the data: (a) bracketing or *epoche*, (b) horizontalization, (c) textual description and (d) structural description (Hays & Singh, 2012). These four processes are the "metaphorical sieve" through which raw data is collected and analyzed (Hays & Singh, 2012, p. 355).

Bracketing, or *epoche*, is the researcher's first step in phenomenological investigation. This means the researcher "brackets" or sets aside his/her experiences, assumptions, biases, and preconceived ideas about the phenomenon under investigation (Creswell, 2012). Bracketing allows the researcher to approach the phenomenon, and analyze the data, with a "fresh perspective" as if s/he is viewing it for the first time (Moustakas, 1994). By bracketing off prior assumptions and beliefs about the phenomenon, the researcher may then understand the essential essence of the participants' experience. This lets the researcher construct a "written representation of the structure of the phenomenon from the participants' experience (Hays & Singh, 2012, p. 50).

Horizontalization is the process by which the researcher reviews broad categories or domains of the transcribed text (Hays & Singh, 2012). From these categories/domains the researcher identifies themes and patterns in the data that emerge from analyzing "nonrepetitive, nonoverlapping statements within the participant's transcripts" (Hays & Singh, 2012, p. 354). The researcher then lists all significant statements relevant to the participants' experience of the phenomenon and assigns them equal value (Creswell, 2007; Moustakas, 1994). From these significant statements, the researcher then looks for clusters of meaning and identifies the salient themes that emerge from the data (Creswell, 2007). By identifying themes and patterns through the process of horizontalization the investigator manages the data more efficiently (Hays & Singh, 2012).

After analyzing the list of salient themes identified in horizontalization, the researcher develops a textural description of the phenomenon's essence. To do this, the researcher analyzes the clusters of meaning and creates a written description of *what* the participant experienced Creswell (2007). The textural description describes the "meaning" of the individual's experience of the phenomenon (Moustakas, 1994). This is an important methodological step in data analysis because according to Hays & Singh 2012), "the textural description always strives to understand the *meaning* and *depth* of the essence of the experience" (p. 355).

Next, the researcher constructs a structural description to identify possible multiple potential meanings from the textural descriptions (Hays & Singh, 2012). The researcher creates a "combination of descriptions" to describe the "overall essence of the phenomenon" (Bloomberg & Volpe, 2012, p. 33). A structural description also helps identify any tension that may exist within participant themes in order to grasp the full essence of their meaning (Hays & Singh, 2012). While the textural description describes *what* the participant experienced, the structural description illustrates *how* the phenomenon was/is experienced by the participants (Creswell, 2007; Moustakas, 1994).

After analyzing the textural and structural meanings, the researcher reduces them to a description of the phenomenon that characterizes the experience of all participants in the study (Creswell, 2007). This description becomes the invariant structure or essential "essence" of the collective experiences of the phenomenon under investigation (Moustakas, 1994).

DEFINITION OF TERMS

Auditor: a person with expertise and interest in the study and is able to determine that the researcher completed a rigorous and comprehensive study. The auditor's role helps to ensure trustworthiness of the results

(Hays & Singh, 2012). Crewell and Miller (2000) observe that the auditor examines both the process and product of the research to determine the study's trustworthiness.

Bracketing: Moustakas (1994) referred to bracketing as a first step in the "phenomenological reduction" of data analysis. This means that the researcher sets aside (as much as possible) his/her preconceived ideas and experiences of the phenomenon in order to grasp the lived experience of the participants of the study (Creswell, 2007).

Clusters of Meaning: as part of the data analysis, the researcher clusters participant's statements into themes or units of meaning and removes extraneous or redundant statements (Creswell, 2007; Moustakas, 1994).

Epoche (Greek): to refrain from and suspend all judgment about a particular phenomenon. Epoche is similar to bracketing in that the researcher sets aside his/her prior beliefs about a phenomena while acknowledging her/his values and assumptions about the phenomenon (Bloomberg & Volpe, 2012; Moustakas, 1994).

Essence: reducing the textual (what) and structural (how) meanings of the participant's experience of the phenomenon to a concise description that characterizes the experiences of all the participants in the study (Creswell, 2007; Moustakas, 1994).

Horizontalization: the process whereby the researcher and research team identify nonrepetitive, nonoverlapping statements within each participant's transcript. This allows the researcher to analyze and manage the data in an efficient manner (Hays & Singh, 2012; Moustakas, 1994).

Lived Experience: each participant's experience of the phenomenon under investigation (Creswell, 2007; Moustakas, 1994).

Member Checking: the process whereby the researcher consults with each participant to check for "goodness of fit" and accuracy to maintain trustworthiness of participant statements (Hays & Singh, 2012).

Nazarene Clergy: ordained Nazarene ministers and graduates of Nazarene Theological Seminary who are lead/senior pastors of a Church of the Nazarene congregation.

Participant: individuals invited and who accept the role as a participant in this research project to determine the lived experiences of Nazarene clergy responses to homosexuality and their interactions with LGBT people.

Phenomenon: an event, or "object" of human experience, e.g., anger, grief, insomnia, homosexuality, etc., that can be described by participant(s) consisting of "what" was experienced and "how" it was experienced (Creswell, 2007; Moustakas, 1994, van Manen, 1990).

Phenomenology: the process of reducing individuals' experience of a phenomenon to a description of the phenomenon's universal essence in order to apprehend the very nature of the phenomenon under investigation (Creswell, 2007; van Manen, 1990). Phenomenology attempts to "discover and describe the meaning or essence of participants' lived experience, or knowledge, as it appears to consciousness" (Hays & Singh, 2012, p. 50).

Structural Description: describes "how" the participant experienced a particular phenomenon in terms of the conditions, context, and situations in which the phenomenon was experienced (Creswell, 2007). The researcher then develops a visual model or a written description that illustrates the framework of the participants' experience of the phenomenon (Creswell, 2007; Moustakas, 1994; Hays & Singh, 2012).

Textual Description: describes "what" the participants experienced (Creswell, 2007). The purpose of the textual description is to grasp the "meaning and the depth of the essence of the experience" (Hays & Singh, 2012, p. 355). Combining the textual and structural descriptions provide an overall picture of the essence of the experience of a phenomenon (Creswell, 2007).

Theme: a general idea or concept that emerges from analyzing the data of participants' transcripts (Bloomberg & Volpe, 2012).

Thick description: a detailed account of the research process, context, outcome and participants. It is more than a simple explanation of one's findings (thin description). A thick description is a strategy for trustworthiness emphasizing both interpretation and a detailed description of the data in order to allow the reader to transfer the information to other settings and contexts based on the shared characteristics of the phenomenon (Creswell, 2007; Hays & Singh, 2012).

ROLE OF THE RESEARCHER

In qualitative research, the researcher is the primary instrument through which data is collected and analyzed (Creswell, 2007). To represent the participants' lived experience accurately, I bracketed (i.e., held in *epoche*) my assumptions and preconceived notions (Moustakas, 1994) so that they did not taint the results of the study. With the assistance of a research team, I analyzed the data seeking relevant/key statements and themes that described the essence of the participants' lived experience of the phenomenon (Creswell, 2007). From these key themes, I constructed thick, rich descriptions of each participant's lived experience as they encountered the phenomenon within their ministry context (Hays & Singh, 2012).

As the researcher, I have received doctoral-level training in qualitative research methodology, and have approximately 20 years of experience as an ordained Nazarene pastor. During my pastoral tenure, I worked with several individuals who stated that they were either same-sex attracted or same-sex oriented. I also have a gay relative who is married and raising children with her partner. Additionally, I have counseled gay and lesbian individuals desiring to integrate their sexual orientation with their spiritual identity. As I interacted with same-sex identified individuals, I did extensive research of various denominational positions on homosexuality.

Researcher Assumptions and Biases

To prevent researcher bias the investigator must recognize and acknowledge the presuppositions that one brings to the study (Creswell, 2007; Hays & Singh, 2012). Because of my experience as a minister in the Church of the Nazarene, frequent interactions with ministerial colleagues, and conversations with same-sex identified people, I presume Nazarene clergy may demonstrate the following attitudes and/or feelings about homosexuality and LGBT people: (a) they will likely hold unfavorable attitudes about homosexuality, (b) they may be reluctant to let gay or lesbian individuals or couples enter into membership, (c) they will be unwilling to allow a homosexual person to function in a leadership role within the church and, (d) they will likely affirm unconditional love for all people but will struggle with its practical application to LGBT individuals and couples.

Researcher Bracketing

To ensure that the aforementioned presuppositions/biases do not influence the results of this study, I utilized the concept of *epoche* (Moustakas, 1994) or bracketing. Hays and Singh (2012) state that bracketing is a critical step in pre-data analysis to guard against investigator bias that may interfere with the results. Bracketing helps the researcher "construct the essential meaning of participants' experience of the phenomenon (Creswell, 2007). Although bracketing one's presuppositions and biases is important in phenomenology, van Manen (1990) argued that is impossible for the researcher to eliminate one's perceptions of the phenomenon. LeVasseur (2003) recommended that the researcher suspend (bracket) her or his understanding in order to investigate the phenomenon from a position of curiosity. This allows the researcher to approach the experience of the participants with a "fresh perspective" (Moustakas, 1994). To bracket my presuppositions effectively I suspended my preconceived notions of the phenomenon and, I set aside my experience(s) of the phenomenon to perceive freshly each participant's experience—as though hearing it for the first time (Creswell; 2007; Moustakas, 1994).

Researcher Objectivity and Subjectivity

Moustakas (1994) suggested that objectivity means viewing reality as it actually is. In qualitative research, objectivity requires that the investigator is true to the object under investigation. In this way, the researcher becomes the custodian of the true nature or essence of the object (van Manen,

2006). Researchers Lincoln and Guba (2000) posit that the criteria for objectivity are met when the researcher maintains methodological rigor, there is a correlation between reality and the data, and when the results are value free. Some scholars argue that true objectivity is unattainable (Rossman & Rallis, 2003) because the subjectivity of the researcher is always present (Hays & Singh, 2012). Sokolowski (2000) maintained that it is impossible to separate objective reality from one's subjective experience of that reality. In phenomenology, objectivity means giving a voice to each participant by fairly and accurately representing each participant's experience of the phenomenon (Hays & Singh, 2012; Lincoln & Guba, 1995).

Quantitative researchers often argue that subjectivity generates faulty findings, biased outcomes, and invalid results (Patton, 2002). Consequently, these researchers attempt to maintain a distance between themselves and their research. They believe that the purpose of distance is to increase objectivity (neutrality) and decrease subjectivity; however, as Patton (2002) observed, distance does not increase objectivity distance simply increases distance. Hays and Singh (2012) argue that efforts to reduce or eliminate subjectivity align qualitative methodologies too closely with quantitative research paradigms. Eisner (1997) proposed that discrete categories of objectivity and subjectivity are a false distinction because there is an overlap between objective reality and the subjective experience of the individual—including the researcher. Moreover, Eisner (1997) argued that investigating the subjective experience(s) of an individual might reveal an undiscovered perspective.

Subjectivity allows the researcher to be closer to one's study and to each participant's experience of the phenomenon under investigation (Hays & Singh, 2012). Rather than maintaining distance, subjectivity provides the opportunity for the researcher to grasp the true essence of the phenomenon as experienced by the participant, and to understand the phenomenon in a way that is deep and meaningful (Hays & Singh, 2012). Here, subjectivity indicates the intimate connection (inseparability) between the investigator and the participant(s) (Patton, 2002). This inseparability allows the researcher to "faithfully represent participants as experts in the phenomenon of inquiry" (Hays & Singh, 2012, p. 145–146). Far from being biased and unreliable, subjectivity offers a positive contribution to qualitative research (Hays & Singh, 2012). Subjectivity allows one to connect with one's participants; it means the researcher is perceptive, discerning, and insightful which helps to illustrate the phenomenon with all of its depth, meaning, and richness (van Manen, 2001). Researcher subjectivity is also beneficial to the study's outcome. Hays and Singh (2012) assert that subjectivity is virtuous and critical to the researcher's role. Moreover, subjectivity "becomes the framework for the study's process" (Hays & Singh, 2012, p. 145).

STRATEGIES TO MAINTAIN OBJECTIVITY AND SUBJECTIVITY

Hays and Singh (2012) recommend several important strategies to address subjectivity and ensure researcher objectivity. These include the following: (a) embrace an attitude of curiosity rather than expertise, (b) utilize regular participant checks to ensure the accuracy of the researcher's interpretation of participants' lived experience, (c) ask other experts in the area of study to review the findings and offer feedback about how the current study compares to similar studies, (d) assemble a research team for assistance with data analysis and consensus about interpretive results, (e) triangulate data collection methods, (f) employ the assistance of a peer-debriefer, (g) counteract "group-think" among research team members and embrace divergent views, (h) note words such as *always* and *never* and *sometimes* and question their use and, (i) use participant/member checks during data collection and analysis to ensure that researcher interpretations are consistent with participants' experience (p. 146).

Lead From a Position of Curiosity

To lead from a position of curiosity I viewed the participants of the study as "experts in the phenomenon of inquiry" (Hays & Singh, 2012, p. 146). I recognized my own assumptions and experiences with the phenomenon. Additionally, I was familiar with the phenomenon of interest as an "insider" of Nazarene culture. Therefore, it was necessary for me to approach each participant as a "naïve inquirer" (Morrow, 2005, p. 254). To do this, I utilized bracketing and reflexive journaling to help me hear the participant's voice from a fresh perspective (LeVasseur, 2003; Moustakas, 1994). Given my experience of the phenomenon and of the Nazarene church, implementing each of these techniques expanded my curiosity and helped me grasp a deeper understanding of the meaning and essence of each participant's experience (Hays & Singh, 2012).

Participant Checks

A key feature of phenomenological research is to protect the voice of the participant (Hays & Singh, 2012). In order to do this I utilized participant checks at four points during the research process: (a) immediately following each interview, I briefly summarized what each participant said; (b) after transcription each participant was given a verbatim copy of the interview to read and review for accuracy, (c) participants were consulted during the data analysis to verify that my interpretations of the data accurately reflected their experience and, (d) member checks were conducted periodically throughout the research and data analysis process to ensure accuracy. This system of member checks ensured I accurately reflected the participants' lived experience of the phenomenon (Hays & Singh, 2012).

Research Team

In order to maintain researcher objectivity, I enlisted the assistance of a research team. The team included two coders, one peer-debriefer, and an auditor. Additionally, I recruited secondary coders so that each transcript was read, reviewed, and coded by two individuals. Of the primary research team members, both secondary coders were female Ph.D. doctoral candidates, trained in qualitative research methodology and analysis. I read and reflected on the interview transcripts and developed a provisional codebook. The research team and I met periodically for consensus coding. During these meetings, we coded the transcripts and operationally defined each code. Research team members arrived at consensus on the operationalization of each code thereby "co-creating new knowledge about the phenomenon" under investigation (Hays & Singh, 2012, p. 308). Triangulation of the data occurred naturally through the cooperative work of the research team.

I also solicited the assistance of a peer-debriefer. The peer-debriefer was a recent Ph.D. graduate serving as church pastor in a sister denomination.

He was trained as a qualitative researcher and utilized a phenomenological methodology for his doctoral dissertation. His professional expertise as a pastor and his academic training as a phenomenologist greatly enhanced the quality of this research. Aside from a peer-relationship, he had no personal investment in the outcome of this study. He and I met periodically for the duration of this study via Skype. This ensured his familiarity with data as well as the process of data analysis. His primary function was to identify potential biases, presuppositions, assumptions, and faulty interpretations of the data. Working with the assistance of a peer-debriefer maintained accountability and helped to strengthen this study's credibility (Hays & Singh, 2012).

I also enlisted the assistance of an auditor. My dissertation chair served in this capacity; she has a Ph.D. in Counselor Education. Although she had no personal investment in this study, she possessed extensive training as a qualitative researcher and demonstrated expert knowledge pertaining to this research topic (Hays & Singh, 2012). As the auditor, she reviewed interview procedures, transcripts, data analysis, memos, the codebook, its codes, and methodological strategies. The auditor reviewed the audit trail to ensure that I completed a comprehensive and rigorous study (Hays & Singh, 2012). Enlisting the assistance of a research team of coders, peer-debriefer, and an auditor promised a thorough, unbiased, and rigorous study.

PROCEDURES

For the purposes of this research, I utilized Moustakas's (1994) transcendental phenomenology to discover the depth and meaning of experience for Nazarene clergy (Hays & Singh, 2012). To accomplish this I set aside my presuppositions about the phenomenon under investigation and implemented systematic methods of data analysis to ensure a rigorous study and confirmable results (Creswell, 2007; Hays & Singh, 2012; Moustakas, 1994).

Data Collection

Participants. I utilized purposive sampling for participant selection (Denzin & Lincoln, 2000); this method built rigor into the sampling procedure (Hays & Singh, 2012). Purposive sampling met the necessary criteria to "obtain information-rich cases" of the phenomenon under investigation (Hays & Singh, 2012, p. 164). Moreover, purposive sampling established that each participant was qualified to respond to the questions of the study. I also utilized snowball sampling when a participant recommended another individual who met the study's criteria. Based on these sampling methods I selected participants who were able to respond meaningfully to their experience as a Nazarene clergyperson and the topic of homosexuality and LGBT concerns. To accomplish the objectives of this research, participants were required to meet the following criteria:

- ordained as a minister by the Nazarene church
- a graduate of Nazarene Theological Seminary
- the lead/senior clergyperson of the Nazarene church where s/he is pastor

Participant selection originated with a list of ordained Nazarene clergy who met the aforementioned criteria (criterion sampling). Potential candidates received an initial contact wherein I described the purpose of the research project and answered their questions. If the candidate agreed to participate, I provided written documentation of the informed consent. The initial screening process yielded a sufficient number of candidates; however, some participants referred other potential candidates whom I contacted thus implementing snowball sampling (Bloomberg & Volpe, 2012). The additional candidates met the selection criteria and were invited to participate.

Although some phenomenological studies are conducted using as few as one participant, phenomenological scholars typically recommend in-depth interviews with at least 3–10 participants in order to generate thick, rich descriptions of the phenomenon (Creswell, 2007; Dukes, 1984). Although my initial list of potential candidates was 15, I estimated that 8–12 participant interviews would provide sufficient data; I interviewed 13 participants. From the collected and analyzed data, I was able to determine Nazarene clergies' lived experience of their responses to homosexuality and interactions with LGBT individuals.

Collection methods. The initial contact and screening of potential candidates occurred by telephone wherein I developed an initial contact screening protocol (Appendix A) and demographic questionnaire (Appendix B) to determine the candidate's appropriateness of fit for this research. If the candidate met the eligibility criteria and agreed to participate in the study, I scheduled an appointment for the interview. Next, I created a file for, and assigned a pseudonym to, each participant. I mailed each participant a research packet that included the informed consent outlining the purpose of the research project, what the participant was agreeing to, and the potential benefits and liabilities of participation in the study.

Prior to beginning the interview, I gave each participant a verbal description of the research project; explained the informed consent document highlighting the importance of confidentiality and the measures used to protect each participant's identity. Next, I invited each participant to ask any questions he had. Once I answered and clarified those questions, I collected the participant's signed copy of the informed consent. Upon completion and collection of those items, I began the interview.

Each interview required approximately 60–90 minutes to complete. Interviews were audio recorded. During the interview, I utilized the interview summary form (Appendix D) to note the participant's nonverbal expressions. On this form, I also memoed my impressions and summarized the interview.

Transcription of the data occurred within 72 hours of the interview. I outsourced the audio recordings of participant interviews to a transcription service. Following transcription, I memoed additional impressions from the typed manuscript and assigned a code to each transcript (Bloomberg & Volpe, 2012). I placed the completed transcription in the participant's file under his pseudonym. Researcher memos and notes were coded with the participant's pseudonym and placed in the participant's file. As a member check, each participant received a typed copy of the transcribed verbatim interview and asked to review the transcript to confirm its accuracy.

Informed consent and protection of privacy. Each participant received two copies of the informed consent (Appendix C). The informed consent outlined participant confidentiality and privacy and explained the potential risks and benefits of participating in the study. I provided a verbal explanation of the informed consent and clarified any questions the participant had. If the participant agreed to continue with the study, the participant signed both copies of the informed consent. The participant returned a copy to the researcher and retained a copy for his records.

I assigned each participant a pseudonym to protect the participant's identity. Information, data, transcriptions, memos, and notes are stored and saved on my personal computer with a secure password. All data was backed-up on a secure flash-drive and stored in a secure, password-protected Dropbox folder. I explained to each participant how the data would be handled following completion of the study.

Setting. Twelve of the thirteen interviews were conducted in the local church setting where the participant is the pastor. This facilitated the recollection of memories, experiences, thoughts, and reflections of the clergyperson's responses to homosexuality and interactions with LGBT individuals. One interview was conducted via Skype. The participant was verbally informed of the potential risk to confidentiality using an online service for the interview. The participant acknowledged the risk and consented to the interview using Skype.

Interview questions. In phenomenological research, interview questions are designed to elicit rich, thick descriptions of the essence of the phenomenon through the lived experience of the participants (Hays & Singh, 2012). To access this information I conducted semi-structured, in-depth interviews with each participant. According to Seidman (2006), "In-depth interviewing's strength is that [the researcher] can come to understand the details of people's experiences from their point of view" (p. 112). In order to discover the essence of the lived experience of Nazarene clergy and their interactions with the gay and lesbian population, I developed the following semi-structured interview questions (Appendix E).

1. Tell me about your perceptions of the church's position on homosexuality.
2. How would you describe your feelings about the Nazarene church's position on homosexuality?

3. How are your own feelings about homosexuality impacted by the church's position?
    a. Have there been times when the church's position and your own position have been in conflict? What happened? What was it like for you?
4. Can you talk about any personal interactions or experiences you've had with a homosexual person?
    a. Personally or professionally have you ever interacted with a same-sex oriented person and if so, what was that experience like for you?
5. Consider a time during your ministry when you were aware that a LGBT person attended, or was attending, your church? Think of a specific situation with them that could demonstrate what it was like for you to work with them.
6. How would you feel about a same-sex oriented person joining or serving in a leadership position within your congregation?
7. What else can you tell me about your experience of serving as a minister in the church of the Nazarene and connecting with or reaching out to homosexual individuals?
8. Describe your feelings about an individual being both homosexual and Christian?

In addition to the in-depth interview questions, I took notes during the interview noting and listed non-verbal expressions of the participant utilizing the Interview Summary Form (Appendix D). Following the interview, I used the Contact Summary Form (Appendix F) to capture reflections about the data as well as highlight salient themes that emerged from the interview (Bloomberg & Volpe, 2012; Hays & Singh, 2012). This provided an opportunity to memo my impressions, thoughts, reflections, and reactions to the interview. After completing these steps, the research team and I began analyzing the data.

Data Analysis

I used Moustakas' (1994) adaptation of van Kaam's (1959, 1966) Phenomenological Data Analysis to analyze the data. Moustakas (1994) modified and systematized van Kaam's phenomenological data analysis into a seven-step format. My research team members and I followed this protocol during data analysis. The research team was given a typed copy of the transcript for each interview; these transcripts comprised the raw data we analyzed. After reading the transcript, the research team listened to the audio interview while following the manuscript. We did this in order to gain an overall sense of the whole of the participant's experience of the phenomenon (Bloomberg & Volpe, 2012). From this, the research team identified broad domains and categories. Once we identified the salient themes, we will implemented Moustakas' (1994) seven-step protocol for data analysis. The following is a list and description of each of the seven-steps.

1. Horizontalization
   Identify non-repetitive, non-overlapping, significant statements in transcripts. I listed every significant statement relevant to the participant's experience and assigned them equal value (Creswell, 2012; Moustakas, 1994). The process of horizontalization allowed me to handle the data more efficiently (Hays & Singh, 2012).

2. Phenomenological Reduction
   Horizontal statements were reduced to invariant constituents. If a statement was necessary and sufficient to understand the experience, it was identified and labeled. Statements that lacked significance or lacked relevance were eliminated. The remaining relevant statements were the invariant constituents of the experience (Moustakas, 1994).

3. Analysis and Clustering into Themes
   Invariant constituents were analyzed and clustered to create textural descriptions for each participant's experience, viz., the core themes of experience.

4. Final Identification of Invariant Constituents: Validation
   The invariant constituents, i.e., significant statements and themes, were cross-checked and validated against the complete record of

the participant's transcript. If they were explicit or compatible with the participant's experience, invariant constituents were retained. If they were not explicit, compatible, or relevant they were discarded (Hays & Singh, 2012).

5. Construction of Individual Textural Descriptions
Utilizing the relevant and validated invariant constituents and themes I developed a textural description (the *what*) (Creswell, 2007) of each participant's experience of the phenomenon investigated. Excerpts of verbatim descriptions were included to describe the essence of participants' experience (Moustakas, 1994).

6. Construction of Individual Structural Descriptions
I constructed an individual structural description of *how* the phenomenon was experienced by each participant within the participant's setting and context (Creswell, 2007). The structural description is derived from multiple potential meanings found in the textural description. The research team and I investigated all possible meanings, considered divergent possibilities, and various perspectives or frames of reference about the phenomenon (Moustakas, 1994).

7. Construction of Composite Textural-Structural Descriptions
Drawing on the textural and structural descriptions of the participants, I constructed a composite description of the essential essence of the experience. This unified description presented the essence or invariant structure of the phenomenon describing the participants' collective experience of the phenomenon (Bloomberg & Volpe, 2012; Creswell, 2007; Hays & Singh, 2012; Moustakas, 1994). According to Polkinghorne (1989), this helps the reader understand what it is like to have the experience.

Utilizing these seven-steps of data analysis helped to ensure the rigor of this study. In addition, the following strategies for trustworthiness were also applied.

Verification Methods: Strategies for Trustworthiness

Strategies for trustworthiness in qualitative research are roughly equivalent to reliability, validity, and generalizability in quantitative research (Hays & Singh, 2012). Rossman and Rallis (2003) suggest that a trustworthy study is defined by how competently and ethically the study is conducted. In qualitative research, the investigator must control for potential biases that may contaminate the "design, implementation and analysis" and unduly influence the study's results (Bloomberg & Volpe, 2012, p. 125). In the sections that follow, I address each of the elements of trustworthiness which Lincoln and Guba (1998) state include the following: credibility, dependability, confirmability, and transferability.

Credibility. Credibility is one of the major criteria used in qualitative research to determine if the findings make sense (Hays & Singh, 2012). Credibility refers to the "believability" of the study (Lincoln & Guba, 1985). Credibility indicates how well the researcher's findings are an accurate representation of the participants' experience of the phenomenon under investigation (Bloomberg & Volpe, 2012). This is similar to "internal validity" found in quantitative research. In order to achieve credibility in this study I utilized member checking, reflexive journaling, a research team, peer-debriefer, and an auditor.

To verify that each participant's voice was accurately represented, participants received a typed copy of their interview and asked to validate the accuracy of the transcript. I also provided each participant with a copy of my notes, impressions, and reflections from the interview to confirm that I accurately interpreted the participant's comments and meaning. Using bracketing and a reflexive journal I limited the ways my biases and assumptions may have influenced the interpretation of the data. The research team pointed out potential and/or hidden biases, sought to provide alternative explanations, and identified emerging themes within the data. The combined training, knowledge, and accountability provided by the research team members ensured a credible study.

Dependability. Dependability in qualitative research is similar to reliability in quantitative research. Reliability indicates the extent to which the results of a study can be replicated in similar studies. However, qualitative research does not usually contain the scope of subjects of quantitative research (Bloomberg & Volpe, 2012); therefore, the emphasis in qualitative methodology is on dependability. According to Lincoln and Guba (1985), qualitative researchers are more concerned with how well the findings are consistent and dependable with the data collected and that "research team members agree with the study's findings" (Hays & Singh, 2012, p. 201). In order to guarantee dependable results I utilized inter-rater reliability by inviting my research team to review and code several interview transcripts. Our goal was consensus in the interpretation of the data and "transparency of method" for data analysis and interpretation (Bloomberg & Volpe, 2012; Merriam & Associates, 2002).

Confirmability. In qualitative research, confirmability is most closely associated with objectivity and neutrality (Bloomberg & Volpe, 2012). This means the investigator's biases and assumptions did not interfere or impinge upon the results of the study (Hays & Singh, 2012) and the findings represent a true reflection of the participants' experience of the phenomenon (Lincoln & Guba, 1985). The research team assisted with consensus coding and data triangulation. Additionally, I developed codebooks (provisional and final) and kept a reflexive journal with memos, impressions, and reflections. Throughout this research, I maintained a comprehensive audit trail and submitted it to the auditor for ongoing examination. The audit trail allowed the auditor, and others, to follow the study's progression and determine that the findings of the study were accurate and confirmable (Bloomberg & Volpe, 2012).

Transferability. Transferability in qualitative research is roughly equivalent to external validity in quantitative research; in other words, how well do the results "generalize" to the larger population (Hays & Singh, 2012). While generalizability is one of the goals of quantitative studies, it is not the goal of qualitative research (Bloomberg & Volpe, 2012). The goal of qualitative research is to help the reader determine the extent to which the results of the study will transfer to the reader's context and setting (Hays & Singh, 2012). Qualitative researcher Patton (1990) discussed the concept of "context-bound extrapolations" (p. 491) wherein there is applicability of the findings to similar but not identical situations (p. 489). To accomplish this task I constructed thick, rich descriptions of the participants' context and experience of the phenomenon (Bloomberg & Volpe, 2012). This allows the reader to draw one's own conclusions about the results as well as determine the applicability of the findings to one's own context.

To summarize, credibility, dependability, confirmability, and transferability are similar to quantitative research paradigms of internal and external validity, reliability, and generalizability. Despite their similarity, however, their purpose is not precisely the same because qualitative research intends to communicate a different type of knowledge (Morrow, 2005). For this study, I implemented these strategies for trustworthiness to validate the accuracy of the findings as best described by the participants and the researcher (Creswell, 2007). Using these qualitative strategies ensured that the findings were credible (believable), dependable (consistent with the data), confirmable (objective and neutral), and transferable (applicable to other contexts) thereby resulting in a rigorous study.

ETHICAL CONSIDERATIONS

I considered several ethical issues as I embarked on this research. Due to the controversial nature of this study's topic and the relational network of Nazarene ministers throughout the denomination, I exercised extreme caution to protect participant confidentiality. To do this, I carefully disguised each participant's identity. All data—recordings, transcripts, memos, codes, codebook, analysis, audit trail, etc.—are stored securely using password protection and under lock-and-key. Each participant was advised on how his data would be stored. All participants were consulted about how their information was to be handled at the end of the study. As doctoral candidate and researcher, I upheld the ethical standards of practices of the American Counseling Association (ACA, 2014) and the Human Subjects Review Committee (HSRC).

I also employed the primary ethical principles outlined by Kitchener (1984) including, beneficence (do good), non-malfeasance (do no harm), autonomy (respect for others choices), fidelity (truthfulness), and justice (fairness). I provided each participant with an informed consent outlining the potential benefits and risks of their participation in the study. Each participant was free to choose whether to participate; moreover, if the participant initially agreed and later changed his mind, or decided to stop in the middle of the interview process, the participant's decision would have been honored and the participant was able to withdraw or stop the interview, although none did. If, at any point following the interview, the participant experienced psychological duress, I was prepared to make professional referrals for counseling services.

Summary

For this research project, I utilized a phenomenological qualitative research methodology.

The intent of this research was to arrive at the essential essence of the question, "What are the lived experiences of Nazarene clergy responses to homosexuality and their interactions with LGBT people?" Participants were selected using purposive sampling procedures. Snowball sampling was also implemented based on participant referrals of other potential candidates who fit the selection criteria.

As the investigator, I was the key instrument in accessing this information. I bracketed my assumptions and biases to represent accurately each participant's lived experience of the phenomenon. I analyzed the data using Moustakas (1994) modification of van Kaam's (1959, 1966) phenomenological data analysis method. Using horizontalization and creating textural, structural, and composite descriptions of the data, I sought to arrive at the essential meaning of the participants' experience.

In addition, I incorporated strategies to maintain objectivity and subjectivity and strategies for trustworthiness, each of which helped to ensure the rigor of the study. The goal for this research was to discover the essence of the lived experience of Nazarene clergy feelings about homosexuality and their interactions with same-sex oriented individuals within the context of their ministry. I hope the results of this study will be a catalyst for dialog between the two groups and build a bridge between the Nazarene church and the LGBT community.

CHAPTER III

Results

———————————

The purpose of this study and the research question it proposed to answer was "What are the lived experiences of Nazarene clergy responses to homosexuality and interactions with LGBT people?" In this chapter, I provide the results of my findings. I begin with demographic data and the participant profile summary. Next, I discuss the processes used to collect and analyze the data. I then transition to the themes that emerged from participant interviews; here, I provide a description of each of the seven dominant themes. These themes and their constituent elements are illustrated with verbatim quotes garnered from participants' transcripts. The results presented in this chapter help to answer the research question that guided this study.

DEMOGRAPHIC DATA

Thirteen Nazarene clergy participated in this study. Their ages ranged from 28 to 61 years old. All of the participants were Caucasian males. Twelve of the thirteen participants reported a heterosexual orientation; one participant reported a bisexual orientation. All the participants were married to women.

PARTICIPANT PROFILE SUMMARY

Each of the participants met this study's selection criteria. Participants were: (a) ordained by the Church of the Nazarene, (b) a graduate of Nazarene Theological Seminary and, (c) the senior/lead pastor of a Nazarene church. Participants held a master's degree—or higher—from Nazarene Theological Seminary. One participant had a Master's of Religious Education (M.R.E.), eight possessed a Master's of Divinity degree (M.Div.), four had earned a Doctor of ministry degree (D.Min.), and one was enrolled in a doctoral program at another university. The length of time participants had served in pastoral ministry ranged from 6 to 33 years. The length of time participants had served at their current church ranged from 3.5 to 18 years. Four participants reported a "conservative" theological orientation; eight declared a "moderate" theological orientation and, one participant affirmed a "liberal" theological orientation. Nine geographical locations were represented among participants including Maryland, Delaware, District of Columbia, Pennsylvania, Missouri, Kansas, California, Washington, and Idaho. Area locations of participant churches were as follows: three urban church settings, seven suburban area settings, and three rural locations.

All of the participants agreed to a 60–90 minute face-to-face, audio-recorded interview. I conducted these interviews at the church where the participant served as pastor in order to assist participant recall of conversations about homosexuality and/or interactions with LGBT individuals. Interviewing the participants at their local ministry context gave each participant greater access to their first-hand experiences of the phenomenon. All participants provided verbal and written consent (Appendix C) to have their results published under a pseudonym.

DATA ANALYSIS

Data for this study was collected during 60–90 minute face-to-face interviews utilizing seven semi-structured interview questions (Appendix E). The interview questions were designed to elicit thick, rich descriptions about participant's beliefs about homosexuality, and the participants' feelings and/or responses to LGBT people. Twelve of the thirteen participant interviews were conducted at the church where the participant was currently pastor. One of the participants was interviewed via Skype. All interviews were audio-recorded. No follow up interviews were necessary; however, member checks were conducted throughout the data analysis to ensure accuracy of the participants' statements.

I began analyzing the data by "bracketing" my personal bias, assumptions, and preconceived notions about the phenomenon (Creswell, 2007). This allowed me to view the participant's experiences from a "fresh perspective" as though I was hearing it for the first time (Moustakas, 1994). I enlisted the assistance of a research team that consisted of two doctoral students who were trained in qualitative research. We analyzed separate transcripts and collaborated in online meetings to develop a provisional codebook of 55 codes with operationalized definitions (Hays & Singh, 2012). In addition to my research team members, I recruited five doctoral students to assist in coding participant transcripts utilizing the provisional codebook. All of my coders were instructed to reflect on the codes and invited to add new codes where needed. My research team members and I met regularly to reach consensus on the codes and their definitions. We reviewed each code, added new codes where needed, and merged and collapsed codes that were redundant or overlapping.

Once the research team and I reached consensus on the codes and their definitions, I constructed the final codebook consisting of 47 codes. I then recoded all of the participant transcripts utilizing the finalized codebook to begin to identify larger meaning units and themes. From this I identified seven dominant themes and compared them to participant transcripts for accuracy. I consulted with my research team members to ensure that all codes were accurately reflected in the seven themes. Next, I e-mailed these seven dominant themes with their operational definitions to each participant as a final member check for accuracy. All thirteen participants returned their member check form verifying that their voice was represented among the dominant themes. I then created a case display for each participant illustrating the textural and structural descriptions for each of the seven dominant themes endorsed by the participants (Appendix G). After demonstrating supporting evidence for each dominant theme, I developed an essence of the phenomenon for each participant (Appendix G). Following this, I combined these individual essences into a composite essence of phenomenon of the lived experiences of Nazarene clergy responses to homosexuality and their interactions with LGBT people.

Throughout the data collection and analysis process, I maintained contact with my research team and peer-debriefer. They provided input to prevent bias and offered feedback about the research process including data collection, data analysis, and interpretations of the data. They were also instrumental in revising the codebook, collapsing and merging codes, and finalizing the dominant themes. I maintained regular contact with my auditor providing routine updates on the progress of my research including data collection, analysis, development of the codebook, and construction of the dominant themes. Working collaboratively with my research team members, peer-debriefer, and auditor ensured accountability and rigor.

I sought to maximize rigor by utilizing several strategies to build trustworthiness. Each of my primary research team members possessed a Ph.D. and were trained in qualitative research methodology. Data collection and analysis occurred simultaneously. With the assistance of the research team, data analysis was triangulated, and rich, thick descriptions were developed. I maintained a reflexive journal, memos, field notes, codebooks, and other documentation to provide a comprehensive audit trail. To ensure sampling adequacy, I interviewed thirteen participants all of whom met the research criteria. I employed regular participant checks for accuracy and to demonstrate that each participant's voice was heard (Hays & Singh, 2012). Member checking occurred at three separate points during data collection and analysis. First, each member received a copy of his transcribed interview transcript. Members reviewed the interview transcript to check for accuracy of the transcription. Second, after the primary researcher and a secondary coder had coded each member's transcript, members were asked to review the coded transcript in order to ensure the accuracy of their voice and experience. A third member check was conducted following the finalization of the codebook and the dominant themes.

Participants were given a list of dominant themes with the operational description of each theme. Members were asked to answer "yes" or "no" regarding whether the theme accurately represented their experience of the phenomenon. At each of the three member checks, each participant affirmed that the data analysis accurately represented his voice and experience. Throughout the research process, I maintained the highest ethical standards established by the American Counseling Association (2014), the Human Subjects Review Committee (HSRC) and Kitchener's ethical principles (1984).

THEMES

In an effort to elicit rich, thick descriptions and to capture the essence of Nazarene clergy responses, I identified seven dominant themes during the data analysis. In the sections that follow, I present each overarching theme drawing on direct quotes from participant interviews. The purpose is threefold: to illustrate the richness of the data, to capture the individual essence of each participant (Appendix G) and to reflect accurately the voices of the participants. Following the presentation of themes, I describe the composite essence that emerged from the collective experience of all participants.

Theme One: The Church of the Nazarene: Denominational and Individual Responses to Homosexuality

The theme refers to the participant's understanding of the Church of the Nazarene's denominational position, and its constituency's response to homosexuality. Whether he agrees or disagrees with the denomination's stance, the participant discusses his feelings about the church's position. As the lead/senior pastor, the participant talked about the cultural climate of the church and the counter-cultural nature of the Nazarene church's position. Some participants discussed perceived shifts in thinking and understanding within the church regarding homosexuality and LGBT concerns. Generational and age related differences were also addressed. Some participants referred to mainline and other denominations responses to homosexuality.

Nazarene position on homosexuality. One of the salient points of this theme is the diversity of opinion among Nazarene clergy regarding the Nazarene church's official position on homosexuality. Nazarene clergy opinions varied widely. Clergy statements ranged from agreement to disagreement, supportive to critical. To illustrate this, participants made the following observations. Matt stated: "The *Manual* position is under review. Its position on homosexuality is solid" (line 35). Kendall commented, "[T]here's been within the position some room for both a gracious and loving response and movement toward this portion of our population as well as a strong support of biblical material and biblical world view" (lines 37–40). Darrell made the following observation, "I think obviously the church's position as a whole is we're concerned about the theological statement and balancing grace with truth. I feel like the statement that the church has made about it specifically tries to balance those" (lines 62–65).

Continuing, Darrell commented,

> I think the church consistently says we understand homosexuality is not part of God's ideal. I think we stand behind that standard and believe in that (948–949). I think the statement of the church is saying we don't affirm this as a Godly lifestyle (lines 954–955).

Harrison observed,

> Fundamentally, as I understand church history, church tradition, [and] biblical teaching, homosexual practice is considered sinful in the scriptures at a point in which the Church of the Nazarene identifies homosexual practice as sinful. I'm in agreement with that (lines 76–79).

While some of the participants focused on the *Manual* statement about homosexuality, some included comments about the church's position papers. The *Pastoral Perspectives* documents, released by the board of General Superintendents, were intended to help pastors "better understand ministry among individuals and families dealing with homosexuality" (Diehl et al., n.d., p. 2). Allen had reviewed both the *Manual* statement and the position papers and remarked:

> I did lot of research that looked at our *Manual* statement, and I took our two Board of General Superintendents position papers; both of those [*Pastoral Perspectives*] and I read them. And I was

very proud of the statements because while condemning the practice of homosexuality, they were very open towards gay people (lines 57–62).

Also commenting on the *Manual* statement and the position papers, Kendall observed, "I think that the position and the statements have, for the most part, from what I'm remembering of them now, represented a value of holiness and love that is healthy and hopeful" (lines 14–16).

Referring specifically to the *Pastoral Perspectives* document, Bradley observed, "I think the document is very well written. I think it helps those in the denomination who may be homophobic or tend to want to push away from people who have homosexual tendencies" (lines 30–33).

Continuing, Bradley said that the *Pastoral Perspectives* helps "those who need a well-thought out position for the church because just the *Manual* statement is way too...too short and so, we needed something a little more involved" (lines 69–72).

Allen remarked that the "position papers take our official *Manual* stance and explain it pragmatically" (lines 74–75). Matt suggested that some of the language needs revision: "[T]he *Pastoral Perspectives* document could easily be given out to even our congregants if the wording was changed, such as 'homosexual.' They're using some antiquated language (lines 75–78). It needs some work linguistic-wise" (line 31).

The aforementioned participants agreed with, and supported, the *Manual* statement on homosexuality. These participants also endorsed the *Pastoral Perspectives* documents. Some of the participants, however, were less supportive of the *Manual* statement and the Nazarene church's position on homosexuality. For instance, Keith made the following observations:

I'm thinking specifically [about] how aggressive our *Manual* statement seems to be; I find that troubling (lines 39–40). No matter how you think about homosexuality where, if you're going to use the label "sin" or "brokenness" or "less than what God desires for us," I don't really feel like where we are right now is commensurate with a gracious attitude toward them, institutionally speaking (lines 69–72). The last time I read [the *Manual* statement], it seemed particularly poignant when related to other behaviors that the church deems as sinful" (lines 105–106). I feel like some of this is we're afraid of losing some sort of battle here and that's why the language seems to be more incendiary than perhaps is necessary to articulate the same thing (lines 110–113).

Harold presented similar concerns:

There's a statement in regards to those who teach the idea that homosexuality and Christianity are compatible, the idea that we deplore any teaching that indicates that. That word "deplore," I just thought wow, can you get any stronger than that? It seemed like a very firm way of saying, "Issue's closed. There's no room for dialogue here." (lines 197–203).

Harold also said,

The way the issue is framed in the Church of the Nazarene is, to use the phrase, "we deplore any teaching." It's like, "Yeah, could you slam the door any tighter on that?" to even a conversation about it (lines 527–530). I think that the language is the most disturbing part to me. I understand most denominations have an anti-homosexual stance, but to slam the door on conversation I think really, really hurts us (1064–1066).

Two more participants shared similar thoughts about the Nazarene church's position on homosexuality. Travis offered the following insights:

Well, I meant to look up this morning what the current *Manual* statement is. You know, I think it says something like uses phrases like while we recognize the depth of the perversion, right? So I thought to myself as we headed towards Assembly like surely somebody's going to bring out a rewrite and say some sentences that are a little more gracious than that (lines 41–46). So you know, the way that it's worded is rather antagonistic, ungracious and we probably don't use similar language to describe other issues that we feel like are scripturally important in terms of human conduct, right? We probably don't use language that's as strong in quite a few other areas. In fact, there's no sin in the *Manual* that describes it with the words depth and perversion, right? Nothing else. So we do special treatment for that one (lines 50–56).

Curtis commented:

[When] you read the [*Manual*] statement on homosexuality, it sounds like we're breathing fire. I mean it just really sounds like we're breathing fire (lines 258–260). The more I think about that, the more that really is true. Before the [*Pastoral Perspectives*] letter came out, just going on the *Manual* statement, there was a pretty big gap because the *Manual* statement is really harsh, it needs to be rewritten (lines 267–269).

One participant shared his opinion about a "white paper" on homosexuality that was published by the denomination. Harrison declared,

I've run head on into the fear mongering...I've run head on into [the] official publication of this most recent white paper that was posted for a period of time that was just—I'm just going to say it exactly as I feel it, it was nothing more than a Fox News right-wing response that just went down the line of gay bashing. A lot of us complained and I think it was finally taken down, but it was out there. It had been out there and downloaded by enough people that it had created the crisis that was absolutely and completely unnecessary (lines 507–515). We didn't give any opportunity by the statement we posted on homosexuality. We just actually said, "We don't love you" (lines 524–525).

Denominational leadership's response to homosexuality and LGBT people. Several of the participants commented regarding their impressions of how denominational leadership, viz., general superintendents, and district superintendents respond to homosexuality and to LGBT persons. There is considerable variation among participants about how denominational leaders respond. Commenting on an experience several years earlier at one of the denomination's quadrennial General Assemblies, Kendall shared the following:

> Probably four General Assemblies ago, I heard a message from one of our General Superintendents that—I think it was Romans 1. Was it Romans 1 or 2 where these issues are addressed? I felt like he kind of drew homosexuality out from the list of sinful behaviors that's listed there in a way that was unfair and kind of unnecessary. That was the one time that I felt like it wasn't written down as Nazarene polity. I walked out of that room that day feeling like I didn't agree at all with what one of my leaders had just said because he just kind of hammered on it, just kind of really… and I just felt like it was more of a political response in that time (lines 43–53).

Kendall continued,

> The sermon that I heard from the General Superintendent, I guess I partly just chalked it up to kind of an over-conservatism that was just, again, trying to give some clarity in terms of leadership to a denomination that maybe some people really needed. I just, again, felt like he went overboard (lines 98–101). I felt like he was just—at least in that Romans passage, as I recall it now, it's in a category, it's in a list of sins, and I just felt like it was kind of let's pull that one out, let's lift it up and let's just shoot at it for 30 minutes (lines 309–311).

Some of the participants indicated that the general superintendents understand the complexity of the issue and attempt to respond accordingly. Curtis said: "Our perspective and our general superintendents' perspective has the potential I think to be very, very welcoming and loving to say you know what, this is what we think, but we still love you (lines 176–178).

Harold talked about a conversation that transpired between his general superintendent and a lesbian who attended the participant's church.

The woman invited Harold to sit in on the conversation. Harold shared the following:

> I had an interesting conversation with _____ _____ a couple of years ago; he was the presiding GS at our district assembly. The reason I had a conversation with him about this issue was there's a woman in my church—she's a _____ grad. Her parents were Nazarene _____, [she] grew up in _____ on the mission field. _____ _____ was one of the missionaries assigned with her parents and so she refers to him as uncle _____. He's like family to her and they went through a lot of things together, those families, and so they've stayed in contact over the years. When Dr. _____ came out to preside over a district assembly, she sent him an email and said, "I'd like to meet with you." They had coffee. She invited me to come along as her pastor. She told me that she was going to come out of the closet to him and so she did. That conversation was very interesting because, again, here is a general superintendent of the Church of the Nazarene having to deal on a pastoral level with her as a human being yet still hold fast to the denominational stance. It was really interesting to watch (lines 252–266).

Following that meeting, the general superintendent met with Harold and gave him instructions concerning what is and what is not acceptable for a Nazarene clergyperson regarding the church's position on homosexuality and how to respond to LGBT individuals. Harold said,

> [The GS's] position was the corporate conscience of the Church of the Nazarene has spoken on this issue and whether I agree with it or not really doesn't matter. He gave me parameters then at that point to say what I could and couldn't do. He said I wasn't allowed to officiate gay marriages; I was allowed to attend them, and I could pray at one if I wanted. He also said that I was not to refuse the sacraments to anyone who is gay. He said if I got any pushback on that I could email him directly and that he would take that (lines 272–280).

Commenting further, Harold said,

> I really agree with _____ _____ and I respected the way he sort of
> framed the issue in saying there's a corporate conscience, whether
> or not we agree with it or disagree with it that we abide by it.
> That's part of what ordination is saying, Hey, I may not agree with
> all of this, but this is who we are (lines 505–508).

District superintendents' responses to homosexuality and LGBT issues also vary. Harrison, whose role encompasses both pastoral ministry
and assisting with district leadership responsibilities, commented about
his colleagues and his district superintendent,

> I have this little enclave here on the _____ district with the dis-
> trict superintendent and with other pastors who are like-minded.
> We're trying to carve out something that speaks in a more bal-
> anced way, but we're fighting against higher ups that just simply
> don't want us to stake out this middle ground (lines 322–325).

Travis has an LGBT couple attending his church. The couple had
asked if he would baptize them. Travis was unsure how to respond to the
couple's request. He contacted his district superintendent for clarification. Travis shared the conversation:

> I called _____ _____ [the district superintendent] and said, "Hey
> I don't know that I'm comfortable with this—from what I under-
> stand my ordination vows to be—but do you think I'm even within
> the bounds of my ordination vows if I baptized someone who's a
> practicing homosexual, you know, sexually active?" He goes, "I
> don't know," if I recall his response right. "Man, good question."
> [I asked,] "So what would the Board of General Superintendents
> say?" I was like, "Somebody going to pull my ordination if I did
> something? Not even saying that I would, not even saying that
> I think I'm within the bounds but what would they think?" He
> says, "I think that would depend on which General you had sit-
> ting in front of you" (lines 840–850).

Blake revealed that his oldest son is gay, and his middle son is wrestling with his sexual identity. As a minister in the Church of the Nazarene with a gay child, Blake often feels isolated and alone. Blake's district superintendent has been understanding:

> I know in my case my oldest son is gay, my middle son is really struggling with his identity. For me, I have nowhere to go with this. I didn't know where to turn. So if I have thoughts or feelings, it was the loneliest place to be—still is. I fortunately have a district superintendent that I've been able to share this with who is sympathetic (lines 61–65).

Bradley indicated that sometimes it is easier not to talk about homosexuality than it is to deal with it. Bradley shared a conversation he had with a district superintendent who avoided discussing an LGBT person seeking ordination. Bradley commented,

> I talked with a district superintendent who told me they ordained somebody who he knew was a lesbian, but they just didn't bring it up. Yeah [it was easier] than for that person to say, "Hey, I'm lesbian and you're going to ordain me, okay?" That just didn't come up, even though some knew. So, it's like we—we just don't want to talk about it, don't want to deal with it, don't know how to handle it (lines 632–640).

Harold remarked that he believes his congregation is ready to dialog about homosexuality and LGBT issues, but he expressed concern about how his district leadership would respond.

> I think we're ready to talk about it here. I think it could become divisive, but I think we're ready to talk about it. Whether the district is ready to talk about it, whether the district would crap a brick if they knew that we were doing that in Sunday school class, That's a whole other thing, but…But I don't think I can do it. We have a tenuous relationship with the district as it is, and I think that it would give them good reason to come down kind of hard

on us (lines 804–813). I wouldn't mind having a conversation on a Sunday morning, but yeah, I would fear for my job (829–830).

Local church board and parishioners' response to homosexuality. Another important aspect of this theme is the participant's views about how their own parishioners and church board might respond to LGBT individuals and/or homosexuality concerns. Some participants spoke specifically about their own congregation, while other participant's reflections referred to conservative Nazarenes in general. One Sunday, while worshiping at another church, Allen observed a transgender individual leaving the worship service. Allen reflected on how the individual would be received at his church:

I thought about how I saw this individual integrated in the life of community, of that church, I began to question how would this individual would have been received in my church? And I talked openly with some people about it and [they] said candidly she or he wouldn't…be accepted. And I could have seen scenarios where people would have had rude things to say and just generally made that person not welcome. And, you know what? As I talk to the leadership—I'm not very proud of that. I've got to come to this place where hopefully my church and someone who might come here searching for…and you can fill on the blank…would not be able to find Christ here because of this condition in their life (lines 303–315).

Bradley made a similar observation about his constituency:

To be honest with you, I'm not sure how welcoming this current church would be [toward] someone like _____. I think it would be okay, but I don't think they would be as welcoming as I would want them to be. I do think that we're fairly open to allowing people to be part of our group. Even, we'll let just about anybody read scripture who wants to read scripture, children, teenagers, [even those] who don't profess faith. I'm not trying to judge them but I'm just making an observation. Maybe they're still doing drugs or whatever, but if they're willing to read scripture and they'd like to, we let them. So, theoretically, to have someone who's part of my church and they're gay and to have them read the scripture and that might bristle some people. This church is probably not as accepting as I would like for us to be. And so, you hope that you're communicating that by what you say but also how you live and that it would rub off on people with, you know, but some people are pretty stuck. But the more people have family members that are struggling in that area, the less they struggle with others in other settings (lines 422–437).

Harrison referenced a Nazarene church, planted in an urban location to minister specifically to the LGBT community. Harrison provided the following information about the church:

We have a church on this district that is specifically planted to minister to the LGBT community and they're doing some really incredible work, but everybody has attacked them for giving in to the liberals. They haven't done that. They're actually sharing the gospel the way in which I've been talking about it and sharing about orientation is not sinful, it's the choices we make in our lifestyles. They're doing really good work. I guess what makes me mad about that is, really good work is being treated as if it's unholy (lines 372–380).

One participant, whose church reaches out to the LGBT community, shared about how a local Nazarene church responded to ministering to gay and lesbian individuals. Matt commented, "When we announced this [LGBT] ministry to the congregation in _____, we subsequently lost 70% of our congregation. That was something they did not want to have a part of (lines 470–472). Matt talked about how a group called "Concerned Nazarenes" reacted to the LGBT ministry. Matt said,

So there's a group called the Concerned Nazarenes and in a matter of about 24 hours they released…a whole blog post—I mean, literally we went to bed on a Tuesday night there was one blog post, just basically hate speech about us. By Thursday morning there were over 60 or 70 blog posts about us on different websites about how horrible we were (lines 514–523).

Discussing his own congregation, Harold talked about the inclusive nature of his church and his congregants. Harold said,

> Our congregation [is]…a very welcoming community. However, there's a real split in terms of the way they think about [homosexuality] in its ethical terms. Some are very progressive and see a real compatibility between Christianity and a homosexual lifestyle, others do not, and it's a very clear sort of understanding to them lines (368–379).

Harold went on to say that there were those among his congregants who left because of the ethical divide that exist between faith and practice. Harold shared,

> I had a family this week tell me they were leaving over the fact that we allowed too much influence from—that we didn't take a hard enough stand against homosexual behavior. They felt like we were welcoming, but let's get them to change (lines 457–460). I feel as if this couple that's leaving, in some ways, it's not fair to them because the rules are changing for them. You know what I'm saying? I think they came with an understanding, and they've been in this church for a long time—I mean, for our church's standards, a long time, ten years; our church is 11 years old. So they've been here for a long time; they're one of our oldest members in terms of time being around. When they came it was a very conservative place and then it changed and became much more progressive and much more open, and it evolved (lines 476–484).

Darrell discussed some of the conversations he has had with people in his church on the topic of homosexuality:

> There've been a few individuals just in conversation about it who tend to be condemning as a whole. I generally find people who

have that kind of position don't necessarily have any interaction with anybody who is gay or lesbian. It tends to be I think the whole thing is an abomination" or "I think it's just despicable." It tends to be much more judgmental, if you would, as whole, but it doesn't deal with the individual necessarily. That's probably the biggest issue, people talk in generalities of a lifestyle rather than the people who may be in that lifestyle, or dealing individually with people that they may not even know in our church family who are in that lifestyle, or struggling with that lifestyle, or trying to figure out what their place is, people who have family members. That's the biggest issue. It's probably just individuals who have extremes, or people who tend to be kind of judgmental by nature, "We have to stand up for truth and condemn what needs to be condemned" type of thing. That's probably the biggest issue (lines 188–204).

Blake talked about his struggle as a Nazarene clergyman, when his oldest son told him he was gay. Blake revealed his uncertainty about whether having a gay son would affect his position at the church:

When my son came out and said he was gay, I went to the church board and said, "Do I need to resign?" Not everybody knew the whole situation then, but I went to them, and I said, "I guess I just need to know where I stand because if I need to leave, the last thing I want to do is hurt this church." There are people who think that the weakness of my kids has hurt the church. I've been told that. The reason some families are not here is because of the actions of my kids. Okay, then maybe it's time I go. I'll wrestle with that. I worked through that, and I didn't go, I stayed, and the board was affirming to say, "You need to stay." I've had opportunities to go, and I chose to stay, but there are times when leaving sounds really appealing, just to get away from the stigma, only to realize that I would still take it with me—more than likely (lines 747–750).

Curtis spoke in general terms about what he has heard and observed from Nazarene laypeople:

People who are part of the Church of the Nazarene and would identify themselves as Nazarenes, have said things either to me or I've seen them in conversations saying things about gay people, I've seen them use "gay" as a derogative, that kind of thing (lines 193–196).

Curtis shared a story about his previous church:

I had a bank robber in my last church. Everybody liked him. But if a gay person had shown up that probably would've been a problem for them. I kind of want to go, "Okay…he willfully did something, and this guy just has an orientation he can't control, how is this worse than that?" (lines 730–733).

Travis also shared a story about the way one Nazarene church responded to LGBT persons in the church. Travis said, "I know a Nazarene church to the northeast of us who if a homosexual left the sanctuary to go the bathroom, the ushers were instructed to follow them to the bathroom to make sure they did not molest any children" (lines 410–416). Talking about the church he pastors, Travis spoke affirmatively about the way his church board has responded to discussions about homosexuality and LGBT people:

I'm really proud of our church board because they have been compassionate and thoughtful, utterly unbigoted while holding true to what they believe is the teaching of the scripture. I mean they've been utterly compassionate and considerate as they wrestle through that issue. I'm very impressed with them. There hasn't been an ignorant word among them. Not an ignorant word (lines 745–753).

Nevertheless, Travis acknowledged that his church board wants to maintain the position of the Church of the Nazarene, uphold biblical proscriptions about homosexuality, while demonstrating love and inclusion to LGBT individuals. Referring to his church board, Travis stated:

Their desire is to keep the door open for people to come to know and follow Jesus. And at the same time, their concern is to not

give the impression that the Church of the Nazarene is an affirming church in terms of gay marriage and gay sexuality. Well, not
even sexuality but gay practice (lines 958–962).

So their concern is to delineate between how do we love these
people and include them in the community of faith so that they
can experience everything you want someone to experience in a
community of faith. They do not want to communicate that we
think that homosexual conduct is biblically neutral or okay. They
don't want to communicate that. They want to stand firm that
they believe that the scriptures indicate that it's not okay (lines
974–980).

Matt offered the following observation about the way the church typically responds to LGBT people: "The church has been really bad about
saying, 'We love you,' especially 'love the sinner, hate the sin' language.
We like to say, 'We love you, but keep your distance'" (lines 208–210). As
the pastor of an LGBT inclusive church, Matt commented:

I see Bob, Suzie, and Mary come through the door. I don't see gay,
lesbian, transgender come through the door. I think the problem
with the church is that's what we see. We see he's gay, she's a lesbian, she's transgender; you got to watch out…The church has
got to do a better job with all people, groups, becoming a loving
presence (lines 260–265).

Matt continued by saying, "the church tends to write people off because of their sexual sin" (line 276).

**Participants' feelings/thoughts about Nazarene position on homo-
sexuality.** Another significant aspect of this theme is the participants'
thoughts and feelings about the Nazarene church's position on position
on homosexuality. What follows are statements that reveal participants'
affective responses and reflections about the Church of the Nazarene's denominational stance about homosexuality. As illustrated in the previous
section, Nazarene pastors' feelings and thoughts vary considerably along a
continuum of "comfortable" to "disgusted" as well as points in between.

Regarding his feelings about the Nazarene position on homosexuality, Bradley commented, "I guess if the question is how comfortable [am I], where I am with the Church of the Nazarene's stance, I would say mostly comfortable" (lines 36–36). Kendall expressed similar feelings:

> The overall tone in terms of what I feel like, [what] I've under-stood anyway the Church of the Nazarene's position to be, I've been comfortable with, and I feel like it's given a helpful place from which to move as a minister in the church in terms of relat-ing to others (lines 24–27).

Echoing Kendall's feelings, Curtis commented that he too felt comfortable with the church's position on homosexuality. Curtis observed, "I think I'm reasonably comfortable with the official position, if you talk about the [*Pastoral Perspectives*] letter from the General Superintendents that went out about that issue" (lines 32–34). Regarding the *Manual* statement Curtis said, "I think I'm pretty comfortable with it" (line 36). Preston expressed a similar view about the church's position. Preston said, "I'm very much at peace with it feeling like it's the biblical approach" (line 27). Blake also shared his feelings about the church's position: "I think that we have taken an appropriate stance on the practice of homosexual-ity. I think our weakness has been in our ability to communicate that in a redemptive way" (23–26).

Some of the participants discussed how well-balanced they believe the Church of the Nazarene's position to be. For example, Derek observed:

> I feel like we have a very solid base, kind of a balance between calling right, right and wrong, wrong, but also having a love for the individual who might be caught up in that. That's our biggest challenge, I think, as a church is not to judge, people will often hear that, but it's to express the love of God and acceptance of the person not their sin. That is quite challenging in our day and age, but in the loving of the person, we cannot compromise the word of God. So I feel like it's a pretty good balance that we have (lines 43–49).

Resonating with Derek's observation, Darrell also felt the church's position maintains an appropriate balance:

My general feeling about the church's position is that we're trying to balance what we believe to be true about theological, spiritual health, what we believe as sin, what is not sin and what is grace, and so, I think [we're] trying to find the balance between affirming the individual who might be in that lifestyle, but also recognizing maybe the concern biblically towards a biblical view. I feel like they're trying to strike a good balance. I think obviously the church's position as a whole is we're concerned about the theological statement and balancing grace with truth. I feel like the statement that the church has made about it specifically tries to balance those and I think they try to help the churches deal with it in a healthy way without being condemning but showing grace and also recognizing the standard of which we try to hold to as biblical believers and Christians (lines 44–55).

Likewise, Matt remarked, "I've been rather supportive of the church's position on the subject" (line 47); however, Matt admitted that was not always the case:

For me personally, yes, there have been times in my life when that has been in conflict considering I've had relationships with both men and women and obviously being in a relationship with a man and being a part of the Church of the Nazarene there's a bit of a conflict there. But like I said, my positions now, after a long process, are in line with the Church of the Nazarene (lines 90–94).

Travis expressed his thoughts about the denomination's position on homosexuality stating:

I don't have heartburn over the fact that we say, Hey look, to the best of our understanding, to the best of the knowledge we have in front of us at the moment, it seems like the historic stance of Christianity has always been to interpret the scriptures to say [homosexuality] is not God's intent for human life and flourishing. So I'm okay with that. Until we have additional information I'm okay with us saying this is our understanding of what the scriptures say. But then, on top of that, where do we go from there (lines 221–232).

Keith commented that he felt "troubled" by the Church of the Nazarene's position on homosexuality:

I would describe my feelings as "troubled." I would say that's the first word that comes to my mind. I'm thinking specifically of how aggressive our *Manual* statement seems to be; I find that troubling. That would be my first response. I think that the reality is that some of the pastors and churches I know do as well as they can at ministering to persons who are homosexual. But I think institutionally, I'm not comfortable with where we sit right now (lines 38–45).

Harold expressed similar feelings:

My feeling about the Church of the Nazarene's stance is that it's unfortunate. It's unfortunate because I think that at the last General Assembly I know there were some modifications made to the statement to make the language a little bit more firm and rigid. I think that's unfortunate because it's really closing off the possibility for conversation around the issue…There's not even room to say, "Hey, there are two ways to see this" (lines 189–194).

Continuing, Harold commented:

I'm not saying that I have it all figured out. I mean I have my own opinions certainly; but closing off the conversation is not the right direction to go with this, I think. That's my initial concern, I guess, in terms of the denomination's stance (lines 204–208).

Later Harold added:

I think in a healthy church you can say, "Look, you have your
opinion and I have my opinion. This isn't central to who we are
as a people, as a movement, this isn't a central issue to what we're
about and our mission and what we want to do. Can we agree
that you can have a position, and I can have a position and we
can respect each other and respectfully disagree on this particular
issue and move forward?" I don't see room for that, for respectful
disagreement (lines 527–537).

Harrison candidly declared his feelings about the Nazarene church's
position on homosexuality:

Just to say [it] directly, I'm disgusted by my church's feelings
about homosexual people. I think that our position theologically
is confused and unhelpful (lines 226–228). At any point in our
history when we were working with drunks and rescue missions
and pregnant teens who weren't married in the early days when
the church was really engaged in that, had we been as pejorative
towards those folks as we are towards homosexuals we would've
done no ministry. I think that my feelings are disgusted by that
(lines 236–241).

Keith spoke about how the church's position on homosexuality is a
barrier to LGBT people. Keith stated: "It doesn't take very much time on
the Internet to find out where the Church of the Nazarene stands in this
issue...And so, that's the barrier, I think, with very little doubt" (lines
558–560). Continuing Keith said, "...as long we have the 'Church of
the Nazarene' on the door, that's going to be a barrier to gay folk in our
neighborhood" (lines 594–595). Keith remarked,

But the Church of the Nazarene, all you have to do is read our
Manual and that's a big old "Don't come in here" sign. Obviously,
there are barriers here that we make, that we create in our institutional identity (lines 622–625)....I think you could paint with a

pretty broad brush and say the Church of the Nazarene, by virtue of what we say institutionally in our *Manual* about the homosexual community, has some pretty high walls for a gay person to want to have to jump over (lines 646–650)....There are persons in the Church of the Nazarene who are themselves obviously barriers to gay people. It's not just an institutional barrier, I get that (655–656).

Summing up, Keith observed, "The truth is that there isn't full acceptance of gay people in Church of the Nazarene because the Church of the Nazarene calls homosexuality a sin" (882–883).

Balancing the Nazarene position with pastoral ministry. Several participants addressed the tension they experience adhering to the denominational position on homosexuality and the practical application of it in pastoral ministry. Most of the participants agreed with the church's stance on homosexuality, but many struggled with how to maintain that position and minister effectively within the church and to LGBT people. Travis provided the following insights:

You know, one of the tensions that is reality for me and every single other Nazarene pastor who is trying to minister to a homosexual folk is that we have to navigate the tension of the possibility that our congregation or our town will think that we affirm homosexual practice as normative and non-sinful. I mean that is the reality every single one of the people that's ministering to homosexual people in the Nazarene church is dealing with (1650–1656).

If there's somebody that's not dealing with that, I would be shocked. You know, because it's one of the tensions. Like how do I minister to them without giving the impression that this is normative and accepted within the theology of the Church of the Nazarene. Right? Regardless of that pastor's particular feeling (1658–1662).

So even if they feel like it's morally neutral and fine, they are still navigating the tension. They know what the perception is. It's accurate that this is considered sinful in the Church of the

Nazarene's theology. So, how do I navigate this without giving, without stirring up a firestorm in my church or having my town— the town—say, "Wow!" gay is fine at the Nazarene Church; that's a gay church, they're cool with it (1669–1674).

Allen also commented on the tension he experiences, "You know, when everything about our denominational stand on this says this [homosexual] practice is sinful, there's a huge tension that I have. How do I respond to that?" (lines 782–784).

Commenting on the church's response to homosexuality, Harrison stated the following: I consider the church's response in practice to be anything but Godly. We pretend like gay people don't exist in our churches and, they're all some evil people sitting out there; when right underneath many of our noses are families with gay children, gay relatives and the incapacity or inability to either acknowledge that, accept that, be loving in spite of the challenges that might be faced by all of that (lines 118–123).

Blake acknowledged that not only do LGBT people exist in the Nazarene church some of them are family members of the clergy. Although Blake agreed with the Nazarene position, he finds it difficult to address it within the context of pastoral ministry. Blake said,

I don't have a problem with the church's position. I think I struggle a bit with how to articulate it, especially with as many people knowing now that I have a gay son and while that's not common knowledge, it's out there and people know. So I probably struggle more with how to address the issue without people thinking that I'm trying to placate it or say it's okay or we need to be more compassionate (lines 116–121).

Continuing his line of thought, Blake stated,

My discomfort's when I try to articulate to you a little bit is how do I navigate through it when I have somebody who's living very differently? I do struggle with that (lines 214–216). We're all kind of looking for some handles of how to communicate this or talk about it or even deal with it (232–233).

Harrison suggested it would be helpful if there were some denominational guidance about how to address the issue. Harrison said,

There are some intimations that some things are being written, but I haven't seen them yet, so I really don't know what—and things can be written. But what happens for the pastor at the local at the local church is a very different matter. How do I bring my people along?" (lines 290–293).

A more nuanced statement and the need for theological reflection. Some participants suggested the need for greater theological reflection and a more nuanced and balanced statement about homosexuality. Harrison observed, "I would have to say officially I think our position on homosexuality is an incomplete and unhelpful position. It is a subject that needs to be more carefully nuanced" (lines 242–244). Keith also felt that more theological reflection needs to done on the topic:

I think that the reality is that some of the pastors and churches I know do as well as they can at ministering to persons who are homosexual. But I think institutionally, I'm not comfortable with where we sit right now. That's my first response. That's the first thing that comes to my mind. I'd really love to see more work done in this area, institutionally (lines 43–48).

Referring to the *Manual* statement, Keith commented,

At the very least it [the *Manual* statement] would sound more gracious—at the very least. I think that further theological reflection needs to be done on this that would lead to even greater changes; that perhaps we will find ourselves in 100 years on the wrong side of history on this right now. What I foresee is potentially the ongoing divide that we find ideologically in our country is revealed in this denomination. And so, I think this particular issue could be one of those increasingly intense wedge issues that divides the church (lines 52–59).

Travis also felt that the *Manual* statement needs work; however, he addressed it with a more practical viewpoint in mind. Travis suggested,

What I think we need in the Church of Nazarene is some language in our *Manual* to at the least, sort of kick start the actual practices that engages the reality that people need ministry including gay people, and what does that look like (162–165).

Travis continued,

So what I think we need alongside our affirmation that this is what we understand the scriptures are saying, I think we need some language that talks about where do we go from here to minister to people who are homosexual or who are gay and married or whatever. I mean you know, because right now we have no language about that at all. Right now, the only thing we have language about is that this is a perversion. But that doesn't really give us a lot to go on in terms of you know, Are these people we try to minister to? Are these people we keep in the church? (lines 186–198).

Curtis shared similar thoughts:

I hope that we can get more of our theologians and folk associated with that working on this issue, processing it, talking to us. All I've got mostly is what I say, but there aren't a lot of Nazarenes out there really helping us think through this other than the crowd that wants to say, "Let's stone them" and they're not very helpful (lines 841–845).

Opportunities for dialog. While some of the participants argued for more theological reflection, others felt there needs to be more opportunities for dialog to openly discuss LGBT concerns. Blake felt that "The Church of the Nazarene could better address this, [by] maybe providing some element, a forum or help to pastors who are experiencing this or maybe some places where there's some confidentiality" (lines 76–79).

Harold observed that there is no room in the church for a conversation about homosexuality or LGBT concerns. Harold remarked, "I know that there are a lot of people that want a conversation around this and there's not room for one" (lines 211–212). Harrison shared a similar thought:

> I would love to be able to dialogue and to express my position more clearly. I do not believe that the church at this point, as heated as it is, has the capacity to listen to a moderating voice. I don't think it's possible. They haven't on any other hotbed issue like that, but that doesn't mean we stop trying to speak into it (lines 362–365).

Harold suggested that what the church is facing and doing with issues related to homosexuality and LGBT people is analogous to segregation during the 1950s. Harold said:

> [I]t goes back to that analogy, in 1954 in Mississippi, at what point do you say I don't want to pastor an all-white church? I at least want to be a part of a church that's going to have a conversation about what it means to be integrated and not say we're never going to integrate, [that] we deplore any conversation about integration (lines 1058–1062).

Darrell said what is needed is a healthy dialog in the context of the local church. Darrell commented,

> I think what's just overwhelming my mind is that the church needs to have the conversation. The church needs to dialogue about this. I think it's obviously a more growing cultural issue. I think there are some views of the church as condemning and intolerant. I think some of that is just overblown. I think some Christians have given the church kind of a bad name as far as what that means. So I think we need to have the conversation.

I'll just speak for my personal church here as the pastor, I think that those conversations need to happen in a place, in an atmosphere of grace but also in an atmosphere of truth and just trying to speak truth and really dialog about what that means. I think we're all a little afraid of it, honestly. I think we tend to be cut-and-dried with it. I think we're just kind of hesitant—I'm hesitant. How do I do that in a productive, healthy, meaningful way? (lines 1264–1280).

Blake provided similar insights:

I think that we have taken an appropriate stance on the practice of homosexuality. I think our weakness has been in our ability to communicate that in a redemptive way. We have, in effect, made some positions pretty clear, but we're a little bit fuzzy on how we communicate that at the local level as well as at a personal level and being able to keep the conversation going with people who may think differently or have different positions on that (lines 24–31).

Blake also said,

I agree with the position of the Church of the Nazarene as I understand it, as formulated by the General Superintendents of marriage between a man and a woman. But I think the practical out-workings of that have yet to be seen, how we dialog about it (lines 53–56).

Darrell shared a story about a Nazarene pastor who did attempt to provide a forum for dialog around LGBT concerns:

I think this conversation needs to happen within the church to deal with it. I know we've talked about it as church staff and with the other pastors on the staff about trying to provide an opportunity and a forum. There've been other churches that have attempted that but has not gone well. It's not been received in the right spirit by a lot of the folks who don't understand why you're having a conversation about it (lines 291–296).

I was thinking about a church specifically in _____ _____
who is dealing with a student leader, actually a point woman in
a Nazarene University who made the statement after one of its
student leaders on the campus came out and said he was gay.
There was a church that tried to have a forum to talk about the
issue with the students and the church that's connected to the
college—it didn't go well; it wasn't received in the right kind of
spirit (lines 300–305).

The pastor was simply trying to open the dialog and begin to
help people deal with the issue and help to articulate the church's
position and where we stand in it, but it got a lot of flack. There
was a lot of feedback on the negative side of why would you even
have a discussion about it (lines 307–310).

The people in the church, they were like, "Why do you need
to talk about it? It's wrong, it's a sin. You condemn it. That's what
we do, that's what the church is about." (lines 317–319).

It sort of blew up and it became more of a point of contention
than it was a point of conversation. It became a conflict rather
than "Hey, can we not talk about this?" A lot of the church said,
"No, there's nothing to talk about. "I mean it's wrong, we know
it's wrong, the Bible says it's wrong, and so you need to just tell
people it's wrong" (lines 326–331).

Denominational guidance for ministering to LGBT people. One participant felt that the denomination has not provided sufficient instruction
and guidance about how to minister to LGBT persons. Travis commented,

> We have really not said anything that I've come across that is in-
> structive in a way as far as how to minister to [LGBT people]. So
> it's sort of an argument from silence. You know, they've said this
> is a perversion with great depth that God can heal people from.
> But they haven't really said much more than that (lines 501–505).

Addressing cultural concerns: church and larger culture. Another significant aspect of this theme includes participant's descriptions of the culture of the Nazarene church and their local congregation. Participants

spoke of the church's religious subculture, conservatism, as well as references to conservative politics. Statements indicating the "counter-cultural" stance of the Church of the Nazarene regarding homosexuality are also included.

Derek stated that the Church of the Nazarene is a conservative denomination. Derek said, The Nazarene Church is very conservative. We live in a very liberal area and our church sometimes speaks to things that the Bible doesn't speak to when we build fences around items that we want to make sure we don't cross—and well-intentioned. Drinking some alcohol really does not send someone to hell, watching a movie—all these things, dancing. These things that are involved in a very conservative church are not always the position that I would hold as a pastor of a conservative church in a very liberal area (lines 125–133).

Kendall said he felt conflicted by the way the church has responded to the larger culture. Kendall provided the following comments:

My conflict has been when we've responded or reacted to the culture as opposed to leading the culture—as I recall, some of that *Pastoral Perspectives* letter I thought was trying to set a positive tone in the midst of kind of a cultural war or whatever.

I realize that's really hard to do, what I'm saying as a church, to always be out front and part of what we do is react perhaps to the things that we're observing around us. I know we can't do that always, but when it's been almost defensive or desperate reaction and like, "We've got to dig our heels in here or we're going to…" (lines 379–389).

While Darrell acknowledged the importance of the church's position, he too suggested that some Nazarenes' response to homosexuality is reactionary:

While I understand we need to have a statement and a stand, we do need to be a voice, as a church. I think it needs to be balanced

in that people just want to say, "Oh, you just need condemn it."
I think that's a reaction, if you would, to a culture that tends to
want to promote that [homosexuality] as okay and we just accept
it, go on with it. A lot of churches are going that way. So I think
there's a tension of trying to balance the other side and sometimes
it gets to an extreme maybe (lines 209–216).

Darrell continued,

I think there's such a wide range of opinion and I do think people
are—maybe some of the reactions of some folks that would, in a
negative sense, are reacting to a society that in some sense seems to
be pushing an agenda, wanting the church to be more accepting
than understand why it is that we would have a biblical standard
that would say we believe homosexuality is not a lifestyle in God's
view is his ideal for us. I think that's not something we've really
probably had and probably need to have a conversation about
(lines 693–699).

Like other participants, Travis understood the need for the church's
position; however, given the current culture, Travis wondered how the
church could better respond to LGBT people where they are in life and
relationships. Travis posed the following questions:

I'm okay with us saying it's our understanding that the scripture
says this is not something that God intends for human flourishing. However I think that given the context that we are in…As
Rob Bell recently said, we're in a cultural context were it's not a
question of, should that guy have been divorced three times? It's
the fact that he has, so where do we go from here?…I think we're
in the same kind of situation with homosexuality in our culture.
It's not a question of the best case scenario, it's more like, do we
think that this is what God intends for this particular person or
couple or whatever. It's the fact that okay we've got married homosexuals in our church. Where do we go from here with them?
Do we hang out a shingle that says no gays allowed? You know,

either literally or, for all intents-and-purposes by how we respond to them, or do we try to find ways to speak the gospel into their experiences? So, I agree that fidelity and faithfulness between the two of them is a better option than the gay bar scene. You know, the sexual promiscuity and no holds barred. So it's sort of a what's the best option that we have open to us right now (lines 108–138).

Blake also posed questions generally and to his parishioners. Blake queried,

I've asked people not if, but when a gay couple comes and sits down next to you in our church, what will you do? Because your love for God is measured by the one you love the least, in my opinion, and that day has come (lines 413–415). If they sit down next to you, how are you going to deal with that? Will you let them? I don't think we know how to deal with that yet (lines 512–515).

As the pastor of an suburban, upper-middle class Nazarene church, Harrison commented that while another Nazarene church may reach out to the LGBT community, his congregation would have difficultly ministering to LGBT people. Harrison said,

I strongly supported the work that our district is doing with one particular church to reach that [LGBT] community and to reach it in a very different way than say my congregation could do and I reluctantly have come to the conclusion that that might be the more effective means. I fear that a suburban congregation like mine, which is still % white suburban, upper-middle class or at least middle class is going to have a much more difficult time with that picture. But I've also not given up on trying to make sure that we minister (lines 912–918).

Curtis suggested that there is a difference between the theological position of the Church of the Nazarene and the religious subculture at work within it. Curtis observed:

What I see functioning in the Church of the Nazarene, I've always kind of divided as…the difference between our theology and our official position and our religious subculture. Our religious subculture gives me a great deal of pause because I think we've adopted way too much from probably conservative politics or something. But I see a lot of Nazarenes who are functionally anti-gay and that's a real problem for us theologically. Ultimately, we're called to love everybody. So I guess I have a mixed set of feelings about that (lines 36–45).

Curtis further explained his understanding of the religious subculture within the church:

My perception of the religious subculture is that if you were to ask them, "Are we supposed to love gay people?" they would probably say, "Yeah, we are, but…"

The "but" is the big thing because we're asking them—sometimes our position as the theologically conservative group is hard to hold together because on one hand we say we think the revelation of scripture is that this is not God's first choice for your life to be practicing a homosexual lifestyle. That being said, we are called to absolutely love you; and by "love" we mean Christian love, which means we will lay down our lives for you.

So it's not for us just a lip service of love, "Yeah, we love them, but…" and they get to the "but" and then we get the long explanation and the "but," but we are called to really—we are loving the LGBT community when they understand that we love them and that's a pretty high standard. That's not just "We love you, but…" That's we have so interacted with you and connected with you and worked with you that a gay person could look at me and say, "We disagree about this, but Pastor _____ really loves me. I know he loves me. I know he'd do anything for me. I know he is for me."

So for me, that's a big deal. I'm not comfortable with "Yeah, but…" kind of statements when it comes to love…the way people talk sometimes sounds right but is wrong functionally in that they say, "Yeah, we love them, but…" and then they want to tell them all the things that are wrong with what they do. That's not really loving someone (lines 61–90).

Some of the participants discussed their thoughts about ministering in a culture where LGBT relationships are accepted, and the church's position is counter-cultural. Participant's feelings varied from confusion to frustration.

Blake felt that the larger culture communicates homosexuality is an acceptable lifestyle, while the church is viewed as judgmental. Blake also said that the media's portrayal of gay relationships has created confusion for many people. Blake shared his thoughts:

I think the message being sent through the media and to our young people today is that it's all okay. We've moved to the side of sympathy and to open expression so far that to now make a decision differently or to give an opinion differently comes across as very judgmental, uncaring, and unsympathetic. The result of that then is, again, we kind of lose the platform on which to speak to it very well.

Part of that has crept in a "culture creep" is what I call it. The culture has crept into the Church to where now we don't know what we should stand on, let alone what we do stand on and so what was once called right is now called wrong and what was once called wrong is now called right. It's very confusing.

Our young people are hearing that. Even some of our middle-aged generation is coming into this and going, "Well, maybe it's not all bad."

Nine o'clock last night I see two men kissing on ABC. On a primetime network station you would never have seen that. It was a very passionate, long kiss. I shook my head, and I said five years ago, ten years ago, we would've joked about it, but we would never have gone, "Oh, that's okay, they're in a loving relationship, it's their right."

Now it's in my home and it's in all of our homes. It's the frog in the kettle scenario, I think. It's fostered confusion. This is such a big issue (261–283).

The Nazarene position as counter-cultural. Preston stated directly that the church's statement about homosexuality is a "counter-cultural" position. Preston remarked that as a counter-cultural position it can be misinterpreted by those outside the church:

I know it's a counter-cultural stance, but I have no problems with it at all. I feel like the church's position is not a—I think it's misinterpreted many times in terms of, I suppose the gay and lesbian community would see it as hate language and I always react against that. Because I think it's a message of love and I think my own ministry has demonstrated that, but that doesn't open the door to it being an acceptable way of life by biblical standards (27–34).

So when we're counter-cultural, we're up against that kind of a presupposition that for us to make a declaration that those acts are sinful acts it's interpreted as being hateful and that's not where we are, that's not the church's position (50–53).

In a similar vein, Harrison commented that the larger culture and the church tend to demonize those who oppose their viewpoint or position. Harrison remarked,

In a culture in which you demonize people you disagree with, and everyone is basically doing that right now—if you're on the left, you demonize the right; if you're on the right, you demonize the left; if you try to stake out a middle ground, you get it from both sides. I feel that that's essentially what's happening (lines 316–320).

Derek pastors a "conservative church" (594) in a "liberal area of the country" (61). He said he and his church are a "minority voice in the community" (61) struggling to make their voice heard. Derek said, "We are outvoted on everything, and the community is like, "Come on, won't you come along? Won't you become modern with us? This is the next century, when are you going to catch up?" (65–67). Derek continued:

We're a part of Chamber of Commerce. We go there and major statements are made opposed to what I personally believe and what our churches stand for and yet here we're standing like, "Okay, now how do we deal with this in a loving way when you are resoundingly outvoted, and your voice is stepped on and you express it through a letter, and it comes back rejected?"

It's very disappointing to see where society is going when you hold it up against the light of the word of God (lines 77–84).

Referring to the cultural war between the church and the larger culture, Kendall posed,

I don't think any of these people who are [reacting to the culture] are hate-filled or mean people. They love the church as well and this is what they think are ways that they can help be a prophetic voice in the church to keep us moving in a direction that obviously they don't want us to go (391–394).

Derek's daughter questioned him regarding the church's feelings about LGBT people. Derek recalled the following:

My daughter who's in college has a friend who's gay and finds out that she goes to church—this is in another city—but they said, "Church? Man, all Christians hate gays." My daughter called me and said, "Dad, that's the perception." I thought, "Well, that's too bad that that's the first impression they get: what we're against rather than what we're for."

I wish that culture would change, that there'd be a sense of loving acceptance of the person and without a change of what's right is right and wrong is wrong and dealing with all of that. I wish there was a little bit more of that, but I just sense there isn't but, we'll do our part to make sure that they feel that from our church in this community (lines 467–479).

Paradigm shift. Three participants intimated that a paradigm shift is slowly occurring in the church about the way in which homosexuality is addressed and LGBT people are received. Travis first spoke of the current attitude of Evangelicals in general and Nazarenes in particular regarding homosexuality and LGBT persons. Travis stated,

> My perception of the general attitude prevalent within evangelical-ism and Nazerenedom is no gays allowed, stay away from us and our kids. It's shifting but I think the prevalent attitude in, certainly in my lifetime, has generally been this is the ultimate abomina-tion like if you are gay you either quit, get saved, or get out of our church. You are going to be nowhere near our kids (lines 403–413).

While that mindset may be shifting, real change may be dependent on the views of the pastor and congregation. Curtis spoke about a conver-sation he had with an LGBT person attending his church:

> They had already identified themselves to me as someone who is homosexual and asked what we believed about that and what that would mean. This was a person that had grown up in an evan-gelical church so they like evangelical worship and they like the evangelical culture in general. I gave them my explanation that flows out of the General Superintendent's thing. I said, "You're absolutely welcome, we love you, you're a part of us," that whole piece of it (438–446).
>
> I said, there's a gap between our culture and where we're at, and there are all of these sorts of things and I think we're mov-ing the right way, we're moving slowly. I can tell you that in this church, in this place with me as pastor, this is the way it will be (lines 454–457).

Matt also commented on the paradigm shift he sees occurring in the church:

> We've got a bit of paradigm shift going on right now in the fact that we really are turning the corner into getting rid of the last bits

of "we need people to look like us." We are really at the point right now where that paradigm is shifting here. That is so far away from what I was taught growing up. I grew up in small town, rural _____ and there you had to look this way, this way and this way and if you could call yourself a Christian, everybody else could (686–703).

Generational and age related differences. Some of the paradigm shift may occur organically as teenagers and young adults move into positions of leadership within the local church and in the denomination. Several participants indicated that generational and age differences account for a change of perspective regarding homosexuality and LGBT people. Travis suggested that one of the differences is that members of the younger generation know people who are LGBT or have gay and lesbian friends. Travis commented,

The big difference between my son's generation and mine is that they have grown up with gay people. These are their best friends at school. These are their classmates, these are the parents of their friends. These are perhaps family members who have come out. So these are dearly loved human beings that they have relationships with. This is a completely different landscape than I grew up with in the Deep South where a kid would have killed himself before he admitted that he was gay (lines 517–524).

Harrison discussed the church's lack of understanding about generational and age related differences in how homosexuality issues are understood. Harrison provided the following:

What I think the Church also doesn't understand is that there is such a massive disconnect between—my son is 16, between his generation, and the people that are in their 20s, and the generation that are our age and older on this issue. Right before our eyes is this wide, wide gap of understanding on this issue.

I think everyone under the age of 30—no, that's a sweeping generalization. The majority of young people in the church under the age of 30 do not see an incompatibility between homosexual practice and Christian faith. The opposite is true for people who are approaching 50 and older, I think, would be how I would say that (lines 141–155).

Matt made a similar observation,

I will say our hardest demographic…are the ages between 30 and 50. That's our hardest, toughest crowd. It seems to be our most doubting crowd. When people go above 50, they tend to be more okay. And under 30? We got them. That's not a problem (460–468).

Harold agreed that the younger generation sees the issue of homosexuality differently than previous generations. Harold proposed,

Younger generations are beginning to see this issue in terms of the way a lot of people saw the civil rights movement in the 1960s that out of conscience there's going to be a lot of young adults who are going to choose not to attend [a Nazarene college] because they have an anti-gay stance. It'd be just like going to a university that is segregated. It'd be like, "Why would I endorse that?" (lines 1107–1111).

Harold continued,

I see, again, that denominations paint themselves in such a corner that it's going to be really hard to find their way out of that and save face. Meanwhile, again, because we have younger generations that are coming in that are just like, "Whatever, I don't get this whole gay thing. Why are they all worked up about…?" (lines 1121–1125).

Mainline and other denominations. Several participants recognized that although the Church of the Nazarene's position on homosexuality presents an obstacle for LGBT people there are other churches, denominations, and associations for whom sexual orientation or identity is not an issue. For example, Keith said, "There are enough welcoming and affirming churches which have made the issue of homosexuality very central to their identity where persons who want to be Christian and are gay [can] go to these churches (lines 709–712). Harold talked about a gay couple he met that "ended up landing at a Methodist church that was a bit more open" (760–761). Harold also remarked, "I know there are a couple of churches in _____ that put out a rainbow flag, Unitarian Universalist and what not" (856–857). Blake commented on one of the churches in his community saying, "We have a Unity church downtown, you can just be about anything you want to and attend there" (lines 558–559).

Travis discussed a Roman Catholic family he knows, whose son came out as gay. Travis shared the following:

> Intriguingly our Roman Catholic neighbors' kid came out. When they were told their response was just that they were just kind of worried about what kind of prejudice he might have to come up against in life. So you know, Roman Catholic but they weren't jumping to the you're going to hell, they weren't jumping to the you've got to stop immediately. They were just concerned what he was going to face in life (lines 1347–1353).

Matt admitted that even though he is a Nazarene pastor, if there are people who are uncomfortable with the Nazarene church he encourages them to attend a church where they will feel comfortable. Matt explained it thusly:

> Another thing we do here with LGBT individuals, with conservative individuals, if you come here and say, "I want to go to church, but this church ain't for me," we have other churches of other denominations that we will send you to.
>
> We have people who used to come here who go downtown to Church of the Resurrection because they have a better fit there. The goal is to bring people to Christ not to the Church of the Nazarene. So if you feel like you can build a stronger connection with Christ being at Church of the Resurrection, go for it.

I used to pick people up and take them down to the Church of the Resurrection and they felt comfortable going. I'm supposed to be making Christians not Nazarenes (lines 479–495).

Derek shared his experience as a Nazarene pastor who interacts with both evangelical and liberal pastor's associations. Derek observed,

There's a pastors' association that I deal with that's quite evangelical, and we all see pretty eye to eye on the biblical view of sexual orientation, and there's also a very, very liberal association of pastors who absolutely don't stand the way I stand on this issue. They do not take a biblical stance of it; they are more of what is popular in the community. They do not agree with me and of course, they think that if I could just read the scripture more thoroughly [I would] catch on (lines 267–272).

Some participants talked about people leaving mainline and other denominations because of softening their position on homosexuality. Some of these people have found their way into the Nazarene church because of the stance it takes on homosexuality. Blake shared the following:

Our mainline denominations who, in the words of many, they've "given in" or "caved in" to gay and lesbian clergy and/or same-sex marriages who come to our church and go, "What is your position on that?" "Why are you asking?" "Because we don't want to be a part of a church like the church we came from that has," in their opinion, "caved in on this" (lines 559–564).

Based on what he knew of the Episcopal Church, Darrel observed, "…in the Episcopal church, I think, homosexuality is not an issue. There are clergy that are homosexual, and they're ordained and that's not an issue" (831–837).

Preston stated that he has had people come to his church because of the Nazarene's position on homosexuality. These individuals felt that their church or denomination had softened its position on homosexuality, and they wanted to affiliate with a denomination that had not softened its position. Preston described it this way:

> Our church has gained—our local church here, and that I would guess it's been so other places too but—a handful of families who have come from so many mainline denominations who weakened their position on it, opened the door even to ordaining homosexuals. As much as they loved the denominations that they've grown up in and been in for years, they've just sadly had to leave (lines 79–84).

Commenting on his interactions with an extended family member who is LGBT, Preston said, "She goes to a Methodist church, or her response would be that she goes to a church that accepts her as the Christian she is (lines 240–241).

Curtis addressed his congregation directly concerning evangelical Christian's response to LGBT people:

> I said to my congregation there is no person who's wrestling with the issue of homosexuality in North America that does not know what the Evangelical Church believes about this, you don't need to tell them again. You don't need to tell them six ways from Sunday, you don't need to lecture them.
>
> You need to love them. You need to just love them. You need to be the guy that they go out and they say wow, that's completely different from what I encountered from the Baptists down the street because we as Wesleyans, it's all about love (lines 92–101).

Theme Two: Homosexuality in Light of Biblical Sexuality

The theme underscores the participants' understanding of human sexuality grounded in one's theological foundation, theological orientation, and scripture. Participants discussed their beliefs about how God responds to LGBT individuals. Participants also shared their understanding of scriptural statements about homosexuality. Some participants disclosed their thoughts about Wesleyan theology and/or ones theological orientation and its influence on their thoughts about homosexuality and LGBT people. Participants addressed efforts to effectively communicate (e.g., preaching and teaching) the Bible's instruction regarding relationships and human sexuality; LGBT responses to sermons are noted. Participants also shared their views about the incompatibility or compatibility of homosexuality and Christianity.

God's response to LGBT individuals. One aspect of this theme addressed participants' beliefs and suppositions about how God responds to LGBT people. While most of the participants agreed that homosexuality and same-sex relationships were not in keeping with God's original intent, participants maintained that God loves all people regardless of sexual orientation.

Derek held to a traditional biblical position on homosexuality, but he also spoke of God's love for people. Derek expressed it this way:

> I'm convinced in how I read the Bible of my position, but I'm also convinced that Jesus loved people, thoroughly loves them, and that His children are not just those who are saved, they are the people who are lost, and they just have yet to clue into this, and so we have a mission [to reach them] (lines 579–583).

Blake acknowledged that he did not have all the answers about the issues and concerns regarding homosexuality; however, he argued that Jesus came for LGBT people too. Blake stated,

> I may not know all the answers about how to address this here or even biblically, but they're people that Jesus came for. Just as He touched the leper, just as He touched the woman at the well, and just as he—this is why I came, and this is what I do, and this is who I am. If we have the opportunity with the gay and lesbian community to be able to have that conversation and point them to Jesus who says, "You're why I came and this is what I can do for you and in you and this is who I am," then I think we've won something (lines 392–401).

Matt said, "Christ hung out with those that the church didn't like...
the woman at the well. Here's Christ saying, 'I do love you no matter what
you've done'" (lines 706–708).

Blake said that if a LGBT person came to his church, he would want
to be able to "look him in the eye and say, 'God loves you and you matter
to him, and I love you, and you matter to me'" (lines 1118–1119). Curtis
had just such an opportunity. Curtis shared the following:

> One of the people that's gay in my church is a young twenty-some-
> thing guy and had some hard things happen to him—people gave
> him a hard time for being gay. I just reached out to him and told
> him we loved him and we're for him and God loves him (lines
> 560–564).

Continuing Curtis said, "God loves them. I'm supposed to love them.
I'll let God sort the rest of that out. He's way smarter than I am" (lines
573–574).

Allen shared a story about a gay individual who attended his church.
Allen said of this person,

> Recently, while I've been here, I had individual. He's deceased
> now. Sad, 26 years old died of colon cancer. A wonderful, won-
> derful young man, struggled with his sexuality all his life and there
> were some people here who hung a gay tag on him. And I think
> that became for him a defining experience. And I know there is
> a period of his life where he was practicing. Towards the end of
> his life, I don't believe that was the case and it's just an amazing
> testimonial of God's grace as God ministered to him through the
> cancer that ultimately took his life (lines 103–111).

Matt discussed the commonality of brokenness in the lives of all peo-
ple. Matt said, "I believe in a God that takes into account our brokenness.
If God doesn't take into account our brokenness, then I don't know how
I feel about a God who doesn't do that" (lines 660–662).

Similarly, Allen said, "The last I looked, the Christian faith is about people. It's about God who loved and gave up everything to redeem a fallen race, to redeem a desperately broken people" (lines 888–890).

Continuing the idea of God's love for all people including LGBT people, Curtis commented that despite a failed attempt to live a celibate life, God continues to love that individual. Curtis observed,

> Someone who has a homosexual attraction and is like, "I'm trying to live celibate; but I fell down." Okay, dust yourself off. Let's come together here. God loves you. You're not going to hell for this. You're in a relationship with God. Everybody falls (lines 657–660).

Blake felt that some "homosexual" persons might "struggle with that for a lifetime and yet, with God's help, choose not to act on it" (lines 885–886). Likewise, Curtis maintained that God can help the LGBT person experience peace regarding the individual's sexual orientation. Curtis commented, "My thought is that at some point God can bring them to a place of Shalom with their sexuality whether that means okay, I'm going to be celibate, whether that means maybe there's some way to reorient themselves" (lines 816–819).

Bradley stated that "We come to Christ as we are" (line 591) and,

> Anybody who comes to Christ, Christ wants them to grow and mature, become like Him. So that could be required of everyone. I think that would happen with people who are gay or—everybody is going to have to sort out what that means (lines 815–818).

Encapsulating many of the participant's thoughts, Darrell said, "God cares about people and that's the key (line 119–120). Curtis responded similarly, "Ultimately, that's what God called us to do is to love the person. So if we do what the Bible says, things work out much better" (lines 549–550).

Scriptural understanding. Another element of this theme relates to the participants' understanding of the biblical standard or scriptural authority regarding sexuality and sexual relationships. Participants expressed their views of the Bible's statements about homosexuality and gay/lesbian relationships. Some participants provided scriptural references as evidence to support their position. Others discussed their understanding of scripture in a more general way.

Commenting on his understanding of scripture, Allen observed, "As I understand scripture, the practice of homosexuality is condemned; that's my interpretation as I understand scripture" (lines 90–91). Referring to Nazarenes, Curtis commented, "We say we think the revelation of scripture is that this is not God's first choice for your life, to be practicing a homosexual lifestyle" (lines 67–68).

Citing history and tradition, Harrison made the following statement: "Fundamentally, as I understand church history, church tradition, and biblical teaching, homosexual practice is considered sinful in the scriptures" (lines 76–77). Travis also referenced Christian history as validating scriptural prohibitions of homosexuality. Travis said,

> To the best of the knowledge we have in front of us at the moment it seems like the historic stance of Christianity has always been to interpret the scriptures to say this [homosexuality] is not God's intent for human flourishing (222–225).

During a conversation with a parishioner in his church, Travis stated, "I communicated that our stance was that we felt the scripture said this [same-sex relationships] is not God's intention for human flourishing, that we think the scriptures identify this with a host of other sins" (592–594).

Kendall spoke of the tension he felt between acknowledging homosexual behavior and scriptural indications that it is less than God desires. Kendall offered the following explanation:

> I have come to this point in my life to understand the scriptural text saying it is something that is short of the Glory of God and that this is something that isn't God's design or God's idea for His creation (lines 820–824).

Curtis provided a similar observation,

For me, the issue comes down to there's a certain sense in which I affirm the authority of scripture. What does the scripture have to say about this issue? As I've pondered that, I can't get to a place where I can say scripture says the practice of homosexuality is okay. I can't get there (lines 622–625).

Some of the participants provided specific or general references to biblical statements concerning homosexuality and/or same-sex relationships. For example, Travis said,

I think we're square with the scriptures—the five verses in scripture that talk about it—that Christian interpretation of that for 20 centuries has been this [homosexuality] is off limits, this is categorized as a sin (lines 1115–1118).

Harrison made a general reference to a passage in Paul's letter to the Romans. Harrison posited,

The six or seven time times scripture even talks about homosexuality…it appears to address it no stronger, than in a place like Romans 1, where in fact what's actually being said is that homosexuality is not the primary sin. The sin is idolatry, and the consequence of idolatry is a whole range of behaviors and homosexuality would be one of those (lines 402–407).

Matt is the pastor of a church whose ministry is primarily directed toward the LGBT population. Referencing 1 Thessalonians, Matt made the following observation:

Paul is talking to people who are in much deeper sexual sin that what my congregation will ever experience and the very first thing he says is, "you're good people." He doesn't discredit them because of their sin, he says, "you're good people and you got some things to work on" (lines 278–283).

Preston struggled with recalling the specific passage but said,

I often reflect on that passage of scripture, and if I was better—it's my memory—I would tell you where it is. Paul was writing and he says, "You know these will not inherit the Kingdom of Heaven and that's what some of you were" (lines 360–363). Homosexual offenders was in that list and that to me is a message that God can change our lives. Now you know, the degree to which such a transformation would take place you know, is that person going to marry and have a heterosexual relationship? I don't know (lines 367–371).

Blake referenced verses in Corinthians saying,

You know the passage in Corinthians, "This is what some of you once were," there are those that think that you're not supposed to change somebody, if they're gay, you're not supposed to change their orientation or whatever. Evidently, there were people who once were homosexual and were not. I think there might be some who struggle with that for a lifetime and yet, with God's help, choose not to act on it (lines 879–886).

Derek said he was given a document that supposedly "proved" that Jesus was not concerned about homosexuality. Derek shared his response:

I received an exegesis on the passage where Jesus is dealing with I think it's a centurion who has a servant back home and just say the word in great faith. The exegesis of that person that wrote me a letter saying hey, here's some New Testament proof that while Paul had a problem with homosexuality, Jesus didn't. I just go, "Are you serious?" because it's a stretch to make it the wording of that person being not just a servant, but a gay servant or a sexual slave of that person. And while that's a remote possibility, it just seems unlikely when you take the scriptures in total where Jesus would bless something that would be against the word. I mean even when He deals with a heterosexual lady at the well, she has her issues sexually, He says, "Go and sin no more" (lines 329–340).

Travis offered his perspective on scripture's position on same-sex orientation and homosexual practice. Travis observed, "The Bible doesn't condemn somebody for having an orientation. It doesn't condemn how they feel, what their instincts are, [or] any kind of that stuff" (lines 969–971). Curtis commented similarly, "We don't believe that feelings of homosexuality are wrong. We believe it's the practice that's not endorsed by scripture" (lines 105–107).

Matt wanted to focus less on homosexuality and focus more on a biblical sexuality. Matt proposed,

> One of the things that we say is when you're talking about sexuality in your church, what if we stick to a biblical sexuality? I know that looks different for a lot of people, but what if we throw in when Paul was talking to people he never specifically pointed out homosexuality, it was always in a list with other stuff. Why aren't we doing what Paul did and keep it in that list? (lines 418–424).

Darrell tied Old and New Testaments together for his understanding of biblical sexuality.

Darrell stated it thusly,

> The model that is given to us from the very beginning in Genesis is echoed in Jesus' words in the gospels to the Apostle Paul are: "For this reason, a man and a woman will be united, and they will become one flesh." Paul even says this is a Divine Mystery, but I'm talking about Christ and the Church.
>
> So I think the model from the beginning of time was essentially a man and a woman. I think that was God's design. But we know that everything from that moment that the sin came is flawed, so nothing's ideal necessarily. I do think that is the model that the Bible gives us as a standard, if you would, or the model that God intended, that God set up from the beginning of time (lines 221–235).

Keith argued that the physical characteristics of sexuality are important and to ignore the physical misses its significance. Keith said it this way,

I am anchored to Jesus' quotes in the Book of Genesis about man and woman and image of God issues and, are we going to say that flesh means nothing? That the physicality of sexuality means nothing? Isn't that a little bit Gnostic? (lines 353–356).

Darrell argued that male and female physical characteristics point to God's design for heterosexual relationships and not for same-sex relationships. Darrell asserted,

I do believe God's standard in the scripture says pretty clearly that homosexuality is one of those issues that is not acceptable before the Lord. God has made us—even just physically the way that He's put us together, men and women, fit together. I think from the simple physical stature or point, I think there are things in there (lines 1077–1081).

Despite participants' views that scripture condemns homosexuality and same-sex relationships, they agreed that they were not to judge those who have a same-sex orientation. Allen said, "Ultimately, as I see scripture, I see Jesus Christ himself saying, 'The Son of Man came not to judge but to seek and save the lost'" (lines 818–819). Allen continued, "I have decided it's not my responsibility to judge anyone's walk with God, but to leave that to God" (lines 822–823). Curtis expressed a similar perspective,

I don't really have any desire to judge them (LGBT people). I don't have any desire to say, "You're not going to heaven." In fact, I don't want to do that with anybody. I tell people all the time it's not my job to tell people they're not going to heaven, that's between them and God. My job is to call them to the life that God wants to give them, to new life in Christ. It's not my job to say you're in and you're out. In fact, scripture is very clear that that's reserved for the Father to do (lines 789–790).

Wesleyan theology and theological orientation. One element of this theme indicated the participant's adherence to Wesleyan theology or the participants' theological orientation (e.g., conservative, moderate, liberal).

Not all participants referenced theology as influencing his perspective on homosexuality and LGBT individuals. A few participants made general comments; these are illustrated below.

Travis argued there are two types of Nazarenes, one group is intellectual and educated, and not rigid. The other group of Nazarenes he described as "anti-intellectual," "anti-educational" and "fundamentalist." Travis stated it thusly:

> This is maybe an unkind characterization, but I think geographically, painting with a broad brush, there are basically two stripes of Nazarene. There are those that draw their theological method from Wesley and Anglicanism, very broad, very open to whatever has been an option within Christian orthodoxy across the planet. They're willing to consider it. They make this very eclectic combination. In classic Wesleyan/Anglican method, right? So if you ask an Anglican what is your distinctive doctrine, what do you believe, they shrug and go whatever Christians have always believed. They refuse to have a distinctive doctrine. So I think there's that stripe of Nazarenes. Which I clearly land within you know (lines 439–452).
>
> So there's the Wesleyan-Anglican type of Nazarene and then there's the 19th century Holiness stripe of Nazarene....The 19th century Holiness Movement was much more anti-intellectual and anti-educational, did not have a lot of access to Wesley's writings (452–454, & 459–461).
>
> I mean this very legalistic version from the 19th century Holiness Movement, and I think that generally Nazarenes in that stream of our movement tend to be no gays allowed, this is an abomination, this is a black and white issue, very black and white issue. I think that Nazarenes that come from more of Wesley's bent you know, more education, a wider general orthodoxy of what's orthodox and what's not. I think those tend to be much more—their attitude towards this seems to be much more yeah let's figure this out where do we go from here rather than black and white like these people are doing something evil and they need either to get saved or get out. You know, protect the church

from them, protect the church's kids from them all that kind of stuff (478–489).

Blake felt the church is losing its mooring and needed to be re-anchored to its basic creedal statements. In an effort to do this, Blake said,

Evangelicalism has gotten slippery, I think, in some of the essentials, even of the things that had anchored us historically to beliefs about hell. Some don't believe there's a hell even in our Nazarene churches. We can't just pick and choose what we want to believe (lines 44–46).

Keith maintained an orthodox position but, has experienced incongruence about how people within the church respond to LGBT persons. Keith observed,

I want to have a high view of scripture in the same—it goes with the tension of being who we are, I think, and our understanding of scripture. So theological inerrancy opens up the door to lots of things, I feel like. I feel like I have a pretty high view of scripture—and at the same time, thoroughly trained as we were not to be fundamentalists, it's the last thing we wanted to be, and have a high view of scripture, theological inerrancy for me begs the question, speaks into this issue, I think, quite significantly for me (lines 374–381).

I hear people in the church who advocate full acceptance of homosexual people, but then I hear the kind of stuff that comes out of their mouth theologically and like, "Oh, I don't think so" (lines 387–389).

In the context of conversations with people in his church about homosexuality and LGBT concerns, Harrison chooses to make clear his position. Harrison said, "I make clear my affinity with the essential teaching of the scripture and of the tradition as I understand it, but this is where the church has gone wrong in the way in which it has responded" (lines 386–388).

Allen shared that he has been a Nazarene since his childhood. Allen acknowledged that this has shaped his theological awareness and personal feelings about homosexuality. Allen said,

I think as I've grown from adolescence, you know, because I've been in Church of the Nazarene—I'm 47 years old. I've been a church member almost 40 years and I was probably seven years old or eight years old when I joined the church. So, I have to say the Church of the Nazarene has formed both my theological and personal perspective. And I think lately that's been more so because of some of the documents I've read [about homosexuality] (lines 265–271).

Harold struggled with the theological implications of having LGBT couples in his church. Referencing interactions he had with two gay men in one of his former Nazarene church's, Harold said,

They were always very welcoming to me. They ended up landing at a Methodist church that was a little bit more open. At that time, I think I wasn't ready theologically to embrace that and what that would look like, and the church wasn't either. It was a small town, and they weren't ready to deal with that issue by any means (lines 760–764).

Darrell felt that finding the balance between affirming the church's position, a Wesleyan theological perspective, and God's grace are important when talking about homosexuality. Darrell observed,

I think finding the balance in that conversation and affirming who we are as a church, what we're all about and the foundations of our theological position and affirming the fact that God is a God of grace; I think that's critical (lines 155–157).

Curtis recognized the challenges of maintaining a conservative position while at the same time demonstrating God's love to others. Curtis made the following comment:

Sometimes our position as a theologically conservative group is hard to hold together because on one hand, we say we think the revelation of scripture is that this is not God's first choice for your life to be practicing a homosexual lifestyle. That being said, we are called to absolutely love you; and by "love" we mean Christian love, which means we will lay down our lives for you (lines 65–70).

Preston felt that the Church of the Nazarene's "primary message is a message of love" (lines 258–259). Preston also described the Wesleyan doctrine of love as it relates to homosexuality:

But to love doesn't mean we accept that [same-sex relationships are] a right way of living and God's way of living. But, and I think that goes back to what I say about the Church of the Nazarene's position, I think that's our church's position (lines 264–266).

When you talk about the Wesleyan doctrine it's a message of love and I think we can communicate that with anyone who's not a person of faith. We are to communicate with them in a Christ-like manner, which is a message of love (lines 280–283).

Preaching and teaching biblical sexuality. One of the features of this theme addressed how participants attempt to communicate the Word of God as it relates to relationships, sex, and sexuality. Two participants provided a brief statement about how LGBT individuals responded to a sermon about homosexuality.

Bradley provided a detailed description about the kinds of topics his congregation wants him to address in his preaching; homosexuality is one of those topics. Bradley explained:

Well, I think sometimes there are certain percentage of my church, and I don't know if it's majority or not but a certain percentage that wish I would preach more against sins of lifestyle (187–189)…such as abortion (line 191). And so, homosexuality is the same thing—they probably wish that I take more as strong conservative stance on that issue, and maybe preach about it more forcefully (197–200).

> I preached a sermon because we had people ask questions and
> they wanted to hear a sermon about that [homosexuality]. I think
> it got the most votes—especially when it was in the news with the
> Supreme Court but—so we preach about it and people appreci-
> ated it although I offended people on both sides (214–219).

During the first year at a new church, Allen asked his congregation
what topics they wanted him to address in his sermons. Allen said homosexuality was one of those topics, "because in this area there is a rather
large LGBT community" (lines 50–51). Allen attempted to address the
topic as he would other important topics. Allen reflected, "So, when I
preached about this [homosexuality] I said, 'You know, this is no different than [an] extramarital affair. This is no different that gluttony. This is
an issue" (lines 95–96). Allen discussed how preparing for sermons have
shaped his thinking on the subject. Allen shared, "As I've researched for
preaching, it's helped me to moderate and really move towards seeing
people rather than this societal hot button" (lines 185–187).

Rather than letting congregational interests drive his sermons. Travis
uses the Lectionary as his guide for preaching. In so doing, Travis explained that homosexuality has only been presented in the Lectionary
passage once or twice during his 19 years of ministry. Travis said,

> I've preached for 19 years through the Lectionary, okay. So there's
> five verses in the Bible I'm told, there's five that mention homosex-
> uality so guess how often you end up preaching about homosexu-
> ality in 19 years. Like once or twice. So when somebody goes well
> how come you're not calling that out, well when it comes up—you
> know, because I follow this regular pattern through the scriptures
> that takes us through the whole bible and in a three-year cycle,
> instead of just preaching my favorite crap or whatever happened to
> be in the news that week, you know, I'm preaching the scriptures
> actually. You know, so it doesn't come up a lot (lines 1687–1693).

> But they expect you to preach on that stuff. So that's part of
> that whole thing of what impressions do you—you know, are you
> avoiding talking about gay stuff? No man, I'm talking about it

when we finally get around to Ephesians chapter whatever (lines 1706–1709). For me it's easy for me to say, No man I'm not evading the subject of homosexuality. When it comes up you'll hear it, make sure you're in church that week if it's so important to you… if you're worried about it (lines 1713–1716).

Harrison also chooses to use the Lectionary as a guide for preaching. Echoing Travis's description, Harrison stated,

In terms of my practice as a preacher, I think I have only addressed the subject twice in 24 years and only because it came up in the text I was preaching from. Generally, I'm a lectionary preacher and so that rarely appears; and on the two occasions in which I did choose to, it came up because I chose to expand the lectionary passage in order to address it (lines 125–129).

Discussing a sermon he preached about homosexuality, Allen declared that the practice of homosexuality is wrong, but the bigger question for Allen was, how will his church represent Christ to the LGBT community. Allen offered the following:

The sermon that I preached I just entitled it simply on homosexuality, I began saying, "Okay, folks. Here's where it is. The practice of homosexual—the practice is wrong. There's no debates in our denomination about that, but that to me is not the issue. The issue to me is how we react to people who are struggling with this issue on their life, and whether we will be truly Christian or whether we will be something less." So, that was the focus of that sermon was how do we—particularly in this community where there are such large communities of LGBT people, how do we represent Christ to that community? (lines 344–354).

Derek also acknowledged that he has preached on the topic of homosexuality; however, Derek stated that when he does, he attempts to choose his words carefully. Derek said,

I have had times when I preached on those issues, and I tried to choose my words carefully. Our sermons are recorded, and they're put on the web. You try to stay on the word of God, you don't want to have somebody call it hate speech or anything, although sometimes it seems like that's the issue or it seems to be interpreted as that way.

So I choose my words carefully, but I always try to bathe it in a loving outreach not in a condemning way. I didn't write the book so they could deal with God. They don't answer to me, they'll answer to God (lines 558–566).

When Preston preached on the topic of homosexuality, he attempted to talk about it with love and concern for LGBT people; however, that was not how it was received. Preston shared the following story about a Sunday when he addressed homosexuality in his sermon:

We had a teenager who's coming to the church who was in a home being raised by two mothers and in the context of a sermon—it wasn't the focus of the sermon but in the context of the scripture I was dealing with, the sermon that I was preaching—I addressed the matter of the biblical position that clarifies that homosexuality is not God's plan. In no way was I communicating a lack of love or care for people in that lifestyle. It was interesting he wrote on Facebook that afternoon, "That was the most hateful sermon I've ever heard" and that he would never come to church again, and he hasn't (40–48).

Harold shared a similar experience about an LGBT couple who had been attending his church. In one of his sermons, Harold talked about marriage and the LGBT couple's response to his message:

They kept coming and kept coming. I was preaching a sermon one week and it was on marriage. I heard this before and I hadn't thought about it in the context of how this might sound to an LGBT person, and I said this stuff that I had heard somewhere and picked up along the way without really reflecting on it. I had said marriage is between one man and one woman for one lifetime. They never came back. I think they felt like it was a safe place until I said that (708–714).

Returning to Preston, he said that he's preached about homosexuality a few times during his ministry. Preston stated,

I have preached on that topic a few times across the years. Well, it's always disheartening because you're up against a cultural lie in terms of what you're saying. And I like people to like me. In my heart of hearts, I'm a people pleaser...and yet, I'm not going to back down from that (lines 63–67).

Although Preston felt strongly about his beliefs about homosexuality he also affirmed,

I've tried, whenever I have addressed that issue in a message, to be mindful of how it would be received by someone in the congregation if they were openly gay or if they were struggling with those issues. So that it's [the message is] always communicated in a redemptive way (lines 329–337).

Darrell shared that when he preaches his messages are "grounded in grace" (line 142); however, Darrell acknowledged that he has not specifically preached a sermon on or about homosexuality. Darrell observed, "I don't know that I've really addressed the issue in a sermon specifically. When we deal with passages that deal with that issue, I would address it, but it's not something I've done a sermon on" (lines 287–289).

Like Darrell, Keith stated that he has not preached a sermon directly related to the "sin of homosexuality" (lines 685–686). Referring to his congregation, Keith explained it thusly,

They might hear a pastor decry hateful behavior to all persons and gay people. They're going to hear that. They've never heard a sermon on the sin of homosexuality. They've never heard that. They've heard sermons about the sin of sexual brokenness, but they've never heard a pastor get up there and start going after homosexuals. And, at the same time, they've heard this sort of call to this extravagant love of God that we're called to for all persons (lines 684–692).

Matt also felt strongly that his preaching admonishes people to love others. Love is one of Matt's essential themes. Matt provided the following statement:

Now when we get up and preach, do we feel called to preach the Word? Yes. But before, after and during you're going to feel nothing but love, that's our goal. And if you don't, let us know within two seconds.

One of the commandments that we have made at this church, we never preach a sermon directly related to homosexuality, ever. If we're going to talk about sexuality, everybody is going to leave feeling convicted, even the person who preached the message. So we're going to hit everybody. It's like one of those whack-a-mole games. Everybody's going to get hit.

I think the problem is we like to have these sermons on homosexuality. The problem is it's just like when you do a sermon on divorce: everybody in your congregation that has been divorced is going to feel picked on—it's the same with homosexuality. One of the things that we say is, "When you're talking about sexuality in your church, what if we stick to a biblical sexuality?" (lines 392–419).

Sin/sins. Also in this theme are participants' statements regarding sin. At times sin is considered hierarchically, that is, some sins are considered worse than others, e.g., murder is worse than lying or homosexuality is worse than gossip. The following participant statements reflect their understanding of the scriptural proscriptions against homosexuality and classifying homosexuality as sin, but not viewing it as worse than any other sin.

Drawing on his understanding of scripture, Darrell said, "I do think the Bible's pretty clear about homosexuality as a sin in God's eyes" (lines

222–223). Commenting further Darrell added, "Personally, I do believe homosexuality is outside of what God says is healthy, good and right, what God made us for. But I also know that we all sin and fall short" (lines 237–239). Travis said it this way, "I think it's fair to say that all of the Christian history of Jesus that we have goes, 'No, this [homosexuality] is categorized as sin'" (lines 1124–1125).

Harrison felt conflicted by how the Church of the Nazarene has responded to homosexuality. Harrison stressed that homosexuality is "treated, in my opinion, as a sin greater than other sins. It's treated quite negatively" (lines 90–91). Other participants said the church has not responded well homosexuality or to LGBT people. For example, Keith stated that gay people do not experience "full acceptance in the Church of the Nazarene" (line 882) because "the Church of the Nazarene calls homosexuality a sin. Not only do we call it a sin, but we also tend to like to point it out as being the big one, bigger than others" (lines 883–885).

Darrell too felt that Nazarenes place homosexuality in a category different from other sins. Speaking about his beliefs and church's response to homosexuality, Darrell said,

> Personally, I do believe homosexuality is outside of what God says is healthy, good and right; what God made for us. But I also know that we all sin and fall short. I think the tendency is we tend to lump this issue, homosexuality, into almost like a different category from other sin, other issues that people deal with (lines 237–241).

Darrell continued saying, "So I think in many ways people have a double standard. I think we tend to grade sins on a curve, and this is definitely high on the curve in people's minds" (lines 252–253).

Echoing Darrell's observation, Preston said, "I think we've put it [homosexuality] on a different plane and I don't think it needs to be on a different plane" (lines 604–605). In keeping with other participants, Allen also felt that homosexuality is considered a greater sin than others. Allen explained, "There's a lot of people that want to make homosexuality the grandmother of all sins. I don't see it that way. I see it as a sin among sins (lines 92–94). Allen followed this saying, "I don't differentiate between

[sins] anymore. You know, there's no hierarchy of sin. So, I think I'm probably more—I think I'm more able to see the person and define them as a person rather than as a sin" (lines 142–145). Blake expressed a similar viewpoint,

> In my opinion, it's not the sin of the decade and it's not the worst sin. It's all lumped together with gluttony, lying, cheating, anger, and malice—all those things are just as bad. It's just very personal. It's very hard because it touches so many people's lives (lines 284–287).

Preston suggested that the church doesn't always know how to respond to homosexuality. Preston urged,

> I think we have to give grace to one another when there are struggles in someone's life. I do think the church doesn't always know how to deal with that well in with this particular issue [homosexuality]. I think a pastor could confess to a lot of other temptations before he could ever acknowledge publicly temptations in that realm (lines 596–600).

Curtis offered an insight regarding why the church responds as it does:

> Again, trying to take homosexuality out of the context of special sins, which is where it tends to be culturally for us. I don't know why we do that, but we do because it scares us probably. We have certain sins that we seem to think are worse than other sins (lines 725–728).

Blake also suggested that "fear" drives people's response. Blake said, "I think the fear factor of, 'Is homosexuality the leprosy of our day?' In some people's minds it still is" (lines 481–482).

Darrell postulated that the church considers homosexuality worse than other sins because it runs counter to heterosexuality. Darrell reiterated,

> As I said earlier, we tend to grade sin on a sliding scale and homosexuality may, for many people, be the worst because as a heterosexual I think it just goes against the very fabric of what

we understand to be right and good or what we desire. So for me to think about a man desiring another man is not a pleasant thought. It's just like, "Oh, that's…ugh." It's that creepy feeling. That's just morally at the very core of who I am and that it is wrong (lines 960–965).

I don't come from an understanding and say okay, pornography, I get that. I get that. I get why couples live together. I can understand that. That's people just being people, normal; but homosexuality is people being freakish, wrong, just an abomination in the sight of God (lines 969–972).

We tend to graduate those things and I think that's, again, why it's such a volatile issue because we tend to like, "It's wrong, they're wrong, and what's the conversation? You just tell them it's wrong and that's the way it is. Get their life straightened out and they'll be okay" (lines 974–977).

Allen expressed a similar feeling, "At the base level, being a heterosexual male, there is still a gut revulsion when I think about the practice. I mean to me it's unnatural (lines 187–189).

Some participants acknowledged the tension that exists within the "hate the sin, love the sinner" language. Kendall stated it thusly:

I think this is the tension that I wrestle with all the time with this issue is that it's kind of the "hate the sin, but love the sinner" idea that I think, especially when it comes to the issue of sexuality, if you hate my sin it sure feels like you hate me too (813–815).

Harold's comments suggested agreement with Kendall's observation. Harold remarked,

Even though there's this idea that love the sinner, hate the sin kind of thing, in practice that really doesn't work very well it seems. They know that if they hate that sin, they're going to hate the sinner that comes in as well (line 996–998).

Blake offered a similar observation,

I think that that lifestyle is sinful, which to a homosexual—I think they interpret that as, "Then you just said I am sinful, not just my..." That's where I struggle a bit—because that's not what I'm trying to say (lines 1066–1069).

Derek stressed that even though he believes homosexuality is a sin, LGBT people are brothers and sisters in need of God's grace. Derek said it this way,

I do call it sin, I don't justify it as I don't justify any other things that the scripture would say this is right and this is wrong and so we would hold to that. But they're not the enemy. They're our brothers and sisters who have not yet got a hold of God's grace in a life-changing way in that area and so they're more prisoners of war (lines 457–461).

While asserting that homosexuality is sin, Darrell also stressed the importance that everyone who strives to live a Christian life must address the sin in his or her own life. Darrell offered the following explanation:

I would say understanding homosexuality is sin, I would trust that anybody on the journey with Christ would deal with that sin ultimately, at least be able to articulate where I'm at in there and where God is at in there. Just like the sin in my life, I would hope that if there is sin issue, immorality, unhealthy thoughts, whatever it may be, that I would deal with that and grow to become like Christ and move away from my sin and (1096–1101)...move more towards the holiness of Christ in whatever way that looks like (lines 1114–1115).

Blake emphasized that one's sin and one's identity are not the same thing. This also true for LGBT persons. Blake explained it in the following manner:

We're not shackled to the sin and our identity is not wrapped up in that sin. Our identity is wrapped up in the one we say we follow and that's who we seek to become like. That's what I hope my position would be with anybody regardless of the label (lines 1112–1115). I struggle with people who say, "I'm a sinner saved by grace." You know what? That's not my identity anymore. I'm not a sinner saved by grace. My identity is not wrapped up in my sin any more than I'm a homosexual saved by grace, I'm an alcoholic saved by grace. I get that. I get that (lines 1123–1128).

Despite their beliefs about homosexuality and sin, some participants expressed compassion and concern for LGBT individuals. When asked how he felt about LGBT people Travis said,

I feel that gay folk are human beings like everybody else and that we're called to minister to them and that they deserve no less love than anybody else. I mean, I really at this point in my life, don't feel any different toward them and their practices as I would somebody who is participating in any other thing categorized as sin in the New Testament (lines 641–647).

Harrison stated that he wants people to feel welcomed; however, sinful practices will not be condoned. Harrison said,

My hope is that we would know that all are welcome here, but not all personal practices are going to be condoned here. I really, really believe that. I don't see this [homosexual practice] any differently than someone who perpetually misbehaves by sleeping around on their wife (lines 437–440).

Allen was interested in helping LGBT people experience the presence of God and communal fellowship. Allen queried,

My issue is, how can we help you experience God? Whatever the sin happens to be, we're here to help people experience God, to connect with God in intangible ways, transformational ways. And if we can't provide community, they may never get the chance to experience that (lines 371–375).

Temptation. Another feature of this theme were participants' comments regarding temptation. There was some overlap in participant statements between the concepts of temptation, sin, and human frailty, i.e., struggle. The following are participants' observations about temptation.

Preston acknowledged that all people, including Christians face temptation. Preston said,

> None of us as followers of Christ are free from temptation and there's all kinds of temptations that besiege us and I don't think Christians are immune from those kinds of temptations at all....I do think that someone who is a new Christian is still going to struggle with those things and they may slip and fall. But in terms of just opening the door to [homosexuality] being acceptable behavior in the life of a Christian, I find no more acceptable than stealing or being vulgar or being unfaithful to my wife or if I'm going to follow Christ those are things that can't be a part of my life (lines 574–583).

Continuing, Preston observed, "If someone does have homosexual inclinations or desires, then I think our calling as a Christian is to be disciplined with those just as would be the case if a heterosexual was single" (lines 377–380). Preston asserted, "The same is true if someone struggled with homosexual desires and temptations and was a Christian, the commitment is to remain pure" (lines 399–400).

Curtis made a bold statement about temptation when he spoke to his congregation about homosexuality. Curtis said, "I have to say scripture says that Jesus was tempted in every way we are. Boy, this blew up when I preached about homosexuality; they got really quiet when I said this" (lines 629–631). Curtis followed by saying, "We have to affirm that Jesus was tempted with homosexual attraction. If we say this is wrong and this is him, that's just the logical outcome of all of that. I believe that temptation is not sin" (lines 633–635). Rhetorically, Derek queried, "Are there temptations? Absolutely. Do you act on them or do you not? Those are big differences" (lines 724–725). Preston also acknowledged that temptation is common to humanity. Preston said,

I suppose we all deal with different kinds of temptations by the way we're made up and by the way we're raised, which goes to the whole thing of, is homosexuality a learned thing or genetic? I don't know that it matters because we're still committed to living lives of purity (lines 588–592).

Derek talked about lust as a temptation and the need for self-control. Derek made the following observation: "I need to exercise self-control because the scripture often talks about sexual sin and sometimes it labels homosexuality, sometimes it's heterosexual stuff—very similar, but [it's] the whole element of self-control" (lines 695–697).

Curtis stressed that temptation does not equate to sin. Curtis said,

Temptation is not sin and everybody has their area of temptation. The difficulty with it being same-sex attraction is that everybody sees it. It's like premarital sex: lots of people get involved with premarital sex and the ones that get pregnant get caught, but they're no worse than the person that doesn't get caught (lines 697–701).

Kendall said he hoped that people would have victory over their impulses. Relating it to homosexuality, Kendall said, "I would hope for someone who feels impulses, I guess, towards homosexual behavior for whatever reason, again, to be empowered and strengthened to not respond to those impulses" (lines 996–998).

Harrison reflected on the temptation of pornography and its deleterious effect on people in ministry. Harrison was an accountability partner with a male missionary who was occasionally tempted to view gay pornography (lines 799–801). Harrison set up regular meetings with the individual in order to help him avoid such temptations. Harrison provided his thoughts about the lure of pornography for people in ministry:

Pornography in itself is the plague of ministers across the world. I can't tell you how many ordained clergy I see continually being disqualified because of their inability to deal with that addictive behavior. It has far greater ramifications than just the sexual orientation or the sexual issues. It consumes their life; it consumes their income…it consumes everything (lines 805–809).

Derek asserted the need for accountability when battling temptation in some area of one's life. Illustrating a mock conversation, Derek said,

"Hey man, I struggle with this." Well, you know what? Let's work at keeping pornography off your computer and out of your life. Let's set up the proper guidelines, protection, and accountability that are going to help walk you through that challenge. I think I would do that the same [way] no matter what the area of sin might be (lines 712–717).

Bradley said one needs to be cautious about putting people in places where in doing so would increase temptation for the person. Bradley referenced pedophilia as an example saying, "not wanting them working with children because [it's] a strong temptation for them" (lines 479–482). Bradley also provided other examples:

Just as if the church had a ministry at the bar—you probably wouldn't take a person who's still struggling massively with alcohol and in recovery. Maybe after they had been in recovery for a long time you would say, "Well now. They're better able to relate. Just as we wouldn't preclude someone's orientation towards kleptomania, we wouldn't be able make them to be the treasurer, but we wouldn't say, "Well, you can't teach Sunday school class" (lines 484–497).

Preston expressed a similar viewpoint about putting people in situations where temptation might get the better of them. Preston commented, "I would think it would be wise not to put them in a situation where they would be further tempted, you know, if they're struggling with temptation. Again, that depends on the maturity of the person (lines 508–510).

Human frailty and the common experience of struggle. One of aspects of this theme included notions about general types of issues with which people struggle. Participants identified some of these as anger, divorce, pornography, gambling, alcohol and tobacco use, and other struggles common to the human experience.

Curtis commented that "Everybody has their areas of weakness" (line 637). He shared a story about working with men who had been incarcerated. Curtis said,

> I used to work with a lot of guys who had been in prison and anger was often their thing. So they grappled with that. That was a hard thing. They'd get angry really quickly and yet they understood that was not God's best for them.
>
> Well, we all fall—we all have. But if he were to go off into the deep end and just be angry all the time and beat people up and do the stuff he did before that would be different than an incident—for all sins, this doesn't hold just to homosexuality, but all sins, same thing applies (lines 637–656).

People struggle with a myriad of issues. Blake stated, "We've got a lot of pain in the seats of our churches, some of it known, much of it not" (lines 523–524). As an example Blake shared that he had "sex offenders" in his church (line 517). He also shared that several years ago, he had a man attending his church who "wore women's clothing under his [clothes] (lines 594–595). Blake shared how he handled the situation:

> He was working with our kids (line 595). I found out about it—I called it a fetish. I said, "Why do you do that?" It was hard for him to talk about the fact that he liked to wear women's underwear. He was actually married (lines 600–602).

Travis recognized how difficult divorce can be. Although the church makes a statement about divorce, Travis said that "doesn't mean that we've hung out a shingle that says no divorcees and no people who are currently getting a divorce (lines 1127–1128). Derek on the other hand had a church board member who was going through a divorce and recommended the person take some time away from his leadership responsibilities. Derek said,

We had a person on our church board who was going through a difficult divorce and all this and I had to say, "You know what? You need some time off right now. Let's take some time off and deal with yourself because there are some issues there of question" (lines 599–602).

Derek talked about how his upbringing helped him avoid certain struggles. Derek explained,

I was blessed to have a good childhood. I've not had a strong struggle in same-sex orientation where some people do. And so, I have to look at them and go, you know what, maybe they struggle with that more than I do where I might have more of a struggle in a different area that would need the spiritual gift of self-control, which we both have to apply (208–212).

Blake had a relative who struggled with his sexual identity. Of the relative's struggle Blake said,

This struggle may be a struggle he has for a season or could be a long time and I feel his pain for that, but I will not say that he's not welcome in the church because he's struggling or anybody else with any other issue for that matter (1104–1106).

Of the LGBT person who might choose to attend his church, Blake said, "I'd like to be able to look him in the eye and say…what you struggle with is no different than what this person struggle with or what I struggle with" (lines 1118–1120). Commenting about a sexually active LGBT person, Blake stated,

I think that falls into the category of any other person who may be struggling with some other issue of promiscuity. Saying that you're a Christian and being sexually active, hetero or homosexual, I think is a slippery slope of seeking to justify one's actions. I think we need to call it what it is and get help, spiritual and otherwise, for that (lines 1150–1154).

Harrison talked about a man in his church who struggled with same-sex attraction. Harrison shared the following:

There's one man who, when he allows himself to be transparent, considers that he acts out in ways that are inappropriate, and they're always in homosexual ways, but he is incapable of acknowledging that he is homosexual. He just sees that these are just these sporadic occurrences, but he's really a straight guy just acting. He's dealing with other issues that are all wound up in this, substance abuse and things like that (lines 828–833).

The Church of the Nazarene discourages the use of alcohol, tobacco products, and addictive substances. Some of the participants discussed these as place of struggle for some of their people. Allen said, "I know a big issue in our denomination is social drinking. I know pastors who make no issue with that (lines 715–716). Kendall indicated that he is not going to make an issue out of something he considers "non-essential" (line 1101). Kendall said it thusly,

I use that a lot with people and alcohol use in our church, I'm not going to judge that, I'm just going to ask that you be willing that the Lord brings that as an issue in your life, that you be willing to respond to Him in faith and obedience. So this would probably be a little bit of a deeper level than that (lines 1101–1104).

Bradley shared his thoughts about some inconsistencies within the church in how some of these issues are addressed. Bradley explained,

A matter of fact we hold like alcohol and tobacco in a higher... higher threshold level than we would—some other things that we say, that's just wrong, you know. So, I think we're a bit inconsistent there. I knew about the Board of Ministry where we would grill with people about, you know, when did you become a Christian or when did you get the divorce and then you got this divorce after you became a Christian. So, you know, it's kind of like there's other candidates who are maybe struggling in another area, or not paying their taxes or, we don't even ask those questions. We don't even ask questions had that have to deal with financial impropriety or you can steal but don't have an affair. So, I find that inconsistent (lines 617–627).

Darrell readily acknowledged that he did not understand other's struggle with addictions. Darrell reflected, "I don't understand somebody who has an issue with alcohol. That's not been a struggle of mine necessarily or that's not an issue that I wrestle with personally, so I don't really understand that" (lines 260–262). Referring to his church, Darrell said, "We haven't said if you have an issue with alcohol or if you're a struggling addict, or if you—we all have sins I think we recognize that; we accept people where they're at" (lines 670–672). Continuing his comments regarding struggle, Darrell added, "Maybe some person might be more wired for alcoholism or other issues. I do certainly think there are things in our lives that we all address, and we all struggle with (lines 769–773).

Allen also recognized the various struggles in people's live but, he is now more willing to accept that a same-sex orientation may not be resolved in the same way an alcoholic may overcome one's alcoholism. Referring to how he would have talked with an LGBT person Allen commented,

I think I would have said to them, "You know, salvation for you means this orientation goes away." I'm much more willing to say, "Now, you may never overcome that struggle in the same way that someone who is an alcoholic may never escape their struggle with temptation to alcohol or someone who is a sex addict may, you know, all of those things. One of the things I think is probably different for me is that I don't differentiate between those anymore (lines 135–143).

Continuing Allen said,

Someone that is struggling with an alcohol addiction may never overcome it, or tobacco. They may never be able to get beyond, "God, I'd really like to have a cigarette today," or "I really need a drink," but that doesn't mean that they need to become a drunk or revert to those old patterns of behavior (lines 163–168).

Harrison reiterated his conviction that every person faces challenges, struggle, and failure. Harrison explained it this way:

Every Christian is a human being who has challenges, weaknesses, and failures of all kinds, I would consider a Christian who understood themselves to be homosexual to be no different than that and I can't bring myself to distinguish that from any other weakness, challenge, failure, or concern that any other human being who calls themselves a follower of Christ would have. I know that sounds like I'm picturing it as a negative issue, but I still think of it the same thing as I'm a heterosexual Christian, but my heterosexuality is still filled with the possibilities of failure, the possibilities of weakness, the possibilities of all kinds of things that have to be addressed in a very similar way. So I think the issue is I take people at the place where they identify as a follower of Christ and then I think I'd just leave it that (lines 964–976).

Allen said of his church, "The issue to me is how [will] we react to people who are struggling with this [i.e., homosexuality] in their life, and whether we will be truly Christian or whether we will be something else" (lines 349–351).

Regardless of the various struggles people face, challenges they endure, mistakes they make, obstacles they must overcome, Blake said he wants his church…

to be a church that provides real solutions to real problems; it's part of our mission statement. And so, the real problems walking into our doors are addictions, the real problems walking into our doors are "My marriage sucks," or "My wife just left me," or "My kid's gay," or "My child's got an eating disorder" (lines 667–671).

Homosexuality and being a Christian. Another facet of this theme was related to participants' beliefs about a person being both homosexual and

Christian. Most of the participants felt that at homosexuality, at least in practice, was not consistent with being a Christian. Moreover, a number of participants commented that a person can have a homosexual orientation or attraction and be a Christian, but the practice of homosexuality was unacceptable. Other participants felt that persons can be LGBT and Christian; these are not mutually exclusive categories.

When asked if a person can be both homosexual and Christian, Travis responded in the following manner:

> Well I'm glad they are. I mean I'm glad they're Christian. You know I can't really change the fact that they're homosexual in their orientation or in their self-awareness. So being Christian is fabulous. You know, I'd rather them be Christian than anything else. Although if they're not going to be Christians, there's other options that I think are better than nothing, right, much better, right. I think you know, so great, fabulous, wonderful right? I mean what would I—okay I guess what would I rather them be if they're homosexual? What would I rather them be than Christian?
>
> Although I guess it goes unsaid that in fundamentalism that would be an oxymoron. They cannot be Christian and homosexual, right? I suspect that there's change coming even for the fundamentalist version of the Nazarenes where they'll be able to separate between orientation and practice (1785–1798).

Like Travis, Derek and others felt that using "homosexual Christian" was an "oxymoron;" that a person can be one or the other but not both. Derek expressed it thusly,

> [Can] you have a sexual orientation and be a practicing homosexual? If you're a practicing homosexual and a Christian, to me is an oxymoron, just as if I'm doing some other sin and I would call myself a Christian. Well, it's a relationship with God that I seem to be breaking and being cool with it. They'll answer to the Lord not to me, but that seems like an oxymoron to me. However, if someone has a same-sex attraction and they're a Christian, I'd get that. But you know, as much as I question that, there are a lot

of people who read the scripture and would interpret it differently based on their bias that also claim to be Christians (lines 805–817).

Curtis commented that same-sex attraction would not be an issue; beyond that, he stated that he chose not to judge people:

If we're talking about what we mean by homosexuality is attraction, I don't have a problem with that at all. With people who are saying if we buy that, will it mean they're openly practicing and Christian? Not my job to sort it out (lines 772–775).

So my feelings are if they're involved in a lifestyle like that, my tendency—if I were given the opportunity to talk to them and you'd have to develop a lot of relationship—would be I think God has something more for you. But I'm certainly not going to judge them (798–802).

Allen also stated his reservations about judging others:

In the issue of homosexuality, it's not my responsibility as a pastor to judge—now, I can see fruit. You know, we all see fruit. But that's not a qualitative judgment. So, largely I do not have an issue of someone saying, "I have a homosexual orientation and outlook, but I'm going to follow Jesus Christ." It's when that becomes the practice...[that it's problematic] (lines 835–839).

Referring to people who are both LGBT and Christian, Derek also said it is not his place to judge them. Derek stated,

Obviously, they don't answer to me. I'm not the judge. But to not live in full surrender to what I know is right and wrong or what the scripture says, that's a pretty difficult stretch for me to say, "You're a Christian, you're a full-out Christian. Really? Okay. Cool" (819–822).

If they have sexual orientation and they know it's wrong, could they be a Christian? Yeah. Could someone who does something wrong still be a Christian? Yeah. But there's not just a continual doing wrong, wrong, wrong...a continual lifestyle (lines 828–831).

Travis felt that being a practicing LGBT person and being a Christian would not fit within the Nazarene interpretation of scripture. Travis explained:

Now how would I feel about someone being homosexual and practicing homosexual sex with another homosexual and being Christian. If they were Nazarene you know, I would feel like they were astray from our understandings of the scripture on that. They wouldn't be the only Nazarene practicing things that were astray of our understanding of the scriptures. You know, the classic thing of what about that guy over that's overeating all the time, you know what I mean? (lines 1802–1808).

But with current Nazarene understanding of what the scriptures say, it would be the same as someone who is hetero having sex with someone they're not married to (lines 1818–1820).

Preston also felt an incongruence regarding same-sex practice and calling oneself a Christian. Preston said,

In regards to a practicing homosexual or a Christian? I don't know that I would use the phrase, I don't know that I'd call someone a homosexual if they weren't practicing. I guess I would be far more inclined to say someone that has homosexual tendencies, or can someone have homosexual tendencies and be a Christian? Absolutely. Do I believe someone can be a practicing homosexual and live a Christian life? I don't think so (lines 547–554).

Blake said he believed there are Christian LGBT people who struggle with same-sex attraction but wondered if one's struggle with same-sex attraction was any different from a heterosexual struggling with pornography. Blake questioned, "I think there are truly legitimate, honest, Christ followers who struggle with same-sex attraction, but is that any different than a person who is a Christ follower who struggles with heterosexual pornography?" (lines 835–837). Blake also commented on how he would approach a practicing LGBT person who professed to be a Christian:

I think I would approach someone who is a practicing homosexual professing to be a Christian, I like to think I would approach them the same way that I would approach someone who professes to be a Christian and is promiscuous in a heterosexual way or is gambling or is addicted to pornography or drug addiction and still say, "I'm professing to be a Christian." I would like to think that in that profession of being a Christian that they could begin to experience the liberation of being set free from the bondage of a sinful lifestyle (line 1058–1064). [But] I don't have a problem with someone saying that they have same-sex attraction (1079–1080).

Kendall said he would take the following approach when talking with the Christian LGBT person:

I'm not going to tell them they're not a Christian. I'm going to keep asking them what they mean by that if I have an opportunity. I guess I'm going to think again back to maybe orientation and practice a little bit at my stage of understanding.
   I'm going to maybe ask them about it, again, the same way I would ask about a Christian who continues to steal or a Christian who continues to commit adultery and just talk to them about the places where these kinds of behaviors may—the jeopardy that they may be causing to their own soul (lines 1079–1086).

Darrell felt that a person can be both homosexual and Christian, but he hoped that eventually the individual would come to understand that was not what God wanted for him/her. Darrell said,

I do believe people can be genuinely Christian and genuinely homosexual, but I would not say—again, I'm speaking maybe in that ideal sense that that would be long term, just to say that's okay that you're homosexual and that you believe in Jesus and God loves you and you just go on. I think God wants to move us, all of us, to deeper levels of understanding of who He is and who we are (lines 1088–1092).

I wouldn't demand they become heterosexual. I would ideally like to see them affirm that homosexuality is not in God's standard and then how do I move from that. I wouldn't expect [him] at some point to say, "I need to find a wife and get married." But I do think there's a standard in which I cannot continue to practice homosexuality in my life and honor God at the same time (1134–1139).

Bradley expressed a similar observation,

Anybody who comes to Christ, Christ wants them to grow and mature, become like Him. So, that could be required of everyone. So, I think that would happen was with people who are gay or— everybody is going to sort out what that means. Some would say, "Well, I'm really trying to be celibate," or some would say, "No, I'll just marry somebody of the opposite sex even though I'm not attracted." And that's happened. And some would say, "Well, I'm not going to fight it" (815–821).

Although counter to the Church of the Nazarene's position, Harold proposed compatibility between homosexuality and being a Christian. Harold stated it thusly,

I guess I see that those two things can be compatible in the same way that heterosexuality can be compatible with—the issue for me is not gender as much as it the way in which we treat each other; the way in which we understand sexuality in the context of covenant sexuality, in the context of empowerment and not abuse or using or manipulation or control or all the different ways it can be perverted and twisted (lines 519–524).

Keith admitted there are people who are both Christian and LGBT, but he had not met them. Keith said,

Here's the thing, I know there exists people who are deeply in love with Jesus, who are Christian in the sense that the Church understands that were in that intimate, passionate, evangelical sense and they're gay, I just don't know any yet. I've never met a person like that. I know they exist. I've never met a person like that (lines 573–577).

When talking about being LGBT and being a Christian, Keith struggled with the "compatibility" of those two ideas. Keith commented,

I think "compatible" is not the word I would use, and I wouldn't say it was mutually exclusive either. It's somewhere else, I don't know. I don't know how to answer that question exactly.

What are my feelings? Ambivalence. I don't know. I mean my lack of experience in this area is telling, I think, at this point. I wouldn't put that on incompatibility. I think it's possible to be a Christian and to be gay, so yeah.

The question though in my mind is: Is the label "gay" going to be the same as adulterer? Or is the label "gay" going to be the same as heterosexual, it just is what it is? There's where, for me, intention lies.

I think this all comes back around to, for me, for how gay people don't want me to talk about their homosexuality being anything other than the way God created them, period. And because I don't believe gay people chose to be gay, then that leads me to—I guess it would become just like the word "heterosexual," but it's not easy for me to get there, as you can hear. (1112–1130).

Matt ministers primarily to the LGBT population. Regarding being LGBT and Christian Matt made the following remarks,

I know quite a few people who consider themselves LGBT and Christian. Here's my feeling—and this is straight from our GS' mouth to mine—if you have read the Bible and you come down differently than I do, I'm not going to judge you. I believe the goal is: Are you looking towards Christ and asking Him every day, "What can I do?"

I always say when people ask me what's the end goal, I say for people to be waking up every day and saying, "Okay, Christ, whatever you want me to do today, however you want me to do it, yes." If you are honestly seeking that out and you come to a different conclusion than I do, I'm going to let God be the judge and I'm going to continue to love you (lines 643–654).

Matt reflected, "Do I think when we get to the other side, there will be those who are in same-sex relationships? Probably" (lines 656–657).

Theme Three: Ministerial Journey

This theme addresses the personal and professional development of the participants related to their understanding of homosexuality and LGBT issues. Several of the participants discussed their developmental journey and the evolution of their thought and feeling regarding homosexuality. Some of the participants referenced their theological education as part of their developmental process. A few participants spoke about the length of time they have served, or been affiliated with, the Church of the Nazarene. One participant specifically referenced his call to ministry.

Developmental journey. Allen talked about how his thinking and feelings about homosexuality have changed during the past two decades. Allen said,

I would say my position professionally and personally is vastly different than it was 23 years ago when I started ministry. I don't think I would have been as open 23 years ago or 24 years ago to say someone who has a homosexual orientation can even be saved. Can even be saved. I think I would have said to them, "You know, salvation for you means this orientation goes away" (lines 126–135)....I am now able to delineate much more between orientation and behavior, the same way I would with anyone else (lines 162–163).

Travis expressed a similar evolution in his thinking about homosexuality. Travis said, "Yeah, so my personal feelings have morphed since I was a kid in where this was like the single worst abomination sin. It was viewed with revulsion and repulsion" (lines 731–734). Travis continued, "I mean wrestling with this issue for seven or eight years has definitely morphed my position" (lines 742–743).

Harrison acknowledged that his response to LGBT people have changed since his childhood. Harrison admitted,

Ignoring homosexuals or treating them with hostility, making derogatory comments about gay people, when I was a kid, you could do that, and everyone thought it was funny. But when you grow up, it's not funny to make those kinds of statements about people (lines 417–420).

Travis reiterated his earlier point when he said,

I was raised in the Deep South. I mean the term gay, for us was a 1980s synonym for stupid, dumb, idiotic. For me to say that is so gay, in my own brain in terms of idiom just means stupid. It was not a reflection in any way, shape, or form towards homosexually oriented people (lines 1175–1180).

Referring to same-sex relationships, Keith shared the following: "I find personally this has been this ongoing sort of evolving issue in my life that I continue to have theological reflection/intention over it within the context of this denominational family" (lines 129–132).

Harold, Harrison, and Curtis each shared stories about how knowing or getting to know an LGBT person or people changed their perception about homosexuality and LGBT individuals. For example, Harold had a gay couple attending his church. They invited Harold and his wife to a party. Harold shared his experience:

They had a party a few months later and they invited us out and we went out and hung out, had a great time. Those gay men throw great parties. That was the first real exposure I ever had where I was friends with somebody who was openly gay. It was really helpful, I think, for me to blow stereotypes. They're just people at the end of the day. They worried about the same things that I worried about, they had the same sorts of issues that I did, it's just they were gay. I think that was helpful for me (lines 750–758).

When Harrison was a child his father befriended a gay co-worker. Although Harrison did not know the man was gay, Harrison said that when he learned of the man's sexual orientation it became a point of growth for him. Harrison shared the following:

There was a man that when I was growing up worked…for a Sears in town. My dad befriended him. We would go fishing with this guy. I never knew until he had died of a heart attack one day in his late 40s [when] my dad told me that he was gay and lived with a man. In those days—we're talking about the early 70s—that was just not spoken about, at least in the part of the world where I was. It was a dark secret no one ever talked about. I remember hearing that as an adult, processing that and I remember distinctly coming to the realization, so what? It didn't change anything. He was still a great guy to be around. He was still a fun, loving person. That was a growing point for me because it enabled me to see someone just as a normal human being whose orientation was different than most of the people I knew, or at least most of the people who I knew acknowledged their orientation (575–594).

Curtis commented on how people are often labeled, and how labeling can be dehumanizing e.g., seeing only the label (gay, homosexual, black, Hispanic, etc.) and not the person. With this in mind, Curtis said,

That's the power of getting to know them as a person first and then discovering these other things or dealing with these other things because when you know them as a person it impacts—so once you've fallen in love with someone that's gay, before you knew they were gay and then you find out they were gay, all of a sudden you start changing your definitions of what it means to be gay or black or Hispanic or whatever it is (lines 542–547).

Seminary/advanced theological education. Curtis's developmental journey was also influenced by his theological education. Referring to the evolution of his thoughts and feelings about homosexuality, Curtis shared the following:

> [As] I was getting more advanced theological education at seminary was the same time I actually started running into and connecting with and working with people who were homosexuals. I was in the grocery business, and we ended up—it was just a number of people that were openly gay. It was kind of a blessing in that my theology stepped up to some of the stuff I talked about at the same time that my emotions were changing because several of those people were people I really liked and connected with and got along with well (lines 139–148).

About the same time Curtis was meeting and getting to know his LGBT co-workers, he was "getting good theology [that] said it's okay, love people" (lines 159–162).

Harrison said that a number of fellow students from seminary "came out" after they graduated. Harrison commented,

> I since have found out that a number of classmates at seminary have come out since I left seminary. I have tried to maintain a speaking relationship with them in a very open way to say, "You're my friend no matter what. [Even though] we clearly have a disagreement on this point" (lines 427–430).

Allen recalled his experience at seminary, "I thank my stars I had Dr. _____ for Ethics and today's moral problems. But there are also days when I just curse that man, because I'm not willing to look at things [as] black and white" (lines 862–865).

In a similar fashion, Keith talked about how seminary influenced his thinking. Keith said,

> I feel pretty good about my seminary education. But they opened the door to this world of theological reflection and many voices

and people I listen to, and I think, all right? I did very well in seminary because of that. And so, my Christian faith was no longer the simple Christian faith that I grew up with—an evangelical, almost fundamentalism, not Nazarene but almost fundamentalism when I grew up—seminary just kind of turned that all upside down (1172–1181).

Time in the Nazarene church. Several of the participants talked about the length of time they have been affiliated with the Church of the Nazarene. A few also mentioned the church's influence on their understanding of homosexuality and LGBT issues. Matt said, "I grew up in the Church of the Nazarene, so I already knew here's where the church stands on these issues" (lines 111–112). Kendall whose father was a Nazarene pastor said,

My life as a son of a pastor and being involved in the life of the church probably since the day I was born, it's probably hard for me to differentiate a little bit what are my own feelings. I guess that's true for anything. We're always influenced by different things, and the church has been a major influence in my life (lines 232–236).

Curtis talked about growing up in the church, and how this affected his feelings about LGBT people. Curtis said, "Growing up in the church, I grew up with some initial fears about people who were homosexual having not really encountered it but just having heard the kinds of things you hear" (lines 134–137). Allen also discussed the length of time he had been in the church and its influence on his thinking. Allen stated,

I've been in Church of the Nazarene—I'm 47 years old. I've been a church member almost 40 years and I was probably 7 years old or 8 years old when I joined the church. So, I have to say the Church of the Nazarene has formed both my theological and personal perspective (lines 266–270).

Derek was also raised as a Nazarene. Derek said of his experience,

Being born and raised in the Nazarene Church, my folks were Nazarene missionaries, the Nazarene Church is all I know and so I'm sure I'm deeply impacted by the theology of our church. But as I examine the scripture for myself, and my faith is my own, I'm absolutely in line with the teachings that I've been brought up with. So I imagine it's had a big impact on me (lines 99–104).

Preston shared a similar story about his life. Preston commented, "I'm a fourth generation Nazarene—both sides of my family" (line 75). Preston also said, "I guess I can't escape the fact that this is the church family that I've grown up in and that I know best. It's the only church family that I've known (lines 100–101). Later Preston acknowledged, "I just know having been birthed in the church and raised in the church and educated by the church in that context that inescapably I've been shaped by it (lines 133–135).

God's call to ministry. One participant specifically referenced God's call to ministry. For Matt, God called him specifically to minister to the LGBT community. Matt stated it this way:

A majority of my time is spent interacting with LGBT individuals. A majority of my friend group considers themselves LGBT. A majority of my congregants consider themselves LGBT. This is where I feel God has called me to. This is the thing that God is blessing in my life. This is the thing that God has said, "I want you here" (lines 140–152).

Theme Four: Beliefs about Homosexuality

This theme highlights the participants' beliefs about homosexuality, including the etiology (origin/causes) of a same-sex orientation. Participants also described their understanding of the differences between same-sex attraction, same-sex orientation, and same-sex practice. Some participants provided descriptions of LGBT individuals. Participants also shared their thoughts about same-sex relationships and gay marriage.

Etiology and beliefs about homosexuality. Participants differed in their beliefs about how homosexuality or a same-sex orientation occurs. For example, Bradley stated, "I think there are people born that way" (line 49). Blake observed,

> I'm probably not as knowledgeable on this as I should be, but I think there's still open debate about this. Is a person born gay? Do they have certain feministic qualities or masculine qualities about them that they've acquired? It may be kind of a moot point, but I think that there are truly legitimate, honest Christ followers who struggle with same-sex attraction (lines 831–836).

Darrell's opinion about same-sex orientation differed; he said,

> I don't believe that God makes us that way. I do believe though that people have a propensity toward that. Again, I think we're all sinful and so I do think there are ways in our lives that we have a tendency (lines 767–770).

Regarding sexual orientation, Keith argued, "I don't think you could choose your sexual orientation any more than you can choose your eye color. I honestly don't think you can" (lines 967–968). Keith added, "I don't believe gay people choose to be gay. I know they don't. I know they don't any more than I chose to be heterosexual" (lines 981–982). Harrison expressed a similar thought:

> I don't think anybody wishes for this or sets out to become this or that. I think that orientation is an orientation. I think there's evidence that people are born with this as an orientation. I don't have any question about that. I also think that there are some folks for whom the orientation is nurtured and [I] have seen both of those cases in my experience (lines 1006–1010).

Like Harrison, Bradley also thought that nurture plays a role in the development of a homosexual orientation.

But then you have some who by nurture would say they're gay. They don't have any, maybe confusion, or ambiguity in their body but they're attracted to men. So, then what does that mean for that person if you know that's how they are? That's where some will say, "Well, they could get help to become straight. Because they got nurtured that way, they could get un-nurtured that way" (lines 755–759).

Keith introduced the possibility of the birth of an intersex person. Keith framed it thusly:

I think it's really telling that there are persons who are born her-maphroditically and that their gender is chosen for them by surgery. God doesn't make mistakes, right? Well, what is that? When I'm there, when I start with: "Do homosexuals choose this?" No, I don't believe they choose this. They've not chosen this (lines 993–998).

Bradley also touched on the idea of an intersex person:

They lean toward homosexuality even though they may not be born with what I call, and there's probably more technical term, sexual confusion at birth to where even the medical doctor does not know whether that person is a boy or a girl because they have sexual organs manifestations of both (lines 51–54).

Bradley continued, "Some people are just born that way, some people never get that; never get convinced, they never get that God would allow that to happen. God wouldn't…but he does (lines 747–749).

Kendall admitted his lack of understanding about the etiology of homo-sexuality and one's sexual identity. Kendall confessed, "The whole nature/nurture kind of conversation in terms of the homosexual lifestyle is one that I have to humbly say, I don't know" (lines 978–980). Kendall also said,

Sometimes I just don't understand the sexual depth, I guess, of [the] interconnectedness with someone's identity. For a homosexual, it seems to be more prevalent, at least those who I've been exposed to and aware of that the sexual identity and their personal identity seems so tightly connected (lines 983–986).

Derek seemed to imply, that a same-sex orientation may result from childhood sexual abuse:

> I think the grace aspect of me in this issue is I just know that everybody's situation is different than mine. I have, for example, not been molested as a child nor have some deformity in how I see the orientation of my sexuality where I'm aware that some people have and that has thrown them off. I just think I haven't had that experience (lines 202–206).

Allen talked about a young man in his church who was gay. Allen revealed his thoughts that the young man may have developed a gay identity because of the environment within which he was raised. Allen said,

> I have a young man who is very close to me…He struggled all his life. He was—his mother was a single parent, so he's never really had a good male influence in his life to a variety of issues and he's always struggled with…Well, he's now in a 2–year monogamous homosexual relationship (lines 192 & 195–198).

Travis reflected that some individuals have been aware of a same-sex orientation from her or his earliest recollection. Travis said that for some people,

> This has been a reality in their self-awareness since their earliest memories. You know, with no trauma attached to it, no abuse attached to it whatsoever. I mean what do you do with that? When you're saying all people are supposed to be straight in the Bible, like what do you do with that (lines 657–661)?

Travis continued his thought, "What do we do with someone who has had this as their self-awareness their entire life? I just don't know that we have access to really easy answers about that right now" (lines 677–679).

Bradley's comment suggested agreement with Travis's observation. Bradley observed, "It's easy to think that we can counsel people out of homosexuality or being gay, but I think the issue is a whole lot deeper than that" (lines 60–62). Regarding a homosexual orientation, Bradley added, "That's how some people are and no amount of drugs or counseling or surgeries or whatever are going to change that about them" (lines 126–128).

Preston felt that regardless of one's sexual orientation, or its etiology, people should be committed to living a pure life. Preston framed it this way:

I suppose that we all deal with different kinds of temptations by the way we're made up and by the way we're raised which goes to the whole thing of, "Is homosexuality a learned thing or is it genetic?" I don't know if it matters because we're still committed to living lives of purity (lines 588–592).

Differences between attraction, orientation, and practice. Participants discussed their views of the differences between same-sex attraction, same-sex orientation, and same-sex practice. Participants made a distinction between same-sex attraction and orientation and same-sex practices. Most of the participants felt that same-sex attraction and same-sex orientation was conceivable; however, most participants also felt that same-sex practice or homosexual behavior was inappropriate and/or sinful. Allen said, "I separate homosexual tendency from the practice of homosexual behavior (lines 98–99). I am now able to delineate much more between orientation and behavior (lines 162–163). Orientation I do not have a problem with" (line 809). Allen also commented, "That's a marked change for me over the years of ministry, I don't have a problem with that [orientation]. I have a problem with the practice in the same way as I would any other sinful practice" (lines 814–816).

Curtis stated, "We [the Church of the Nazarene] don't believe that feelings of homosexuality are wrong. We believe it's the practice that's not endorsed by scripture" (lines 106–107). Commenting on his personal beliefs, Curtis said,

I would divide between attraction, orientation, whatever you want to call that and the actual practice of the lifestyle (lines 627–629). If we're talking about orientation and not practice, I'm good (line 707). If we're talking about what we mean by homosexuality is attraction, I don't have a problem with that at all (lines 772–773).

Derek argued that there is a big difference between having a same-sex orientation and adopting a "homosexual label" (lines 658–660). Derek said, "Sexual orientation…you [may be] struggling with that…but you're nowhere near being labeled a homosexual" (lines 662–664). Derek continued, "A non-practicing person who's attracted to the same-sex, I don't see that as being someone who's a practicing homosexual at all—very different" (lines 699–700).

Blake shared a similar view: "I think a person can have a homosexual orientation and have that be a point of 'I'm attracted to a same-sex person.' But the decision of acting on that is really—that is a willful choice that a person makes" (lines 843–847). Blake also acknowledged, "I think there might be some who struggle with that for a lifetime and yet, with God's help, choose not to act on it" (lines 885–886).

Regarding orientation and practice, Darrell provided the following observation and admitted the dilemma this presents for LGBT people:

I do think there is a difference there [between orientation and practice]. I think the way that we're wired does play into that. I think that that's maybe my biggest struggle with this issue that I don't think I've resolved or really had a conversation about is, Okay, so if we believe, which I do, that homosexuality is not a biblical standard, so then what does that mean for somebody who lives that lifestyle, who has that orientation? What does that mean for them moving forward with Christ? (lines 798–804)…I don't know, I haven't resolved that (line 808).

Harrison also recognized the challenges same-sex oriented people face. Harrison said,

I see homosexuality as an orientation as a challenge to those who live in this world because by the virtue of that orientation and as the way in which I understand the biblical, theological underpinnings of the Christian faith, persons who are oriented as homosexuals are limited in the ways in which they can properly express themselves (lines 994–998).

Travis acknowledged the predicament for gays and lesbians. Travis argued that for,

The heterosexual guy there's always the chance he's going to meet someone and get to express his sexuality but in terms of the homosexual person, you're basically throwing out something that's understandably a deal-breaker. They're like, I'll will never be able to express my sexual orientation physically (lines 1440–1444).... The hetero guy is always holding out, you know, maybe I'll find someone that will accept me...and you're asking the homosexual person to never express their sexuality (1449–1452).

Darrell too addressed the complexity of the situation for same-sex oriented individuals:

A complication that I feel in my spirit is I recognize when you begin to talk about (lines 1153–1154) an orientation in our life with people and intimacy...it's a little different plane because it's relational, not just these are the choices that I make in my life. That's why I'm saying it's complicated and not just a one dimensional thing (lines 1156–1160).

In addition to orientation or practice, Kendall added a third consideration: sexual "identity." Kendall observed,

The identity issue is...a place, I think, where the Church can begin to land in terms of trying to minister or work with people who are so deeply engaged and enmeshed in this lifestyle and maybe for reasons they completely understand [or] that they don't, and to potentially talk to them about the difference between orientation and behavior (lines 1002–1007).

Derek suggested that people are often too swift in labeling others and that identity and orientation are different. Derek argued, "Just because you're same-sex oriented doesn't mean you're homosexual, and we're pretty quick to label in our community. Having an identity like that is a little different than having an orientation like that" (lines 214–216). Continuing his thought Derek said, "There's a huge difference between sexual attraction and homosexual orientation. I think we label people too quick" (lines 629–630).

Curtis felt that there was a difference between same-sex attraction and same-sex practice. Curtis observed, "Differentiating between the attraction and the practice, that's a nuance most laypeople don't make" (lines 119–120). Curtis continued, "I would distinguish between orientation, attraction, whatever you want to call it and practice and even within practice, I would distinguish between an incident and a lifestyle" (lines 667–669). Harrison argued a similar point stating, "Most people don't recognize or distinguish what I would call orientation from practice (lines 157–158). Bradley went a step farther and recommended clarifying the terminology to minimize the confusion about homosexuality. Bradley proposed,

Part of the confusion is we use the same word to describe a person as to describe an act. So, we say homosexual: "they are homosexual." Often we mean that they are acting out on that tendency, not just describing their disposition. So, if we could clarify the terminology just a bit and it's confusing in the culture too, it's not just in the church, to where when we talk about a person who is gay, we should be able to mean by a term that that's their disposition or that's their tendency. It doesn't mean they are gay in lifestyle, but we don't make that distinction (lines 153–161).

Harold offered an alternative viewpoint. Rather than limiting his insights to same-sex concerns, Harold discussed sexuality as part of what it means to be fully human. Harold stated it thusly:

I think that practicing—again, it seems like a false dichotomy to me. It's like—I'm trying to give a good analogy of what that'd be like, I don't know. You can like doughnuts, you just can't eat them. I don't get that. I think that human sexuality is such an important part of what it means to be human that to deny that to another person is not very loving. I wouldn't have a problem with it and again, the issue for me isn't orientation or even practice but how we practice, how do we love? Are you in a committed monogamous relationship or are you an alley cat? That to me seems to be a bigger question than body parts or who you're attracted to or what you're attracted to. How are we treating our sexuality with respect and dignity and loving towards another person instead of exploiting and those sorts of things? And that's not a gay or straight issue, that's a human issue (lines 952–974).

Descriptions of LGBT people. In this section, several of the participants provided descriptions of LGBT individuals. Keith said, "These are intelligent, savvy people" (line 558). Harold echoed Keith's observation saying, "I think they're a lot more savvy than I realized" (line 1020). Allen shared several instances where he observed an LGBT person and his perception of the person. For example,

One of the younger girls in the church has a friend. She came and helped out with Bible school, volunteered, came to church a couple of Sundays. I don't 100% know her orientation. I have suspicion. She has a very butch look about her (lines 316–320).

Allen shared another experience:

I went in to this one store and the manager there, there was something that just didn't—that was odd to me. I don't want to say odd to anybody, but it was odd to me. I couldn't put my finger on it, dressed very much the same, very long straight, stringy hair, an ankle length kind of a dress turtleneck shirt (lines 401–405)… On the way out of the store, the phone rang. And when the manager picked up the phone, the voice did not match the persona.

It was a very deep, gravelly voice, definitely masculine and as I walked past, it was very apparent—when I heard that voice—that I was looking at, a transvestite, it was very unsettling (lines 408–413).

Allen detailed an account of working with an LGBT individual:

We had a manager—I worked for a rental car agency, and it was widely known that the manager was a long term monogamous homosexual (line 427–428)…There were days he came to work, and I didn't even notice. The other guys…that I worked with noticed that he'd come visibly lame and of course then the jokes, you know, about _____ (lines 431–433). He was walking very, very slowly. Sitting very gingerly (line 435). And of course for all the guys in the van, it was an illustration that there had been a rough night at home (lines 439–440).

Allen also observed an LGBT couple when his children were with him. Allen shared the following story:

About a year and a half ago, my three kids and I went…to see the U.S. Women's National Soccer team play.…And as we are standing in line waiting for the park to open up, there was an adolescent homosexual couple in front of us. And they were very demonstrative (lines 470–474).…I was more put off by the fact that, you're in line with a thousand people, why are you hanging all over each other? (lines 476–477).

Travis talked about an LGBT woman that he and his wife had known for several years. Travis said,

We've probably known her for most of the 17 years we've been here. She's fabulous. I mean we adore her. She babysat our kids, whatever I mean you know. She's just sort of a masculine-ish gal but I mean we adore her (lines 1277–1280).

One of Bradley's relatives struggled with his sexual orientation. About his relative, Bradley said, "He's a musician. He's a singer. He sings with opera, and he sings in other ways too; he teaches music so that the people he would be around have a greater percentage of homosexuals and the people he interacts with" (lines 334–336). Bradley also talked about an LGBT person who occasionally attended his church. In describing this individual, Bradley observed,

It's sometimes hard for men to know how to relate to another man. Who you know struggles in an area. Just how do you greet him? Give him a hug? A hand-shake? You know, how close do you and personal space, how close do you get to them? What do you talk about it? Not to use a stereotype, but sometimes, they're [gay men are] not interested in sports and guys want to talk about sports or whatever. So, you know that's not something they care anything about (lines 401–408).

Keith's church is located in an area with a relatively large LGBT population. Keith provided an example of what he's observed:

The way gay men greet one another, I just noticed that there is—I don't know how to articulate what it is, but from just looking at things anthropologically, I'm like, "Wow, there's a whole culture here that I just have no access to," and you get a little glimpse of it, and I find that interesting (lines 483–486). [Then] there've been times, just really honestly, like when I was friends with _____ and _____ and I was walking—they were at a parade right by our house—I was walking up, they didn't know I was there, and I watched their interaction. It was just like a husband and wife interaction (lines 488–491).

Keith also said of the LGBT people in his neighborhood, "The gay people I know in this neighborhood are crazy drunks. I mean they're really addicted to alcohol. It seems like the big thing I notice these days" (lines 631–633). Keith continued by describing one of the gay men he knows: "[He] seems pretty gay to us. He's very effeminate" (line 758).

Harold shared an encounter he had with a gay man. Harold said, "He would introduce himself as, 'My name's Babe, you know like Babe Ruth.' I thought, 'Okay.' He wasn't like really effeminate, which is kind of funny about the whole thing" (lines 746–748).

Harrison talked about three gay men with whom he has interacted. Harrison described each of the men:

> One who was a Roman Catholic priest and left the priesthood and married a woman, then divorced the woman and finally came out late in life and is almost 80. He's a very sad individual, a brilliant mind, successful…but emotionally and relationally a wreck, and that's always saddened me (lines 564–569).

The second individual was a man his father had befriended. The participant and his father and the man fished together. It was following the man's death that Harrison's father revealed to him that the man was gay. When Harrison heard the news he said, "I remember hearing that as an adult, processing that and I remember distinctly coming to the realization, so what? It didn't change anything. He was still a great guy to be around. He was still a fun, loving person" (lines 587–589).

The third individual was a gentleman whom Harrison has encouraged him to go to therapy to help address his feelings of guilt. Harrison described him:

> The guy that I keep trying to get to go to [therapy] has grown up in a Nazarene family, spent all of his life in the Church of the Nazarene but has hidden his dark secrets. He's unwilling to talk about them or acknowledge them. I think it would emotionally devastate him to actually have to say, "I'm a homosexual." He's distanced himself from the help I've tried to offer and is not ready to say, "I need help" (lines 848–853).

Travis shared a story about a young girl with same-sex attraction. Travis said,

Okay this is an amazing story... _____ was a little girl....Her parents died when she was six or seven and she was raised by an aunt and uncle. When she was eight, her uncle taught her firsthand through raping her repeatedly about human sexuality. From that point on she had very strong same-sex attractions (lines 788–780). She got married when she grew up, had two or three daughters and her marriage dissolved...because of relational issues including physical abuse...she was attracted to her own sex and finally came out when she was maybe in her late 30s or early 40s (lines 803–807).

Preston had an LGBT individual attend his church occasionally. Preston offered the following description of the man: "He'd come to church here and there. He knew, I knew how he was living, but he seemed kind of, he was a lonely guy and he seemed to be reaching out for something" (lines 166–169).

Travis also described a lesbian couple who attended his church. Recalling the couple Travis said,

The first six months they were here, most of the people in the church probably didn't realize that [she] was a chick. Had no idea she was a girl right. She had concealed that in every conceivable manner. Then when they slowly did figure out, Oh, that's a woman, then they—because she dresses and looks and acts and cuts her hair like a trucker, a male trucker right. When they finally figured out that she was a woman, it didn't dawn on any of them that they're gay, right (891–898).

Darrell provided a description of lesbian couple that his wife had assisted. Of these women, Darrell observed,

There was another young couple that [my wife] dealt with that came for a brief time and actually moved out of the state, I think. I think she got transferred, a work transfer or something, but a young gal, was in a homosexual lifestyle, she had some kids and I think divorced, probably around 30 and had met a gal and they were living together here in town. I'm not sure that she was more bisexual, and her partner was very tomboyish, very butch in her appearance, very short cut hair, plaid shirts, very nondescript, not feminine in any way, so it was pretty obvious (502–509).

Travis shared a similar description of a LGBT woman he knew. Travis said of her, "She's an ex-Navy vet and she's boyish and doesn't hide it. She's very stereotypically you know, works in construction, you know what I mean?" (lines 1264–1266).

Matt lives in, works with, and ministers to a primarily LGBT population. His church is located in a section of the city with a large population of LGBT individuals. Matt welcomes LGBT people to worship. Matt recalled an evening just before the service began:

Nothing you can say to us, I think, shocks us or surprises us at this point. Sometimes it gets a little strange, but you know…For instance, we had one night where it was like a clown car; a van pulled up out front and drag queen after drag queen after drag queen after drag queen got out of the car, and they were coming to church. That's the type of place that we're trying to put together, a place where anybody can feel welcome (lines 267–272).

Gay marriage and same-sex relationships. In this section, participants shared their views about same-sex relationships and gay marriage. Participants recognized the tension between upholding the church's position and state and federal government legalization of same-sex marriages. Allen said that the legalization of same-sex marriages will present new questions for pastoral ministry. Allen shared the following:

_____ is a state now that recognizes homosexual marriage (lines 762–763). There are some pastoral issues coming with that shift in our legal system (lines 765–766). We are going to have people who are coming to our churches who are legally married in the eyes of law. That's going to pose a unique set of pastoral tensions and issues. For instance, you have a legally married gay couple come, they're part of your church for whatever reason. They're having marital difficulty. They are coming to you for counsel. How are you going to deal with that pastorally? (lines 767–773). Or they are on the verge of divorce and there are children involved. How do you deal with that pastorally? (lines 775–776). There's a theological tension I'm wrestling with particularly, you know, as it pertains to marriage. Does a legal marriage necessitate a spiritual marriage? (lines 780–781).

Referring to the church's response to LGBT people, Harrison made the following observation, "We have to be better because it will be the law of the land before I die that all states have same-sex marriage—it will just be the case" (lines 247–248). Harrison declared,

The Church has committed itself to being in bed with the State for so long on this; whereas I could see the fact that the State may begin to try, or someone may begin to try to force back on the Church, "Well, if you're going to be an agent of State to certify marriage, then you're going to have to do all the marriages." I can see that as a possibility, and that would be unfortunate as well (lines 250–254).

Curtis discussed how his people—and he—responded to a bill legalizing gay marriage in his state. Curtis said,

I've had people want me to be involved in anti-gay sorts of things that are Nazarenes. We had that come up in the State of _____ with the gay marriage thing. There were people that really thought we should have a petition out there and get that signed and I put it right there [motions to trash can] when I got it (198–201).

Regarding his own feelings about gay marriage, Curtis stated, "I'm neither for nor against gay marriage. What the state does is different from what the church does in my opinion. But I'm not going to swing a dead cat that's going to hit some people that Jesus loves" (lines 215–217).

Kendall attended the denominational General Assembly where the issue of same-sex marriage was a topic of discussion. Kendall said, "During

General Assembly the Supreme Court ruled on the same-sex marriage issues" (lines 319–320). Kendall continued,

> There was a statement kind of made from the front that seemed a little out of place, but then the statement that "This is 'the issue' of this General Assembly" just made my blood boil and just made me kind of sad. I think it was the same-sex marriage or preserving marriage as being between one man and one woman. I think he was basically saying that if we don't give our churches and our pastors clear directives on how to respond to this then we're doomed to fall away from the mission of the church. And [it] was the statement that was wanting to be introduced into the Covenant of Christian Conduct, I think. It was going to be much more even explicit than it is now in terms of a response to homosexuality and to same-sex marriage (lines 324–346).

Harrison felt that the issue of gay-marriage presents a dividing line. Harrison said,

> We're being forced into two camps. We're being forced into the camp on the left that demands that same-sex marriage ought to happen without question and there should be no issues and the camp on the right that just wants to decry how horrible it is (lines 276–279).

Sharing the following story, Keith revealed his struggle about same-sex marriages:

> A Nazarene pastor in another country, in the Netherlands, asked me, "Would you provide same-sex union for a gay couple if you didn't have the constraints of the Church of the Nazarene?" I didn't know how to answer that. I still don't know the answer to that question (lines 135–140).

Of performing a gay-marriage, Keith said, "I've never been asked to do that. I've never been in that position" (lines 157–158). Keith continued,

I think that if the denomination did not provide this constraint I probably would, in the right circumstance, provide say, a civil union—no, that's not true. Perhaps I would in a certain sense provide space for a civil union. I have not gotten to the place theologically for sacramentalizing a gay union or have been able to get past that particular barrier for me (lines 171–176).

Harrison said of same-sex marriage,

To date, I can find no sufficient biblical warrant for that in my mind. I have tried. I have worked through this on multiple occasions, but ultimately Richard Hays and others like him...have convinced me that the scriptures actually teach something other than that (lines 164–166 & 168–169).

Reiterating his point, Harrison stated, "I don't have a theological position or any kind of a position that supports same-sex marriage" (lines 210–211).

Returning to Keith's struggle with same-sex marriages, he reflected,

If I came to the day where I thought I had to, for example, provide marriage for a gay couple, then I need to think about another denomination—although, I'm not sure anymore if that's even the case. I've never been in that particular situation where I've been asked to do that (lines 315–318).

Keith shared some of his dilemma with gay marriage:

The reason I hesitate when it comes to the whole marriage thing is because I know my experience has been that I've never met a gay person that if they were straight I would have married. Will there ever be a day when I meet a couple that are deeply committed to Christ and want to enter into covenant? That's when the test is going to come, but I've never had that test (lines 586–592).

Regarding marriage, Harrison declared,

Marriage is not anyone's right. I don't have to marry anybody. Marriage from the Christian perspective is the coming together of a man and a woman before God and witnesses, but the pastor has the responsibility to certify that these two people should be married (lines 256–259).

Darrell shared a similar perspective about marriage stating, "There's this [biblical] pattern I think that is healthy and right and good and it's a man and a wife…it's that intimacy that I think changes when it becomes the same-sex" (lines 1196–1198).

Bradley confessed he had difficulty using the word marriage to describe a same-sex relationship. Bradley admitted, "I have a hard time dealing with the word marriage attached to those who are not men and women. To me, I want to keep that word for a man and woman" (lines 687–698).

Blake admitted concerns about the church losing its identity if it begins to embrace same-sex marriage. Blake said,

I think we lose our identity if we think that if we—maybe what I mean by that is we stopped standing on something that we should stand for. Marriage, for example, two loving couples should be able to do what they want, but we stand for marriage as being between a man and a woman. How do we stay in a compassionate relationship with another person who is in that relationship who, now by law, has been made legal? If we start allowing that in our church, are we going to lose our identity for what we believe and stand for as followers of Christ? (lines 556–574).

Travis said he understood why same-sex couples want the right to marry; however, same-sex marriage concerns him. Travis commented:

I completely understand why they're like, "Hey, we want some sort of legal protection that if something happens to my kids I want them to go to _____." I agree with them they should (lines 698–701). So, I understand completely why gay people would want to have the legal protection of marriage (710–712). I remember when gay marriage was really getting talked about the most, I wasn't thrilled with the idea of my kids growing up in a culture where that was normalized and just seen as morally neutral. Because I wasn't hoping for that experience for them (lines 715–719).

Bradley recognized the limitation placed on LGBT individuals by telling them that same-sex relationships are prohibited. Bradley explained it thusly,

I struggle with saying to someone who—that's who they are, that's how they were born, to say to that person because you just happen to be born that way. You could never be married or never have a relationship even though it's with the same person. I struggle with making that so hard and fast, because I do believe there are people who are genuinely gay. That's who they are and that's how they are (lines 553–560).

Bradley also observed, "And to say that you can't be part of all the other benefits that other people have who are born straight or nurtured straight, I just find that to be unfair and not fully appreciating that person's position or predicament" (lines 763–766).

Harrison stated directly that the church does not have the "capacity to speak to" same-sex unions. Harrison asserted,

The Church doesn't have the capacity to speak into this subject because it has not adequately: (a) addressed the subject biblically and theologically, (b) it has not pastorally accepted its responsibility to minister to people who are homosexual and, (c) its own political leanings and its own incapacity to separate itself from the far right or the Republican Party, for example, has made it impossible for it to speak with any integrity into this—it simply has no integrity to speak into it, and this is the problem for all of us (lines 266–272).

Harrison posed a thought-provoking question:

Certainly anybody on either side of the equation—those who are for same-sex marriage and those against—would both, I think, agree that promiscuity of any kind is sinful within the church. I think we're all in agreement on that. The question really is, "Are same-sex, monogamous relationships genuinely Christian and can the church approve of that?" (lines 1016–1020).

Theme Five: Clergy Response and Disposition toward LGBT People

In this theme, participants described their interactions with LGBT individuals. Participants also revealed that knowing an LGBT person influenced their views about homosexuality and/or their understanding of LGBT people. Participants shared their affective (feeling) responses for LGBT people as well as their behavioral and attitudinal disposition toward same-sex oriented individuals. Several of the participants provided insight regarding attempts to help LGBT people feel welcomed and/or included in their church.

Interactions with LGBT people. In this section, participants discussed interactions they have had with LGBT individuals. These interactions are not context specific, i.e., not limited to the church or in the participant's role as a clergyperson; rather, these interactions occurred in a variety of settings. Several of the participants acknowledged that their interactions with LGBT persons have been limited. Derek admitted,

I have not had a lot of interaction with that, thinking personally as well as professionally. There's been you bump into somebody or that kind of thing. It happens all the time here and the fact that it's [LGBT people are] a part of the community—seemingly a very strong part of the community (lines 369–372).

Kendall also said that his interactions with LGBT people have been limited. When asked about his interactions, Kendall stated,

Not a lot. I mean, not a lot of people that I can point to as folks that were a known homosexual to me. I can think of some that

I've related to quite a bit in the past that I have since discovered were homosexual at the time. And people are a lot more bold on Facebook than they were in person and so some of that interaction has been post personal closeness and contact. I haven't had a lot of people in terms of my pastoral ministry come to me with this issue. I don't think I've ever had anyone personally come to— I'm trying to remember—have a significant conversation about this (lines 411–421).

Kendall continued,

Other than that, some folks in our community, some parents of kids that have come to our youth group (lines 456–457)....So more kind of casual relationships and conversations with folks, but I can't point to a lot of one-on-one or interpersonal relationships with a lot of folks and homosexuality (lines 461–463).

Darrell also said that his interactions with LGBT people was but mentioned a brief conversation with the son of a family that attends his church. About this person Darrell shared,

He was in college, so he wasn't here very much. But when he was here, when he visited, I tried to have conversations with him, ask him how college was going, just regular conversation (lines 463–466).... But the conversation was fine, it was natural, there wasn't any hesitation or anything awkward, just regular conversation as I would with anybody else on a Saturday night or Sunday with the limited amount of time that I might have in that dialog (lines 470–473).

Darrell followed with,

But personally, I really have not had a large amount of interaction on a personal level interacting with somebody's who's made the statement that they're homosexual, honestly. My personal contact on a regular basis has been limited, quite honestly, it really has been (lines 488–491).

As with Kendall and Darrell, Bradley acknowledged that his interactions with LGBT people had been limited. Bradley commented, "I would say in my own personal experience it has been sparse" (lines 290–291). Bradley continued, "I guess personally, I've not had to work really close with someone who is gay, in church especially" (319–320). Blake expressed a similar thought: "My exposure has been a bit marginalized partially because of what I do and maybe exposure to people" (lines 439–440).

Whereas some of the participants expressed limited interactions with LGBT individuals, other participants talked about several interactions they had with LGBT people. For example, Curtis commented, "I was in the grocery business and…there were just a number of people that were openly gay" (lines 142–143). Curtis continued,

> I've worked with tons of them when I was in the grocery business. My very first exposure was to a gal that—back when I was running freight crews and in the production end of it was a gal that was on my freight crew that was really good and so we became good friends, she was a good worker. And I've worked with them in other contexts where someone would identify [as LGBT] (lines 289–311).

Keith said there is a significant population of LGBT people living in his neighborhood. Keith provided the following illustration:

> Our neighbors, the house beside us, [my wife] and I became pretty good friends with this particular gay couple. I don't know if they were civil union or not, but they were living together, they were together, _____ and _____. And over the course of time, they became pretty good friends (lines 252–255)....They were some of the best neighbors we've ever had (lines 291–292).

Keith also affirmed: "We have lots of gay people in our neighborhood with whom we have really good relationships" (lines 301–302).

A few of the participants reminisced about friendships they had developed during college. Some of these friends had revealed a same-sex orientation. Curtis recalled the following:

One of my very best friends from college actually came out as gay about ten years ago. I've actually had a lot of contact with him. He's a very close friend. If he comes out, he would stay at my house. If I'm out there, I would stay at his house. We've done all kinds of stuff together (lines 515–523).

Bradley shared a story about one of his college friends and the friend's attraction to Bradley:

He came out to visit us [me and my wife]. He was a guest in our home, and I had to go off to work, and he got to talking to my wife. And he told her that he had a crush on me when we were in college. Well that didn't set too well with my wife. I didn't' know anything about it. I mean we were friends and…Would it surprise me that he was attracted to me? Probably not but…I mean I don't know what women are thinking much less what men might be thinking about me. So, he told her and when I got home from work that morning after working all night. She said, "We need to talk. I want to know exactly your relationship with him." I asked, "Well, what do you think?" You know. But she had a hard time processing that (lines 248–262).

Keith's interactions with LGBT people began during his college years as well. Keith talked about his experience,

Really having a relationship with gay people began in college when my roommate came out to me as gay. We were part of an honors music fraternity, which, of course, in the Nazarene school, and he was my little brother in the fraternity. It's kind of a sordid story how it all unraveled, but that's sort of where it began. He had to confess to me that he was a gay and there was some sort of inappropriate relationship happening between him and another fraternity member. Anyway, he continued to be my roommate and we continue to be friends (lines 403–412).

Some of the participants discussed their current and ongoing interactions and friendships with LGBT individuals. Harrison, for example, talked about an LGBT person, with whom he maintained a current friendship,

I maintain relationship—what I would call friendships and not just acquaintances—with eight to ten—I'm trying to count in my head, and it sounds very impersonal to just try to quantify it like that, but somewhere in the range of that—folks that I regularly interact who have openly told me that they are homosexual. In doing so, I've done my very best to assure them that doesn't change anything about our friendship or my feelings towards them. To this point, I have enjoyed the interaction with them in the same way that I would enjoy the interaction with anyone else (lines 555–562).

Harrison continued,

I've had many interactions, continue to have ongoing interactions, but don't see them in any way any different than the interactions I have with other friends or other acquaintances or other people in life. If I am visiting with a man who is homosexual, I don't feel the need to have to guard myself in any different kind of way (lines 633–637).

Travis shared a story about a man he had known for some time. The man told Travis that during an earlier period of his life he was actively gay. Travis shared the following story about that experience:

I was sitting in a car one time with a guy that I've known for years and he just kind of blurts out you know, from this period of my life to that period of my life, I was an active homosexual. So like it just got thrown out there like out of the blue right, you know? So

I was sitting there, and I said, "Oh, okay. I said it doesn't change anything about how I feel about you" (lines 1212–1217).

Harold shared several interactions he had with LGBT individuals who attend his church. Harold said,

> We had six lesbians or three couples who attend here that we know of and that are out of the closet (lines 381–382)....[My wife] and I invited all six of them over to our house. We just had dessert and wine, which, in light of them being lesbians, we thought wasn't that big a deal, from a Nazarene perspective anyway. I just asked them, I said, "Tell me about your experience in real life" (lines 417–420). They talked about how they felt like it was a safe place and that they appreciated, and they understood the tension that I was in, between the Church of the Nazarene and my own personal beliefs and they appreciated that, appreciated me going to bat for them and making it a safe place for them (lines 422–425).

Harold also discussed another LGBT person who attends his church. Of his interactions with her, Harold commented,

> _____, this woman who I was talking about, who's an NTS grad, who attends my church, she and I have had some really great conversations surrounding this. It's kind of an interesting thing because she was attending, she was married to guy and they split up, they divorced, and she and _____ became roommates (lines 593–596). So I called [her] up and I said, "Let's have coffee." We went for coffee, and I said, "Tell me about your journey and what it's like to be a lesbian in the Church of the Nazarene." (lines 614–616). We talked for a long time about gender identity; about sexual orientation; her own journey, about what that looked like for her; the responses that she got as she came out to her parents—Nazarene missionaries, you might imagine how that went—and then her ability to pick out [identify] other people in the congregation (lines 633–637).

Matt, also talked about his interactions with LGBT people in his church and the local community. Matt said,

As far as my individual interactions with people…my job is to build a bridge, so my goal with anybody—we're really big about not asking people['s] sexual orientation. Obviously we live and interact in the gay community so it's pretty obvious (lines 313–316).

Blake revealed that his son identifies as an LGBT person. When asked about his interactions with LGBT people, Blake shared his experience:

My son—he's probably been the one I've had the most conversations with. His sexual identity and his confusion began probably long before I knew it. We started having conversations when he was a senior and leaving out of the house and I had concerns that he was struggling with some aspect of his identity and who he was (lines 296–300).

Blake continued,

This summer he came home—first time in five years—for the wedding of a high school friend and he was at it. I said, "Love to have you here." He came home for three or four days, had a great visit (lines 340–342).

But the interaction did not end there; Blake decided to visit his son. Blake provided a description of his visit:

I went to where he lives, and I asked him if I could come down and ski with him for a day. He said, "Yeah, I'd be good with that." And so, I was on the plane the next day. "I'm coming, I'll come tomorrow." That was the first window that was ever opened in five years and so I went, I'm down. We spent the day together. I went to his bar, went to his house. I was introduced to the guys he works with. I think they all thought we were in a relationship; it was kind of awkward. Yeah, that's right. He said, "Dad, I never thought you and I would be sitting in a bar together, let alone a bar like this." I looked at him and I said, "I love you. Where else would I be?" (lines 355–370).

Personal knowledge of LGBT individuals. In addition to describing their interactions with LGBT people, some participants talked about how knowing an LGBT person reduced prejudice and helped the participant view the LGBT individual as a person rather than a nameless other. Commenting about this Darrell said, "I think oftentimes people hold a view that's very domineering or very strict until they meet somebody, until they personally have interaction with somebody who's struggling, whether it'd be homosexuality, [or] whether it'd be other issues" (lines 1024–1027). Darrell also said,

So it's engaging in the conversation with people and the journey of their life that makes a difference. I find most people hold that view pretty strongly until they have contact with somebody like that. All of a sudden, a moralistic view of a lifestyle becomes different when you deal with people who are struggling and identify [as LGBT] or acknowledge that or try and figure out what the next step is or what the journey is all about (lines 1032–1037).

Allen reflected a similar thought when he commented,

I would be dishonest if I didn't say internally I get conflicting feelings about the lifestyle, but from a pastoral perspective and of course, the more regular, the more experience I have with gay and lesbian people in conversations with them, the more compassion I feel about them (lines 64–68).

As with Darrell and Allen, Bradley shared a similar insight about knowing an LGBT person. Bradley reflected,

I think the closer you are with someone who struggles in the area, or has come out as gay, the more you're forced to deal with the issue because you have someone, either a family member or a close friend or work associate or somebody that you see on regular basis, for whom that's an issue (lines 347–350).

Blake talked about how after finding out his oldest son is gay; Blake developed more compassion about LGBT concerns. Blake shared, "I know in my case my oldest son is gay; my middle son is really struggling with his identity" (lines 61–62). As a result, Blake said,

> I have become much more compassionate. I think this was easier for me to speak to when it wasn't so personal. Now that it's become personal, I'm more compassionate to the issue and maybe more able to speak to it, yet I haven't really done a very good job of doing that in this forum (lines 156–159).

While not quite so close to home as it was for Blake, Curtis also acknowledged that knowing an LGBT person made a difference in the way the people of his church would respond to LGBT people. Curtis observed,

> If the people in my church fall in love with you and then they find out you're gay, that's going to really challenge some of their thinking because [if] their idea of a gay person is this person I don't like…(lines 496–498). Then they look at you who they've already fallen in love with and they're gay and that creates that dissonance in the thinking that helps them move the right way to go. [So the] next time they hear somebody say, "All gay people are…" my parishioner goes, "Not all of them, I know a guy that…he's really a great guy, I really like him (lines 500–503).

Continuing this line of thought, Curtis said,

> That's the power of getting to know them as a person first and then discovering these other things or dealing with these other things because when you know them as a person [it] impacts… so, once you've fallen in love with someone that's gay, before you knew they were gay and then you find out they were gay, all of a

sudden you start changing your definitions of what it means to be gay or black or Hispanic or whatever it is (lines 542–547).

Earlier Harold discussed the three lesbian couples that attend his church. Like Curtis, Harold observed that their presence among his congregation, revealed the humanity and personhood of LGBT people rather than just a controversial issue. Harold stated it thusly:

I think the longer that their presence is here, the more the human aspect of that is felt—this isn't an abstract issue for people in San Francisco; this is _____, _____ and it's not "those people out there," it's _____ and _____ and it's _____ and _____ and it's those people that we love and care about (lines 449–452).

Travis recognized that dichotomizing LGBT issues as right or wrong, or black or white negates the humanity of LGBT people. Travis argued,

By that black/white separation, you perpetuate the cultural milieu within your church that I grew up with where I didn't know a single gay person. Right? So this is the classic case of the faceless other that you could legislate against and talk about. But since you didn't know any of them, like there was no real humanity involved. Right? Well you perpetuate that if you have a black/white approach to this issue and there are no gays in your church, and you know no gays and so you eject them from your family the moment someone affirms that they're gay. Then you perpetuate that. The big difference between my son's generation and mine is that they have grown up with gay people. These are their best friends at school. These are their classmates; these are the parents of their friends. These are perhaps family members who have come out. So these are dearly loved human beings that they have relationships with (lines 509–522)....I think that's what changes the conversation, that these are people that you know and love (lines 531–532).

Affective responses to LGBT people. Here, participants talked about their affective (feeling) responses to LGBT people and about homosexuality.

These affective responses ran along a spectrum of revulsion to love. Harold felt that addressing homosexuality and LGBT concerns from an affective perspective was "appropriate" (line 226). He suggested that homosexuality is emotionally charged. Harold said, "I think that part of what makes this a difficult conversation is that it's a very emotional issue on both sides. If you have friends that are part of the LGBT community, it becomes a very emotional issue" (lines 226–229).

Two participants talked about caring for LGBT people but not approving of same-sex relationships. Referring to a gay individual who attended his church, Preston said, "I think he knew I cared about him as a person, but I also cared enough that I wouldn't put a stamp of approval on how he was living" (lines 191–193). Similarly, Derek commented,

> If I really care about them, if I truly care about them, I would lovingly point it out and say, "You know what? I would disagree with you. Doesn't mean I don't like you or we can't hang, I just don't agree with you" (lines 568–570).

A few of the participants discussed their feelings about homosexuality or the idea of same-sex relations. Allen said, "I would be dishonest if I didn't say internally I get conflicting feelings about the lifestyle" (lines 64–65). Later, Allen said, "At the base level, being a heterosexual male, there is still a gut revulsion when I think about the practice. I mean to me it's unnatural" (lines 188–189).

Keith recalled a moment when he saw a gay couple interacting with one another and the feeling he experienced about their interaction. Keith said, "I watched their interaction. It was just like a husband and wife interaction. There was something in me that turned a little bit. I responded slightly viscerally in a negative way to seeing that" (lines 490–493). Keith admitted that the environment in which he was raised was disparaging of LGBT people. Keith said, "I was raised in a home that hated gay people. Hate is maybe too strong, but yeah. I mean, my mom still calls them "homos." So I have that part of my story as well" (lines 1061–1065).

As part of his internship, Kendall worked with an HIV-AIDS hospice ministry. Kendall and the ministry team attended a gay rodeo to distribute flyers detailing their ministry. Kendall said of the rodeo, "I observed some behavior that was probably beyond anything that I had personally been around (lines 632–633)....it was pretty eye-opening" (line 635). Kendall continued,

It broke my heart on a couple of levels. One, that there were men with AIDS who were dying—friends of these men, lovers of these men, potentially—and that there wasn't a real sense of wanting to deal with that (639–642).

Kendall continued,

I don't know what it stirred in them, but I know it stirred in me, again, those extreme kinds of dynamics of that community and I think grew my heart perhaps in terms of compassion for men in that setting involved in a homosexual lifestyle (lines 652–654).

Kendall confessed his discomfort in that atmosphere, "It was very uncomfortable; that's what I primarily remember about it" (lines 676–677).

Travis described a scenario detailing how he might feel in the presence of certain types of gay men:

There's just this wide a range of gay as there is straight, right? So over here you've got a guy wearing pink feathers, a black leather thong and chains at a gay rights rally, right...he's dancing down the street and he doesn't have a good bod, so not like yo, he's cut you know? Having a conversation, sitting down [with him]...I would be leaning towards revulsion especially if the guy is coming on to me. Right? That would be like a very different experience for me sitting down with some guy that's just acts like a normal member of society and is gay. Understandably. You know, if the guy is in feathers and black leather, and you know, acting like he's coming on to me, that would be uncomfortable for me right. And if the guy was acting like a regular human, let's talk stereotypes who just dressed really nice, right and was soft in his relationships, I mean just had a very relational hand in ways that we typically classify as feminine...I'm not uncomfortable with that guy right (lines 1198–1231).

Travis admitted that his feelings about LGBT persons run along a continuum, depending on how the LGBT individual behaves. Travis stated, "My feelings would run, my personal feelings would sort of run a spectrum depending on who I'm sitting with and how they present themselves and act and all that kind of stuff" (lines 1235–1237).

Allen was introspective about LGBT people. He pondered how he might prevent his feelings from becoming a barrier to relationship. Allen reflected,

> With this particular issue, it unsettles me either because of the longtime societal stigma that this is deviant or because—I don't know. I've had to come to consider if a person is a person of value, if they're a person who is uniquely made and loved by God, why does their public appearance or persona cause just that gut negative reaction? Or, or how can I appropriately redirect that, so that my reaction isn't the barrier to a relationship (lines 463–469).

Commenting on his feelings when he started to become aware of LGBT people, Bradley said,

> Early on it was hard to process, because you can see the real struggle in their life and that you'd like to fix it or cure it or help it go away. My heart goes out to them sometimes because of the treatment, the torture they seem to be going through (lines 307–310).

Bradley provided an example to illustrate how he felt:

> One time over the holidays at [college] we were [there]—because some of us didn't go home for the holidays—we were all thrown into the same dorm and so we were with people we didn't even know with six to a room. It was just some place to stay over the holidays. Our campus was pretty much shut down. One guy we knew was gay came home drunk one night and turned on the music, start dancing around the room. It made me uncomfortable but, you know, my heart went out to him more than my

uncomfortableness that he was just was trying to figure out who he was (lines 311–318).

Derek talked about his feelings about a young man who had been part of the youth group when Derek was a youth pastor. Derek said of the young man,

> I know one guy in particular who is a homosexual and is [in]—I don't know if it's official marriage that he's in. He keeps in touch, like [on] Facebook with me, and he knows my position and I know where he stands on it and of course, I pray for him (lines 235–237). That's probably the one that's closest to my heart because I love that kid. He's a great guy. He's a young man who's just caught up in that lifestyle (lines 244–245).

Travis said he had a lesbian couple attending his church. The couple went to New York to be married. Travis talked about the conversation he had with them and his feelings for them. Travis reflected,

> I had to explain to them when they went to New York and got married that wouldn't make them married in the eyes of the Church and the Nazarene. So like whenever we talked about marriage type stuff, we weren't saying since you guys are married now you guys fall within the bounds of it's okay. I mean only the fact that they knew that I loved them and was committed to them as their pastor, made that anything less than a horrific conversation. I mean that would have been a grueling conversation for anybody that loves people that isn't an ass, you know (lines 603–610).

Blake shared that his oldest son is gay, and his middle son struggled with his sexual identity. As a Nazarene pastor, Blake talked about his feelings of isolation: "For me, I have nowhere to go with this. I didn't know where to turn. So if I have thoughts or feelings, it was the loneliest place to be—still is" (lines 61–63). Blake's beliefs and his son's sexual orientation strained their relationship. Nevertheless, Blake attempted to communicate his love for his son. Blake said, "I say it every time we talk now; we're texting. I always say, 'I love you.' He hasn't said it back yet, but I know he does. I know he does" (lines 375–376).

Matt discussed how he responded to LGBT people who attend his church. Matt commented, "My job in that situation was to say, 'I don't care who you are, we're going to love you no matter what. You can tell me whatever you need to tell me, we're going to love you no matter what" (lines 381–382). Allen had a similar response to a LGBT individual who attended his church during the summer. Allen said he wanted to "let her know she's loved, no qualifications" (lines 570–571).

Harrison talked about one of his former classmates who had expressed a same-sex orientation. Harrison said,

> One of [my] classmates came out, not to me, but when I recon-
> nected with them after years of losing track, they told me that
> they had come out, told me their experience and it was a very sad
> story for me to hear. I felt like the way the church had betrayed
> them had required them then to take such an extreme position
> against the Church of the Nazarene that there was no capability of
> mediating or finding a way to love one another (lines 598–603).

Curtis discussed his feelings about how he has witnessed Nazarenes respond to the LGBT community. Curtis said, "My heart is also broken by having seen Nazarenes do and say things that just is not the way Christ would call us to be and we've burned some bridges" (lines 180–181). Curtis continued,

> That breaks my heart that they're [Nazarenes] not catching on to
> that. That would be hurtful if other people were to see them do
> that and I have no doubt that gay people have seen them do that
> and probably identify them as Nazarene (lines 203–205).

When describing his feelings about the LGBT people in his church, Harold said, "I guess I feel sorry for them. The other side is they're just grateful people. They just seem to be really thankful, thankful people" (lines 1055–1056).

Keith provided a tangible expression of feelings when he talked about how he would want the church to respond if one of his children were LGBT. Keith became tearful when shared the following:

When I start thinking about my girls and I think about what if one of them were gay, how would that change this for me and what would I want for them? Well, I'd want them to still be able to have a relationship with Christ, and I'd still want them to be part of a Christian community, and I'd want a pastor that would minister well to them and would accept them and love them. I would want that. [*Tearfully*] I would want that for them. I don't know where these emotions come from, talking about my girls mostly, but it does kind of make it so much more—I don't know, it just gives it a whole different sort of place when you think of it in those terms (lines 1044–1055).

Blake provided an example of how he would like to respond if an LGBT person began attending his church. Blake said,

[For] the homosexual who comes that that would be—I think I'd like to be able to look him in the eye and say God loves you and you matter to Him and I love you and you matter to me and what you struggle with is no different than what this person struggles with or what I struggle with and say that together, with God's grace and help, we can grow and we can encourage each other along in that journey (lines 1117–1122).

Darrell admitted he was wary of talking about homosexuality and LGBT concerns with his congregants. Darrell acknowledged,

It hasn't demanded that I take a look at it and address it; maybe we just haven't as a church, we haven't asked that question. And so, even asking the question to me [there] is a little trepidation because it's like, "Do we really want to have that conversation?" (lines 1012–1015)....I believe we need to as a church and I believe part of my responsibility as a pastor is to help that conversation take place (lines 1018–1019)....I guess I just have a little trepidation even beginning the conversation because [there] is such a diversity of opinion (lines 1021–1022)....I think we're all a little afraid of it, honestly. I think we tend to be cut-and-dried with it. I think we're just kind of hesitant—I'm hesitant (lines 1278–1279).

Behavioral and attitudinal disposition toward LGBT people. Participants also talked about their behavioral and attitudinal reactions to homosexuality and LGBT individuals. Some of the participants discussed their difficulty with homosexuality and/or LGBT persons. Darrell acknowledged that it was difficult for him to understand the attraction of one man to another man. Darrell said,

As a heterosexual, I think it's difficult to understand the attraction, like me attracted to another man just—that's not going to happen, you know? It's hard for me to understand somebody that would be. So there is a barrier, if you would, I think just in understanding (lines 255–258).

Darrell continued,

In my own personal feeling as a heterosexual, I don't understand the mindset that is attracted to the same-sex. So there's a barrier there because there's got to be some compassion and some understanding beyond what I personally may hold to as a viewpoint or an understanding or a life perspective (lines 1083–1086).

Travis declared, "Unless the guy is coming on to me you know, I'm not repulsed by being around them—gay folk" (lines 738–739).

Keith admitted, "I think it continues to be a struggle for me to say that I love and accept gay people when I know good and well that's not altogether true. Because I know what gay people want from me" (lines 229–231). On the other hand, Keith also confessed,

I think it would be really good for me to have a relationship with a Christian who happens also to be gay, like a real friendship where

I could just say okay, help me understand—although, I've talked to enough gay people, I think I can understand their reality to some degree (lines 1092–1095).

Harrison indicated that he has maintained relationships with several former classmates who acknowledged a same-sex orientation. Harrison shared how he has responded to them: "I have tried to maintain a speaking relationship with them in very open way to say, 'You're my friend, no matter what'" (lines 428–429). Harrison also declared, "I don't want to lose relationship with anyone over sexual orientation" (lines 527–528).

A young, gay man attended Preston's church. Preston talked about his response to this person:

I would always go out of my way to just be kind and gracious to him and from time to time he'd ask if I would have time to I don't know I think we had lunch or coffee. There was a little café there in the heart of town and I had to work through the thing of fearing that others might presume that that meeting was something that it wasn't (lines 160–164).

Preston also discussed an extended family member who revealed her same-sex orientation. Preston talked about his reaction to her,

I would always be kind and gracious [to her]. I admit that when my children were growing up I really didn't want them to have to deal with that issue when we would have large family gatherings and as they've grown up they've learned what it was. We've more recently kind of reconnected with her and I'm glad for that (lines 233–237).

Preston continued by affirming, "I'm not going to try and alienate [her] and I'll try to love and care for her, but..." (lines 301–302).

Allen talked about how he responded to a young LGBT woman after some of his parishioners made derogatory comments about her. Allen said,

I went out of my way...to make sure that when I saw her, I went to her and we talked, "How you doing? How is this week in school for you?" Those kinds of things to [let her] know that someone here cares…" (lines 583–585).

Curtis also talked about how he how he responds to LGBT people who attend his church. Like Allen, Curtis said he goes "out of his way" too to make sure they know he cares about them. Curtis commented, "I go out of my way because I know it's easy for them to perceive me as not loving them, it's easier for communication to break down" (lines 323–324). Curtis also shared about an LGBT person in his church. Curtis revealed how he chose to respond to a young, gay man who attended his church:

> One of the people that's gay in my church is a young twenty-some-thing guy and he just had some hard things happen to him.…I just reached out to him and told him we loved him and we're for him and God loves him and that kind of thing (lines 560–564). Darrell said he tries "to receive people where they're at" (line 446) but also thought that LGBT people have their guard up when talking to him because he is a pastor. Knowing this, Darrell said, "I always want to go out of my way and try to be outside of that stereotypical idea of what they might perceive me as or our con-versations (lines 607–609).

Harold stated that did not treat people differently because of their sexual orientation.

Harold commented, "My own feelings are to look at persons with a sexual orientation different than mine—my own feelings are not treat that any differently than I would anyone else" (lines 309–311).

Although earlier, Allen said he experienced a "gut-revulsion" (line 188) to homosexual practice, Allen acknowledged that he was "not will-ing to dismiss the people because of that feeling. I'm much more willing to try and see the person" (lines 191–192).

Keith recounted an LGBT man who did an internship at Keith's church. Keith supervised his internship. About that relationship Keith said, this young man "was really struggling with his sexual identity and I tried to walk him through that" (lines 441–442).

Kendall also shared as story about a young man who had revealed to Kendall what he was gay. Kendall said he, "had a chance to have a brief conversation with him...I just tried to tell him, 'Love you man'" (lines 429–431). Kendall continued, "He's one, I guess, that I've tried to come around and support" (lines 452–453).

Kendall also recounted that approximately 20 years earlier, he attended a gay rodeo as part of an HIV-AIDs hospice ministry. Kendall shared his response to what he observed at the rodeo:

> There wasn't a reaction of, "Oh, this is gross. This is disgusting. That guy's chaps, that's all he's wearing," you know? There wasn't in me this gross reaction or this, "I'm here with the AIDS ministry and you're all going to get it." None of that raised, it was more of—and obviously, this is coming from my upbringing, but I think there was more compassion and awareness of humanity behind this issue that was really significant (lines 699–706).

Blake talked about his response when greeting an LGBT person when she attended his church. Blake said,

> When [she] walked into our church, I made a point to go right to her. She's been here on a couple of occasions, and her partner. I sincerely—and it was genuine—shook their hands and was so glad that they were here. I wanted them to see that from me, that I was really glad they came (lines 187–190).

Derek said that if an LGBT person came to him for guidance he would respond in the following manner:

> I would welcome them in, let's talk. This is how I understand scripture. How do you understand it? And go from there. There wouldn't be a wall between us; I don't think there should be, but just one brother [to another] (lines 916–918).

Derek also stated that if an LGBT person were in a same-sex relationship and wanted out, Derek said he would,

Come alongside them and say, "Okay, what's the next step?" Let's help you. That's what we exist for as a church is to help people come close to the Lord, and I believe this is keeping you at a distance from the Lord. It's not acceptable; it separates. And so, let's look at how we can get you out (lines 938–941).

Harrison recognized that, "we live in a broken world and sometimes that painful reality happens, and we have to be loving and that are ways to overcome that for people who genuinely want to heal" (lines 519–522).

Kendall said he wanted to be "gentle and loving and firm, but open to peoples' personal experiences" (lines 107–108).

Travis said of LGBT people,

Gay folk are human beings just like everyone else and that we're called to minister to them and that they deserve no less love than anybody else. [I] don't feel any different toward them and their practices as I would somebody who is participating in any other thing categorized as a sin in the New Testament (lines 641–647).

Matt pastors in an area with a large LGBT population. Matt described how he responds to LGBT people in the community, "Our job is not to ask anybody's sexual orientation, our job is to love people and because of the radical love that we show, they respond with, "Why are you different?" (316–318). Matt admitted that he has to remind himself that, "the process of loving the LGBT community is a slow process…you can quickly love somebody, but these are people we're going to need to travel with for the rest of our lives" (lines 622–626).

Attitude of inclusion. Here participants described the way in which they attempt to help same-sex oriented individuals feel welcome in their church. While some participants were openly receptive to LGBT people, others demonstrated caution about how they would respond to an LGBT individual attending their church. For example, Preston said, "I wouldn't tell them they couldn't worship here, unless they were making an issue of it" (lines 437–441). Harrison commented, "My hope is that we would know all are welcome here, but not all personal practices are going to be condoned here" (lines 437–438). While worshiping at another church, Allen saw an LGBT person in attendance. Allen began to question whether an LGBT person would be welcome in his church. Allen said, "I began to question how this [LGBT] individual would have been received in my church? I talked openly with some people about it, and [they] said candidly, she or he wouldn't—would not be accepted" (lines 305–309).

Other participants' comments revealed an attitude of inclusion and openness toward LGBT people. Matt said, "Our job, we believe, is to be a nonjudgmental, loving presence in the community" (lines 217–218). Situated in a primarily LGBT part of the city, Matt remarked about when people attend his church,

I see Bob, Suzie, and Mary come through the door. I don't see gay, lesbian, transgender come through the door. I think the problem with the Church is that's what we see. We see he's gay, she's a lesbian, she's transgender; you got to watch out. That is not who we are by any stretch of the imagination (lines 260–263)…we're trying to put together a place where anybody can feel welcome (line 272).

Curtis shared a similar view:

I've had a number of them attend my church here. They know where the Church of the Nazarene was at, but I went out of my way to make sure that they understood that I love them and that they are welcome and that I was for them, and God was for them in the same sense that I would anybody else (lines 295–299).

When discussing how he wanted his church to respond to LGBT people, Curtis stated,

The way it will be [here] is that you're welcome in this place, you're a part of us, you can do stuff with us. I can't get you elected to the board if you're openly living in a homosexual lifestyle. You can't be a teacher, if you will, of our theology. But you can participate, you can be a part, you will be loved (lines 461–464).

Allen said he was intentional about making people feel welcomed when they attended his church. Allen commented, "I go out of my way to make—to help people feel welcome in this community of faith—this issue aside, regardless of whether they'd be low economic status or high, whatever" (lines 609–613).

Bradley shared a story of a LGBT person who attended his church for a brief time. Bradley recounted how he and his congregation responded to the man:

We tried to include him in things like when having men's groups and things and I think we were successful at that. But now, I don't know where he is. You know, but we definitely ministered to him for a period of time, and we helped him, and my hope is that when he reflects upon those times of his life, he saw a church that loved and embraced him and cared for him (lines 441–446).

Travis talked about how he responded to an LGBT couple who attend his church. Travis remarked, "I've been very forthright with them. I've also been very forthright with them that I love them; I care about them; I want them to be here (lines 866–867). Travis also provided a description of the type of youth group his youth pastor has attempted to create. Travis described it thusly:

[The youth group's] become known as this place where you can explore like a version of Christian spirituality, like not the version of the church they left and swore never to go back to. Right? Where they weren't even allowed to ask questions. But these athe-ist kids, these gay kids, these Wiccan kids, all these kids that fall outside the boundaries of what people typically think of church doing, right, these different categories in life where people are like well they don't go to church because they're atheist or they're this or that. They come to our youth group and the youth pas-tor has created a very safe place where remarkably he's able to affirm what we believe but open up like this totally accepting space for people to come be like belong before they believe (lines 1335–1345).

Keith said he wanted to create a gracious attitude toward all people, including LGBT people. When asked what he meant by "gracious," Keith responded by saying,

Gracious means a predisposition towards mercy, kindness, well-being, [and] love toward the other. It is also an invitation, an invitation that we try to extend as a community [of faith] to persons no matter where you are in life's journey, no matter what brokenness you're dealing with…that this community can be a place where healing can happen (lines 76–80).

Harold said his church has developed an "inclusion statement" that welcomes everyone. Harold shared the following:

We have an inclusion statement that we have here that everyone is welcome here, we don't care where you've been, what you've done, we don't care if you just got out of jail, we don't care if you were out drinking too late last night, we don't care if you're gay or straight, we don't care if you…we just go on and on, Republican or Democrat. Everyone is welcome (lines 368–372).

Harold continued, "This is a really welcoming community and not just in terms of the LGBT thing, but I mean we talk a lot about what it means to be inclusive of everyone (lines 871–873).

Kendall reflected on what an LGBT person might think or feel about the Nazarene church. Kendall offered the following:

If somebody's driving by a church and would see our name, a homosexual who's need of spiritual help and saw our church's name, would they feel welcome to come into the church for that spiritual help? I've always hoped to pastor a church and be the kind of person who would be seen in that way (lines 1018–1022).

Commenting on his personal strengths, Kendall said,

I'm kind of driven, whether it's sexual orientation, color or language and background and economic status, to be welcome and
hospitable to anybody wherever they are in life and to create an
environment where folks who come as they are would leave as
God would want them to be (lines 1025–1029).

Kendall admitted though, "As a pastor, I wrestle with that as how
we best provide hospitality and warmth and love to someone who is so
closely identified with what we call sin" (lines 1036–1038).

Referring to how his church will respond, Matt said, "It doesn't matter who are, or what you identify as, we're going to love you no matter
what" (lines 389–389).

Theme Six: LGBT Presence in the Local Church and Community

In this theme participants describe the presence of LGBT people in the
local church and the local community where the participant ministers.
Participants shared their experience of how LGBT individuals respond to
the church and/or the Nazarene position on homosexuality. Participants
also discussed the manner in which LGBT people have responded to
them. A few of the participants provided a description of the brokenness
found in the LGBT community and/or the people who comprise it.

LGBT individuals in the local church. Many of the participants commented that there were LGBT individuals who attended the participant's
church. For some of the participants, LGBT people attended regularly;
for others, LGBT individuals visited but had not integrated into congregational life.

Harrison observed that during his ministry a few LGBT people had
attended his church. Harrison said, "In the 13 years I've been here—there
have been people who have a homosexual orientation come through here.
There hasn't been a gay couple or children. There hasn't been anything like
that, that I can think of" (lines 494–497).

Derek said he did not have a lot of experience interaction with LGBT people in within his local church:

To be honest with you, I don't know of a lot of experience that way. I'm trying to think back if we've had a person come—we may have, and it's been cordial. I'm trying to think of a face, but the times that I've been aware that somebody has come—actually, I do know one. It's the daughter of a person in our church. We do our very best to love her; although she would like to be called by a different name, a man's name, and is going through the hormonal changes and stuff, so it may be even deeper than same-sex orientation (lines 524–533).

Allen also spoke about an LGBT individual who attended his church. Allen reflected,

While I've been here, I had an individual—he's deceased now…A wonderful, wonderful young man; struggled with his sexuality all his life and there were some people here who hung a gay tag on him. I think that became for him a defining experience (lines 103–107).

Allen continued, "I had an opportunity to minister to him and to say, 'God loves you for who you are.' And I don't know if that ever resolved, you know, the struggle. I know the practice did" (lines 118–120). Allen also said of one other young LGBT woman that attended his church, "She came and helped out with Bible School, volunteered, came to church a couple of Sundays. I don't know her orientation; I have a suspicion" (lines 317–319).

Preston said there was a young LGBT man from the community who asked Preston if he could come to the church to play the organ. Preston admitted that he knew the young man was in a gay relationship, but Preston agreed to let him play the organ. Preston said,

In my first pastorate, I had a young man who'd been in the community many years and I got acquainted with him through another family in the church…[He] would come by the church. He loved to play the organ and he'd come by the church and just ask if he could play the organ, which he did (lines 152–158). He'd come to church here and there. He knew, I knew how he was living, but he seemed to be kind of, he was a lonely guy and he seemed to be reaching out for something (166–169).

Curtis also had LGBT people who attended his church. Curtis said, "I have actually a couple of gay people attending my church" (175–176). Curtis continued,

One of the people that's gay in my church is a young twenty-some-thing guy and he just had some hard things happen to him. I just reached out to him and told him we loved him and we're for him and God loves him and that kind of thing (lines 563–564).

Bradley spoke of an LGBT person who occasionally attended his church. Bradley said that the LGBT man was,

A gentleman by the name of _____ who was gay (line 386)….he would come to church. He would try to get out of the lifestyle. We prayed a lot together and we talked a lot together. We tried to encourage him to remain celibate and then he would fall away for a while (lines 393–396), And he'd come back into our lives, and we would have him in our home and over for dinner and we would talk to him and be his friend and try to include him in the church body (lines 397–399).

Darrell said there was a lesbian couple that attended his church. Darrell shared the following:

There was only really one instance personally that I know of probably in the last three or four years that I can think of where there was an obvious lesbian couple who became part of the church; they put their kids in the nursery, they sat together in service (lines 626–629).

Darrell provided some general observations about LGBT people who had attended his church:

There's only one couple that I know came to our church where you could obviously see that she was lesbian, and it wasn't anything that they were trying to hide. The others that I've been aware of are people that have not made it really publicly known, whether it'd be fear of condemnation, whether it'd be not being accepted. So yeah, it just is very limited (lines 1006–1010).

Travis had a married lesbian couple regularly attending his church. Travis said, "There's a pair of married lesbians in our church and what they're doing seems a lot less damaging to me than a whole list of other sins that people in my congregation are involved in" (lines 652–654). Travis said that some LGBT individuals have brought their partner to church. Travis said,

When [these] two girls walked into church together, I don't immediately go they must be gay right? So these girls were coming to church, I mean we have girls bring girls to church all the time. We have guys bring guys to church all the time. Never even entered my mind that these girls were gay. I had no idea, right? (lines 908–913).

Travis also said that a couple of the teenagers at the church revealed their same-sex orientation. Travis commented, "We had a couple of kids come out in our teen group" (lines 888–889). Travis went on to say,

I have not gotten involved in gay kids in the youth group whatsoever. For many of them, our youth pastor is their pastor and many of them wouldn't even hardly know me (lines 1326–1329). Our youth group is one of those places in town where gay kids, atheist kids, Wiccan kids, etc., are all welcome (1332–1333).

Blake talked about a gay couple that attended his church briefly. Blake said,

> We had a gay couple that was here in our church for a little while and I had a chance to have some conversations with them (lines 496–497)....The person who invited them said, "How are they going to be received?" I said, "Let's find out" (lines 502–504).

Although Keith lives in a neighborhood with a sizable LGBT population, Keith confessed that there had not been much of an LGBT presence in his church. Keith commented,

> There's been very little of that here, so I don't have—we've had gay people come, we've had gay couples come, but mostly it was special kind of things like special services like Christmas Eve. It's interesting, we had, I think, two or three gay couples at our Christmas Eve service one year, and the only feedback I got from folks in the church was it was so nice to see the gay community represented so well (lines 531–536).

Matt's church was situated in an urban location with a significant population of LGBT people. Matt said of himself and his church, "A majority of my friend group considers themselves LGBT. A majority of my congregants consider themselves LGBT. We immerse ourselves into the gay culture here in _____" (lines 143–144). Matt also stated, "Our church is mainly LGBT" (lines 214–215).

Harold also had LGBT people attending his church. Harold provided the following comments about these individuals:

> There's a woman in my church who is actually a [Nazarene college] grad. She came out of the closet; she's a lesbian. She attends our church (line 244–248)....She and I have had some really great conversations around this (line 594)....We talked for a long time about gender identity; about sexual orientation; her own journey, about what that looked like for her; the responses that she got as she came out to her parents—Nazarene missionaries, you might imagine how that went—and then her ability to pick out other people [LGBT persons] in the congregation (lines 633–637).

According to Harold, this woman has also worked with one of teen girls in the church who identified herself as LGBT. Harold commented, "We have an adolescent girl in our congregation who's gay and she's been working with her to help her process what it means to be an adolescent in _____, _____ who's gay, as well as what it means theologically" (lines 641–643).

Commenting on other LGBT people who attended his church, Harold remarked, "We had six lesbians or three lesbian couples who attend here that we know of and that are out of the closet" (lines 381–382). Harold provided a description of the LGBT people who have attended his church:

I think back to the first couple, the first gay guys in my first church and then the lesbian couple in _____ and then the lesbian couples here, any amount of grace that's extended to them has just opened up like flowers and they're just amazing people. They're amazing people to be around and [they] are probably the most loyal people here" (1036–1042).

LGBT people in the local community. Participants also discussed their awareness of an LGBT presence in the local community. Matt pastors a church in an urban community with a large LGBT population. Matt made several comments about his, and the church's involvement in the gay community. Matt said, "A majority of my time is spent interacting with LGBT individuals" (line 140). Referring to his church, Matt commented, "What we do as a group here is we immerse ourselves into the gay community" (lines 212–213). Matt also said, "We live and interact in the gay community" (line 315).

Keith's church is also located in an urban area that has a sizeable population of LGBT persons. Keith said, "I'm a pastor in _____ and lots of people in my neighborhood are gay" (lines 161–162). Despite the number of LGBT people in his neighborhood, Keith confessed, "I've never here, in this context, become the pastor of a gay couple" (line 297). Keith went on to say, "We have lots of gay people in our neighborhood with whom we have really good relationships, but that's as far as that has ever gone" (lines 301–302). Keith speculated, "Currently our neighborhood is probably comprised about one-third of gay people" (line 430).

Allen indicated that where he pastors, "there is a rather large LGB, LG—gay and lesbian—yes, LGBT community" (lines 54–55). Allen said, "The issue to me is how we react to people who are struggling with this issue in their life, and whether we will be truly Christian or whether we will be something less" (lines 349–351). Allen then queried, "How do we—particularly in this community where there are such a large communities of LGBT people, how do we represent Christ to that community? That has posed a struggle for me" (lines 351–354). Allen went on to say,

> The difference between this area and the other areas I've pastored [is] the LGBT population is very much more open here. The only place that would have been remotely like it was when I lived in _____ the same way that there's a large population in _____. The _____ area is another large population of LGBT people. Every place else I'd been it's been largely underground, and very much a social stigma to come out (lines 387–395).

Curtis, referring to other places he has lived said, "I've worked with [LGBT people] in other contexts where someone would identify—[but], more so here because people are more likely to identify themselves and be openly gay here than in the Midwest" (lines 310–312).

Kendall said he did not have a lot of contact with LGBT persons but was aware of their presence in the local community. Kendall commented, "[There's] not a lot of people that I can point to as folks that were a known homosexual to me" (lines 411–412). Kendall continued by saying that there are "some [LGBT] folks in our community, some parents of kids that come to our youth group" (lines 456–457).

Derek observed that there is a considerable LGBT population where he lives. Derek said, "I know of [LGBT people] in the community, I've talked to them, but they don't come to my church" (lines 250–251). Continuing, Derek commented, "There've been times you bump into somebody or that kind of thing. It happens all the time here and the fact that it's part of the community—seemingly a very strong part of the community" (lines 370–372). Derek gave the following example: "Down at the farmer's market we'll have the gay and lesbian booth and then a church booth right next to it or something else. It's quite interesting how that works" (lines 374–376). Derek also shared that there is a "church in town that very much supported [LGBT people]; it's a very liberal church and it's got the rainbows and obviously it's for [the] gay and lesbian group and I understand that the minister is a gay man" (lines 421–425).

Blake said there was a gay bar in city where he lives. Blake commented, "I've toyed with the idea of going cold turkey down here to the gay bar and just having conversation with people, but I haven't done it because I'm not quite sure what to say" (lines 424–426). Blake also knew that one of the city officials was LGBT. Of him Blake said,

> Our city planner is openly gay. I've toyed with going over there and talking to him about "Help me understand," but I wasn't sure I'd be received well, to tell him I have a gay son and I'm trying to understand him, help me understand him. Is that a good thing to do with people? I don't know (lines 428–431).

During a conversation with the LGBT women that attended his church, Harold wondered if there were LGBT men in the community. Harold recounted the conversation:

> I asked the lesbians when they were at my house, I said, "What's the deal with—we have all lesbians, where's all the guys in all this?" The response I got from them, to summarize, and we kind of laughed about it, the way they responded was they said, "If you were a gay man, would you live in _____?" I said, "There's no way, man. I'd be fearful for my safety." They said, "Uh-huh, red neck men are a lot less threatened by lesbians than they are by gay men. There may be some gay men at _____, but they'll never come out of the closet, not in _____" (lines 648–656).

Harold observed, "So getting them to come out, out to church and come out of the closet, I mean, it's like walking into a lion's den, right? (lines 658–659). They have no idea, and rightfully so. They should be very concerned about their safety in a church in _____, _____" (lines 663–664).

Commenting on the LGBT population in his community, Matt said, "The process of loving the LGBT community is a slow process" (lines 623–624). Matt continued, "You don't see a lot of overnight changes, but you do see people growing closer to Christ" (lines 634–635).

LGBT responses to the Church and the Nazarene position on homosexuality. Participants shared their views of how LGBT individuals respond to the Church or, in some cases, how they respond to the Church of the Nazarene's position on homosexuality.

Keith commented about how the LGBT people he has met have responded to the Christian community. Keith stated,

> The gay people that I meet are either in this neighborhood that I know, or, in some cases, I can tell there's a real—I don't know if animosity is the right word. There's a barrier there, there's no doubt. These folks are not people who—the ones that are very close by who I sense aren't interested in being part of a Christian community (lines 579–583).

Keith continued,

> The truth is there are some gay people that they have bought into the caricature of what Christians are like from the media and therefore there is, on their part, a real resistance to Christian community (lines 616–618).

Blake provided the following description of how his son embraced his same-sex orientation and disconnected from the church. Blake said,

> [He] is a very smart young man. He's probably one of the smartest of my three sons. His way of dealing with his homosexual orientation was to say, "I can't believe in God because I know what the Bible says and what God says about this and so my way of dealing with that is that I'm now going to become an atheist because I can't justify the two that if the Church, God, and my parents

don't agree with this, then I think God's wrong or if there is a God, I can't believe in him." That's where he's landed (302–308).

When he attended a Nazarene leadership conference Kendall said the issue of LGBT adult children was discussed. Kendall recounted that during that conversation, someone commented that "you can go to any gay bar and hear story after story of [LGBT people] who had been basically chased away by the church" (lines 1034–1038).

Derek said that while his daughter was at college, she had an LGBT friend. When the LGBT friend found out that Derek's daughter attended church, the friend exclaimed, "Church? Man, all Christians hate gays!" (lines 468–469).

In conversations with LGBT individuals, Harrison acknowledged that in his experience many LGBT people feel angry toward the Church of the Nazarene because of the way the church has treated them. Harrison shared the following:

> One of [my] classmates came out…they told me their experience and it was a very sad story for me to hear. I felt like the way the church had betrayed them had required them then to take such an extreme position against the Church of the Nazarene that there was no capability of mediating or finding a way to love one another. Unfortunately that's what I'm experiencing with people who I know who've been in the Church of the Nazarene or whatever. I'm finding them years later so angry and so bitter that the damage has been done, there's no capacity to mediate that (598–608).

Referring to the Nazarene church's position on homosexuality, Preston indicated that it can be interpreted as "hate language" by the LGBT community. Preston said of the church's position, "I feel like the church's position is not a—I think it's misinterpreted many times in terms of I suppose the gay lesbian community would see it as hate language" (lines 28–31).

Curtis acknowledged that an LGBT person almost left his church because the individual had read the Church of the Nazarene's *Manual* statement on homosexuality. Curtis intervened:

I about had a homosexual person leave my church because they read that before talking to me and said, "Is there a place for me in this church? I understand I can't preach but,..." I had to come back and say, "No, no, no, let's talk about this" (lines 262–265).

Curtis stated that because the *Manual* statement sounds "fire-breathing," (line 449) that is "one of the reasons we don't start with Nazarene" (line 434). Curtis elaborated:

By the time this person read the statement, the only reason they looked it up in fact was because they had been coming, they liked the church, they liked my preaching, they liked me, they had already identified themselves to me as someone who is homosexual and asked what we believed about that and what that would mean (lines 436–440). It wasn't until later when they went back and said, "Let's see what Nazarenes really believe in," and read that and it's pretty fire breathing. But on the good side, they didn't just leave; they came back and said, "I'm really concerned about this, give me some explanation," and gave me the opportunity to talk about it and then they were comfortable (lines 448–452).

Darrell said, "I find maybe the church isn't the place they [LGBT people] come typically just out of curiosity. I think there's a stigma, if you would of the church and how we receive people like that. I think that they would find a church that makes a statement that they're going to be received there" (lines 995–998).

Keith admitted that the Church of the Nazarene's position on homosexuality does not feel like "love or acceptance" (line 235) for people who are sensitive to LGBT concerns. Keith said,

[It] sounds like you're not welcome here, which is probably why we don't have any gay people at [our church]. All they [LGBT people] have to do is take a look at what the Church of the Nazarene has to say and they're not going to come to this church because they've got plenty of options here in the city of welcoming and accepting congregations (lines 236–240).

Keith continued by stating, "Gay people do not have to come to a denomination that questions their sexuality at all" (lines 554–555).

As a Nazarene pastor, Harold said he was "amazed at how much [LGBT people] know about what our official stance is; there's not a lot of mystery to it" (lines 1000–1001). Moreover, Harold expressed surprise by how knowledgeable LGBT individuals are about denominational positions about homosexuality. Harold commented,

> I think what surprised me when I had these conversations with really everybody that is in the LGBT community, I've always been amazed at how much they know in terms of the different denominations stance on stuff. They must have a website or something because they're all very aware of what places are safe and what places are not (lines 990–994).

Derek acknowledged that he had not had many interactions with LGBT people. Derek summarized it thusly:

> I think there's a distancing between us. I mean they probably think that I know what they believe, and [they may think] "I'm not going to go there," and "This won't be a welcoming place for me," which is quite unfortunate, but I sense that is the mindset. "I'll go there to be judged? Well, I'll not go there." There are churches they can go to that would be more in line with that and hold that as a biblical position (lines 382–388).

Matt said that at his church they tell both LGBT people and conservatives alike, that if they are not comfortable worshiping at his church, they will help them locate another church where they can worship. Matt stated,

> If people want to leave because they don't feel comfortable— [what] we do here with LGBT individuals, [and] with conservative individuals, if you come here and say, "I want to go to church, but this ain't the church for me," we have other churches of other denominations that we will send you to (lines 479–482).

A few of the participants discussed how some of the LGBT people in their church have responded to the church or the Nazarene position on homosexuality. For example, Darrell said of one LGBT person in his congregation:

> [One] gentleman in church tends to get connected to the church when he's not practicing. I find the cycle in his life is when he establishes a relationship or begins a new relationship—[with] a homosexual man—he tends to fade away from the church. Maybe it's a perception of his own or perception of the church, perception of what many people believe the church condemns anyway (lines 272–281).

Darrell continued,

> I think there's a part of him that understands the church believes it's wrong. I think he understands that and feels that and is aware of that and yet there's a part of him that wants to be a part of the church, the Nazarene Church specifically. He's connected when he's not really practicing the lifestyle, and then again, when he comes into a relationship of that nature, he tends to step away (lines 361–368).

Matt's church ministers primarily to the LGBT population. As a result, his church had come under fire from conservative Nazarenes. Matt described how the LGBT people in his neighborhood rallied to support him and his church:

> The community here, the LGBT community got word of what was going on. I thought that was the end of our ministry here. But what happened was they showed up at church to support us. People who had never been to church and never been to church since showed up here to support us (lines 524–527).

Travis shared a story about an LGBT woman who, because of several bad experiences related to her sexual orientation, had sworn never to return to church. Travis said,

She said would never darken—wanted nothing to do with Christianity because of her experiences. So somewhere along the line, she meets _____ who had four children, who was divorced from her husband, and they end up best friends, eventually lovers, and then partners. So _____'s kids had gone to church here and somewhere along the line, she got interested in God. So she started coming here and there and got [her partner] to come with her. This is the [woman] who said, "I'll never darken another church's door." And like just over time [she] came to want to be here really badly and [her partner] was like "Do you have any idea like how huge that is, like how radical that is. Like she wants to come to church, she wants be here. She wants to hear about God and Jesus" (lines 819–830).

During a conversation with an LGBT person who attended his church, Harold said she talked with him about the spiritual hunger of LGBT people. Harold stated in thusly:

[She] told me at one point, she said, "If you want to be a welcoming community then just say, 'We welcome you no matter what your orientation is.'" She said put a rainbow flag on your website and you get 50 people the next week. She said you would not believe how many [LGBT] people are hungry, just starving for spiritual connection but don't know if [the church] is a safe place to go or not. A lot of them have gone to those places where—there's no shortage of them, of people that are just bashing homosexuals and "Those gays and their agenda and blah, blah, blah…" There's no shortage of that (lines 1003–1011).

LGBT response to the participant. Participants also commented on how LGBT people have related to or responded to the participant. Blake, whose oldest son is gay, said that his son has distanced himself from Blake as well as God and the church. Blake shared the following about his son's responses:

"Don't tell me that God loves me"—these are the conversations I've had—"and hates the sin because I identify with my homosexuality and if you say that God hates the sin, then you're in effect saying that God hates me. I have a hard time accepting the fact that you can say you love me when I know you don't agree with who I am" (lines 310–315).

Blake continued, "[My son's] way of dealing with this was, 'I'm not going to believe in God, I don't believe in my family,' and he just went off the face-of-the-earth. He chose to just disassociate himself with our family" (lines 324–326). Blake said,

As much as we try to make a relationship, it was one way, he would not reciprocate. He changed his name. He took a different last name. It was really hurtful—not because he's in a relation-ship, he just said I don't want the name _____ anymore because I know what it stands for and I don't agree with that anymore (lines 331–335).

During a conversation with his LGBT son, Blake asked why he changed his name. His response to Blake was, "Because I don't believe in anything you stand for" (379–380).

Harrison reflected LGBT individuals' responses to him during his 24 years of ministry. Harrison said, "I would say that over 24 years of minis-try, two or three dozen individuals have wanted to talk about this subject. Some clearly were saying this was their struggle or their journey" (lines 171–174). Harrison continued,

I know of no situation that I'm aware of in which I've had a neg-ative encounter where I felt poorly about, "Oh, I did the wrong thing here." I can't recall that I've never had a gay person attack me just because I was a pastor, I've never had that experience, or because I was a Christian, which, here in [this area], could be just as easy for most people to do is to react negatively that way (lines 624–628).

Kendall said there was an LGBT person who brought his son to church activities. Of this man, Kendall admitted that,

He never tried to rub it [his sexual orientation] in my face or he'd never be like, "Here's my partner, Pastor." He would always be very respectful if he thought that was a concern to me. I don't know what he thought of me or what he thinks of me..." (lines 545–548).

Kendall also said, "He faithfully brought his son to youth group. I think he recognized that the church was and is a good thing in the life of his family and wasn't anti-me or anti-the church" (lines 570–572).

Preston discussed an LGBT person who, years later, called Preston. Preston said of the phone call, "He was just calling me to thank me for caring for him and being his friend and standing beside him during those years" (lines 184–185).

Harold discussed the lesbian couples that attended his church. Harold invited them to his home to learn about their life experiences as LGBT individuals. Harold said,

They talked about how they felt like it was a safe place and that they appreciated and understood the tension that I was in, between the Church of the Nazarene and my own personal beliefs and they appreciated that, appreciated me going to bat for them and making [the church] a safe place for them (lines 422–425).

Harold stated that while they felt loved and accepted by Harold, they also felt "impatient in terms of where the church's stance is" (line 454). Commenting further Harold said,

The [LGBT] women that attend here, I think they're very reticent to come out of the closet obviously and they were very reticent to get involved. But once I assured them that it was a safe place, I really felt like they would have my back until I died, they were loyal (lines 842–845).

Working with LGBT people Harold realized that,

They're human beings, they have the same foibles and strengths and weaknesses as anybody else and there's no difference there.

But in terms of their experience, their unique experiences as an LGBT person, especially within the Church, I think they operate out of a huge amount of gratitude to have a safe place (lines 848–852).

Travis talked about a lesbian couple that began attending his church. The couple said to Travis, "We don't want to blow this church apart. We love this church. We don't want to do things that are going to blow the place wide open. We don't want to wreck what we found here" (lines 832–835).

Curtis also had LGBT people who attended his church. Curtis said they had responded favorably to him. Curtis observed, "They felt good enough with me that they continued to attend my church even though they knew the position of the church, so they certainly weren't feeling heavily rejected or anything like that" (lines 306–308). About the LGBT people in his church, Curtis added, "They get along well with me, and they come to my church, and they listen to me every Sunday" (lines 584–585).

Referring to the LGBT people who have come to his church, Darrell thought LGBT persons might have a preconceived idea of how he would respond to them. Darrell commented, "Maybe they might anticipate what I might feel or think. I know there's an expectation there" (lines 441–442). Regarding one LGBT individual who attended his church, Darrell said,

I felt like there may have been a perception on his part of how I would respond to him. He was a little guarded at times…(lines 590–591). I just think that the guard there is that maybe perceiving a minister, or a pastor would be condemning of people in that lifestyle (lines 606–607).

Derek felt that he started at a disadvantage with LGBT people because of his position as a pastor:

Sometimes I feel like since they know who I am and I know who they are, it's almost like we start at a disadvantaged relationship. I don't try to create that myself, but I just sense that, "Oh, you're a pastor" and so immediately I'm questioned or I'm on the shelf (lines 258–261).

Derek also thought that "if they took the time to know me, I think it would disarm them and realize I'm not here to judge you" (lines 300–301).

Brokenness in the LGBT community. Some of the participants commented on the brokenness found among LGBT individuals and/or within the LGBT community. Matt observed, "When you start working in an LGBT community you find massive levels of brokenness" (lines 666–667). Keith commented about two gay men who have become his "really good friends," but Keith said, "[I am] also very aware of the brokenness in their lives" (line 425).

Keith continued, "I know enough gay people to know that they're not all just really wonderful folk. They're just as broken as everybody else. They also happen to be gay" (lines 628–629). Keith commented further,

I had a friend one time whose dad was gay, and he said this to me, I'll never forget, he said, "My dad's biggest problem has nothing to do with him being gay." I feel like that's true about some of the folks I've made relationships within this neighborhood. So there are barriers within their own life narrative that has something to do with being mistreated maybe, but not altogether (lines 635–643).

Harrison talked about a gay man he knew who "came out late in life" (line 566). Harrison said, "he's almost 80, is a very sad individual, a brilliant mind, successful...but emotionally and relationally a wreck" (566–569). Harrison also discussed an LGBT person who had,

Grown up in a Nazarene family, spent all of his life in the Church of the Nazarene but has hidden his dark secrets. He's unwilling to talk about them or acknowledge them. I think it would emotionally devastate him to actually have to say, "I'm a homosexual." He's distanced himself from the help I've tried to offer and [he is] not ready to say, "I need help" (lines 848–853).

During his internship, Kendall attended a gay rodeo as part of an HIV-AIDs hospice ministry. Of the men at the rodeo, Kendall observed,

> It just kind of reminded me that there was, at least among some of those men who were there that day, some degree of hurt and some degree of confusion and some degree of trying to figure out really what they were all about (lines 644–647).

Keith acknowledged that one of his assumptions about LGBT people was, "When gay people hear the words "welcoming" and "accepting" they don't expect to hear the word "sin" to be said anywhere near them [or] their sexual identity or brokenness or whatever word you want to use" (lines 872–875).

Allen observed, that beyond the "issue" of homosexuality (line 882), "behind all of that there's people, incredibly hurting, incredibly damaged people who are desperately seeking something; whether it be acceptance, whether it be love, whether, you know, whatever. It all boils down to people" (lines 883–887).

Harold spent some time talking with an LGBT woman who attended his church. Harold said of the woman, "she has lots of theological training and so she really understands [LGBT concerns] from a theological framework" (lines 249–250). According to Harold, she was also knowledgeable of the LGBT community about which, "She said you would not believe how many [LGBT] people are hungry, just starving for spiritual connection" (lines 1006–1007).

Theme Seven: Challenges Facing Nazarene Clergy

This theme illustrates the complexity of homosexuality as it relates to upholding the Nazarene church's position and providing ministry to LGBT individuals. Here Nazarene pastors talked about the challenges of balancing the denomination's position on homosexuality, their congregants' expectations, and the participant's desire to minister effectively to LGBT people. In this theme, participants discussed the complex nature of the church's position and LGBT concerns. Participants also described communication challenges as well as the resistance of both Nazarenes and

LGBT people to dialog about same-sex relationships. Participants addressed opportunities—or the lack thereof—for membership, leadership, and/or ordination for LGBT persons in the Church of the Nazarene. Participants shared their overall purpose of ministry as well as their efforts to reach out to LGBT people and the LGBT community. A few participants discussed the multi-cultural/cross-cultural experience of ministering to LGBT people.

Awareness of complexity. Participants commented on balancing the complexity of the Nazarene church's position on homosexuality and LGBT concerns. Travis made the following observation concerning the church's position and LGBT people:

> It is a difficult area to navigate right now because we're trying to figure out what does this look like in ministry. So you know, it can be a conundrum to figure out how to navigate loving people and yet not communicating to a culture or a church that this is morally neutral or okay in our theology (lines 572–576).

Blake shared a similar feeling, "My discomfort's when I try to articulate to you a little bit is how do I navigate through it when I have somebody who's living very differently? I do struggle with that" (lines 214–216). Referring to homosexuality, Blake observed, "I think there's confusion on it, frankly, all across the board" (lines 256–257). Blake explained,

> "[C]ulture creep" is what I call it. The culture has crept into the church to where now we don't know what we should stand on, let alone what we do stand on and so what was once called right is now called wrong and what was once called wrong is now called right. It's very confusing (lines 267–270).

Like other participants, Darrell acknowledged the complexity of pastoring a Nazarene church and dealing with LGBT concerns. Darrell said,

> There's a whole complicated dynamic that I just don't think I've quite resolved or really know how to respond to, and that's maybe

the conflict in my own mind is I don't know that I've done a good job personally of saying here's what I believe and so here's what it means for us, the church (lines 816–819).

Darrell also said, "It's such a complicated issue; it's not a cut-and-dried thing" (line 865).

Allen provided a comparable observation saying, "It's terribly complex. I know they [LGBT people] are coming and I'm thinking about it, but I don't have any, any ideas" (lines 796–798). Allen added, "It's an immensely complicated, complex issue" (line 882).

Kendall acknowledged the complex nature of the same-sex debate:

This isn't easy stuff for me, for the church, anyone who has—I just kind of think if anyone has easy answers to this subject on either side within the church, especially, all-inclusive love, embrace, toleration, tolerance of whatever sexual lifestyle you choose, and to the other extent to say, "Boom. This is the way. Walk in it, and there's no going to the side. I just think we have got to watch out (1057–1061).

Kendall also said, "I don't want to make this fuzzy for people, but I don't want to make it too easy" (lines 1136–1137).

Preston made a similar observation: "It can be a complicated thing and it seems to me; it does get fuzzier when families are impacted by it" (lines 109–112).

Harold commented, "I think that part of what makes this a difficult conversation is that it's very emotional on both sides. If you have friends that are part of the LGBT community, it becomes a very emotional issue" (lines 226–229).

Keith said that loving people unconditionally creates a tension, especially regarding LGBT people. Keith said it thusly,

I have declared this unconditional love for all persons and this real desire to not be a people who are hateful in any way, but there's still tension. I am living in that tension. Tension is the first word that comes to my mind when this issue is what we're talking about (lines 906–909).

Communication challenges. Participants described the potential communication difficulties that arise with the LGBT population and/or the participant's congregation when attempting to address issues related to homosexuality and LGBT concerns. Participants also acknowledged their personal struggle to know how to communicate effectively about same-sex issues. For example, Travis said, "We're all kind of looking for some handles of how to communicate this or talk about it or even deal with it" (lines 230–233).

Darrell felt that the church needs to have a conversation about homosexuality and LGBT concerns, but admitted that attempts to do so, have not been well received. Darrell said, "I think this conversation needs to happen within the church to deal with it" (lines 291–292). However, Darrell also stated that, "There've been other churches that have attempted that but [it] has not gone well; it's not been received in the right spirit by a lot of folks who don't understand why you're having a conversation about it" (lines 294–296). Darrell said, "There was a church that tried to have forum to talk about the issue, it didn't go well; it wasn't received in the right spirit" (lines 303–305). Darrell admitted, "So there's a real hesitation as a minister that I don't want to begin a conversation in an unhealthy way so, you just don't have the conversation" (lines 851–852). Continuing Darrell said,

> So, even asking the question to me is a little trepidation because it's like "Do we really want to have that conversation?" I believe we need to as a church and I believe part of my responsibility, as a pastor, is to help that conversation take place. I guess I just have a little trepidation even beginning the conversation because it is such a diversity of opinion (1017–1022).

Harold believed his congregation is ready to talk about homosexuality and LGBT concerns; however, he too expressed apprehension about the potential for division. Harold observed,

> I think we're ready to talk about it here. I think it could become divisive, but I think we're ready to talk about it. Whether the district is ready to talk about it, whether the district would crap

a brick if they knew that we were doing that in Sunday school class, that's a whole other thing, but I don't think I can do it. We have a tenuous relationship with the district as it is and I think that it would give them good reason to come down kind of hard on us (lines 804–813)....I wouldn't mind having a conversation on a Sunday morning, but yeah, I would fear for my job (lines 829–830).

Darrell acknowledged that homosexuality and LGBT concerns are a "hot topic" (line 844). Because it is a "hot button" issue (line 844) Darrell confessed, "By default, maybe we just avoid it. We really haven't addressed it. We really haven't dealt with it in an honest conversation" (lines 844–846).

Blake provided another example of the challenges of talking about homosexuality:

What do you say to a parent whose boy just committed suicide? What do you do? You don't say anything. You just avoid the conversation. You avoid eye contact. You don't know what to say. I think we're doing that in this context too (lines 820–824).

Bradley said he has tried to have conversations about homosexuality, but it resulted in conflict. Bradley shared,

There's been conversations where I was trying to articulate the church's position and that person either didn't understand what I was trying to say or didn't accept it and there was a bit of conflict—on both sides. But I tend to pastor in it in area that's conservative. So, most people's arrows would be coming from thinking I was too liberal and not thinking I was too conservative (lines 175–182).

Curtis expressed concern that someone in his church might say something that would be offensive to one of the LGBT individuals who attends the church. Curtis said, "There's always this little worry that somebody's going to say something stupid because there's always—in a church this size, there are some very traditional kind of people, but they are probably unaware that those people are gay" (lines 318–321).

Derek believed that the biggest challenge facing the church is to balance adhering the word of God while loving others regardless of their sexual orientation. Derek stated it thusly,

> That's our biggest challenge, I think, as a church is not to judge, people will often hear that, but it's to express the love of God and acceptance of the person not their sin. That is quite challenging in our day and age, but yet in the loving of the person, we cannot compromise the word of God (lines 45–48).

Travis said that at present the church's language about homosexuality is insufficient and lacks direction about how to effectively minister to LGBT people. Travis commented,

> What I think we need alongside our affirmation that this is what we understand the scriptures are saying, I think we need some language that talks about where do we go from here to minister to people who are homosexual or who are gay and married or whatever. I mean you know, because right now we have no language about that at all. Right now, the only thing we have language about is that this is a perversion. But that doesn't really give us a lot to go on in terms of you know, are these people we try to minister to, are these people we keep in the church? We really need some language because left unspecified you know; you and I both know that what we probably have is a geographical divide between the coast and the center of the country (lines 186–200).

Keith said his church occasionally mails invitations to the community inviting people to attend the church. Keith described the mailer:

> Every once in a while we'll put out mailers introducing our church to folk. I think one of the first ones we did we tried sort of tongue-in-cheek binary invitations to Democrats, Republicans, cat people, dog people. We named these binary sorts of divisions,

but we didn't say gay and straight. We didn't say gay and straight, but that's [because] (lines 855–859)…I don't want to set them up. I don't want to set up their expectations. I feel like if I put gay and lesbians, I would be misleading them. I would be misleading them as far as the institutional realities that I have to deal with (lines 868–870).

Blake felt that there is discomfort for both Nazarenes and for LGBT people who may want to attend a Nazarene church. Blake observed, "The reason our churches aren't full of people like that is because they're not comfortable and neither is this side of the seat. We don't know how to have conversation" (lines 817–819).

Keith expressed a similar thought about the bi-directional discomfort between Nazarenes and LGBT people. Keith commented,

It goes both ways. It's not just me protecting the unity of this church, it's also me knowing—I feel good and well that it's going to be an ill-fitting suit in the Church of the Nazarene for gay people. It's going to be a difficult place for them to be (lines 863–866).

Foreclosed dialog. Foreclosed dialog indicates participants' implicit or explicit comments that the Nazarene church and/or LGBT people are reluctant to enter into conversations related to homosexuality or same-sex orientation concerns. Preston had a cousin who was LGBT. Preston admitted that he does not converse with her about her same-sex orientation. Preston said, "If there was openness, I would dialog with her about it, but I'm not one who feels I need to go [to her]. I've never felt very fruitful to impose your opinions and perspectives on others, if there's not openness" (lines 288–292). Preston added, "If someone is not open to your input then there's not really much use, you're wasting your time" (lines 296–297).

Derek suggested that for some LGBT people in his community there was a preconceived idea of how he—an evangelical pastor—would respond to a person with a same-sex orientation. According to Derek this perception created a barrier to dialog. Derek explained: "In general, running into [LGBT] people in the community, there's not a lot of warmth there. I don't know if it's pre-judgment going either way or both ways—I don't know" (lines 292–294). Derek said, "It's hard to get past your title" (lines 307–308)....Sometimes when you're [asked] 'What do you do?'...you could feel the wall, 'Okay, we'll not be hanging...' and that's too bad" (line 318–320).

Darrell referred back to a Nazarene church that had tried to have an open dialog about homosexuality. Darrell said, "it did not go well" (line 304–305). Darrell provided the following description of what transpired:

The pastor was simply trying to open the dialogue and begin to help people deal with the issue and help to articulate the church's position and where we stand in it, but it got a lot of flack. There was a lot of feedback on the negative side of, "Why would you even have a discussion about it?" (lines 307–310)...."Why do you need to talk about it? It's wrong, it's a sin. You condemn it. That's what we do, that's what the church is about" (lines 317–319).

Darrell continued,

It sort of blew up and it became more of a point of contention than it was a point of conversation. It became a conflict rather than "Hey, can we not talk about this?" A lot of the church said, "No, there's nothing to talk about." "I mean it's wrong, we know it's wrong, the Bible says it's wrong, and so you need to just tell people it's wrong." That's, again, one extreme of the pendulum to say this is not something we need to be having conversation about (lines 326–331).

Darrell added,

I think that's, again, why it's such a volatile issue because we tend to say, "It's wrong, they're wrong, and what's the conversation? You just tell them it's wrong and that's the way it is. Get their life straightened out and they'll be okay" (lines 974–977).

About the church, Blake declared, "We've lost the ability to engage in conversations with people" (lines 199–200).

Harrison felt that the church is unwilling "to listen to a moderating voice" (line 364) on the issue of homosexuality. Harrison said,

> I would love to be able to dialogue and to express my position more clearly. I do not believe that the church at this point, as heated as it is, has the capacity to listen to a moderating voice. I don't think it's possible. They haven't on any other hotbed issue like that, but that doesn't mean we stop trying to speak into it.... does this make me more reluctant to speak up? No. Does this make me weary in trying to stake out what I think is the right path? No, but I just have to recognize when I can and can't push a point and those are really hard places to be (362–370).

Harold echoed a similar concern stating that the Nazarene church has closed off "the possibility of conversation around the issue" (lines 192–194). Harold argued, "There's not even room to say, 'Hey there are two ways to see this'" (line 194). Harold admitted,

> I'm not saying that I have it all figured out. I mean, I have my own opinions certainly but closing off the conversation is not the right direction to go with this...I know that there are a lot of people that want a conversation around this and there's not room for one (lines 205–212).

Harold also said,

> I think in a healthy church you can say look, you have your opinion and I have my opinion. This isn't central to who we are as a people, as a movement, this isn't a central issue to what we're about and our mission and what we want to do. Can we agree that you can have a position and I can have a position and we can respect each other and respectfully disagree on this particular issue and move forward? I don't see room for that, for respectful disagreement (lines 532–537).

Membership, leadership, and ordination for LGBT people. Participants commented on the opportunities for LGBT people to hold membership and/or leadership responsibilities and positions within the local church. A few participants discussed their thoughts about the possibility of ordination for LGBT persons in the Church of the Nazarene. For many of the participants, either implicitly or explicitly, these opportunities were contingent upon same-sex orientation verses same-sex practice. For example, Harold stated, "I think it's the Nazarene position that orientation is one thing, practice is a whole different deal; they like that separation" (lines 920–922). Harrison commented, "I'm of the opinion that homosexual orientation does not disqualify you from ministry in the church or from participation in the life of the body any more than a heterosexual orientation" (lines 186–188).

Travis reflected on the *Manual of the Church of the Nazarene* regarding the possibility of membership for LGBT individuals. Travis observed,

> I think the *Manual* is pretty clear up to like there's a shorter version of the do's and don'ts about membership towards the front of the *Manual* and it is listed in them. You know, along with a bunch of other sexual or other things that are about sexual practice. So it wouldn't be orientation that would be the issue (lines 1423–1427).

Matt too referred to the *Manual* as he discussed the possibility of membership for LGBT people in his church. Matt commented,

> The *Manual* says we can't offer you certain things like full membership, but we're going to love you. Our district has specifically given us permission to—which now is called fellowship membership, it used to be called associate membership. For anybody who comes to our congregation and basically believes in the Apostles' Creed and the basic beliefs of the Church, we welcome them into associate membership (lines 433–438).

Preston offered a different viewpoint regarding a "practicing" LGBT person joining his church. Preston stated, "I couldn't knowingly do it" (line 416). Clarifying his statement Preston said, "I could not in good conscience open the door to membership to someone, and thus to leadership, if they were a practicing homosexual" (lines 427–429).

Derek expressed a similar opinion: "Any leadership or membership would not be available, as it wouldn't be to anybody else who's practicing a sinful behavior" (lines 595–596). Derek also stated, "If you're a practicing homosexual, that is not something that will make into our leadership or our membership" (lines 685–686).

Of a same-sex oriented person participating or joining his church, Kendall said, "I think if they were involved in the practice of same-sex relationship, then I would probably invite them to participate wholeheartedly, but wait on membership" (lines 857–859).

Darrell indicated that the margin was wider for membership than for leadership in his church. Darrell suggested, "Joining the church we try to receive people with grace and welcome them into the fellowship. We don't feel like you've got to get all your issues worked out or nobody would be able to join the church" (lines 674–677). Darrell admitted however that, "the leadership standard would be a different issue" (line 680). Darrell explained, "I would say strongly that if somebody was engaged in a same-sex relationship we would not want them involved in leadership. I don't feel like that's an appropriate lifestyle to be in leadership" (lines 944–946).

Like Darrell, several of the participants commented on opportunities in the church for leadership for LGBT individuals. Allen said, "Official leadership, church board that kind of thing, I don't see any way around that polity in the same way that someone who's practicing extramarital affair could serve in leadership" (lines 661–663).

Travis expressed a similar feeling about an LGBT person serving in a leadership role in the church. Travis commented,

> I don't feel like I can allow it given current Nazarene polity. In terms of my own understanding of the scriptures, I have to have more work in my own mind on this issue before I could even allow it even if it was up to me, you know what I mean? I'd have to process some more stuff before I came around to saying yeah okay. It might depend on what that leadership kind of thing was (lines 1386–1391).

Harold felt that an LGBT person would be able to serve in a leadership role within the church as long as Harold's church board was supportive. Harold said it thusly,

> I have no problem with it as long as my board can agree as to what leadership is and how much [LGBT people] can serve; then I think we can move forward with having them do that. But that's going to be tricky (lines 889–891).

Curtis emphasized that LGBT people were welcome in his church and that they could participate in congregational life. Curtis admitted, however, "I can't get you elected to the board if you're openly living in a homosexual lifestyle. You can't be a teacher of our theology. But you can participate, you can be a part, you will be loved" (lines 462–464). Curtis followed by saying, "There would be no limitation, like any other thing, so long as their practice falls within scriptural parameters" (lines 735–736). But he added,

> I would say that a homosexual practice would be over the line. You can fall, but once you move to okay, this is what I'm going to do, I'm living with someone else—all of those sorts of things, and I don't know exactly how to draw that line, but the practice of a homosexual lifestyle would be where I'd say okay, that's it (lines 740–743).

Similar to Curtis's experience, Harrison also had LGBT people attend and serve in his church. Regarding LGBT persons presence and their service, Harrison said,

> We have had folks who are oriented gay and lesbian and have served in the church and I don't have any issues with that. Those who would be in committed relationships, same-sex relationships, who are promiscuous in a homosexual way, would, in my mind, be disqualified for serving (lines 869–873).

Matt is the pastor of a primarily LGBT congregation. Even so, Matt stated that he had to follow the *Manual of the Church of the Nazarene*. Matt said,

For us, we obviously have to go by the *Manual*; but we have positions such as the people who read scripture. Our church is at
the size where it's all hands on deck or it's not going to make it, if
that makes any sense. So we have people of all sexual orientations
doing pretty much everything except for preaching. They serve
communion. They help lead music. They cook because we always
start out with a meal every time we meet (lines 560–568).

Matt commented further saying, "This church is mainly run by people who identify as LGBT. But as far as full membership, membership on
the board, preaching position, I have to stick with what the *Manual* says.
I'm okay with doing that" (lines 574–576).

Blake stated, "If someone is knowingly practicing (line 915)…we won't
put them in leadership" (line 917). Kendall declared, "I can say with great
confidence that our church would not have a homosexual on the church
board (lines 957–958). I think that would be my own decision—and the
constituency of the church" (lines 967 & 971).

Commenting more on his own concerns and his church's response to
an LGBT person in leadership, Keith commented,

I'd be concerned about the disunity [it] would cause if an openly
gay person were here and wanted to be in leadership.…I would
probably lose some people—maybe. I think I would. I'm not sure
about that. Be interesting to find out. (lines 741–744).

Three of the participants referenced the possibility of ordination for
LGBT individuals. As with leadership, sexual orientation verses sexual
practice was an important distinction. Curtis said, "I would not ordain
someone who's openly practicing" (line 113); however, Curtis continued,
"If someone came to me and said, "I'm attracted to the same-sex, but I
believe God's calling me to live a celibate life and I'm not participating in
that," I would ordain them" (lines 114–117). Curtis also said,

"Oriented" being the key word, so long as they're not actively
practicing, I'm fine with that. I'd lay my hands on them and

ordain them. So long as they're saying, "I'm going to live celibately, I'm not going to practice," I'm good (lines 693–696).

Harold articulated a similar position, "I would have no problem with them sitting on my board. As far as I'm concerned, if I were on the Board of Ministerial Credentials, I would ordain them" (lines 928–933).

Like Curtis and Harold, Bradley also stated that ordination should not be withheld from an LGBT person because of one's sexual orientation. Bradley observed, "I don't see why they could not serve, and I personally don't see why that person could not be ordained just because that's their disposition" (lines 523–525).

Some of the participants stated that celibacy and/or sexual abstinence would be required of LGBT individuals as a condition for membership, leadership, or ordination. For example Travis stated that if an LGBT person said, "I'm willing to live a celibate life because I think that's what the New Testament calls for" (lines 1429–1430) then, Travis argued,

> To me that's no different than to me that's no different than a heterosexual single guy going I'm celibate and you know, until I get married, until something changes, you know what I mean? I've often argued that celibacy for a homosexual is no different than celibacy for a single heterosexual in terms of Christian commitment (lines 1431–1435).

Preston speculated about an LGBT person who might want to join his church. Preston said,

> If someone said to me I'd like to join the church, but I need you to know I've dealt with homosexual desires all my life, but I also need you to know I understand that's not acceptable by God's word and I'm committed to living a life of celibacy and, but I want you to be aware. I just wanted you to be aware and if it's okay I'd still like to join the church. I could welcome someone into the church (lines 469–473).

Kendall expressed a similar viewpoint:

Someone who felt this orientation but was committed to, by the grace of God, a chaste lifestyle, I think, again, would receive positions of ministry and depth of participation in the life of the body would be opened up more freely (lines 1009–1011).

Darrell spoke of the commitment to abstinence as a condition for involvement in ministry for the LGBT person:

If somebody came to me and said, "Hey, this has been my orientation, this has been a struggle for me, but I'd like to lead the ministry and I'm making the commitment to live a life of abstinence or just live single and committed to the Lord," I don't think I'd have a problem with them being involved in ministry. I think a practicing homosexual would because I think the church would not embrace that obviously, I don't think I would embrace that as a God-honoring life (857–863).

Harrison said he has tried to help LGBT people, who feel called to ministry, understand how they can live a celibate life in the same way that an unmarried heterosexual person remains celibate. Harrison said it thusly,

I've done my very best to help persons who feel called to ministry, who feel that they have an orientation that they believe disqualifies them to understand how to live and function in that in the same way in which many heterosexuals who are not married have chosen to live celibate lives in service to the Kingdom (lines 201–206).

Bradley posited that the church could do better at communicating with LGBT people that they are not precluded from service or ministry because of sexual orientation, so long as the LGBT person commits to a life of celibacy. Bradley encouraged the church "to go on and say, that person could then serve in ministry and be ordained knowing they're going to live a celibate life." However, Bradley said, the church "needs to say 'Yes, they could,'" but heretofore [the church] hasn't said that" (lines 146–149).

Purpose of ministry. Here participants discussed their purpose of ministry, e.g., being called to love others, making the church a welcoming place, and demonstrating grace regardless of sexual orientation. Harrison said,

> I have ministered to the best of my ability in a loving, compassionate and "as helpful as I can" way to those who have, on the journey, talked to me about these things, who've I've encountered and become aware that that's who they are (lines 907–910).

Allen commented that his "fellowship needs to be a place where anybody, regardless of race, color, creed, or sexual orientation can come and be received into this community, because that's what it means to be part of the community of faith" (lines 324–327). Allen continued, "We are here to represent Christ and to offer that hope to whoever comes. And for us to be gatekeepers to that grace is, to me, one of the grossest sins anywhere" (330–332). Allen questioned,

> How do I help my congregation be that kind of a group, where anybody can come and experience the love of Jesus Christ, experience genuine community and experience or have the opportunity to experience the transformational character of the gospel? Whether that ever means a change of orientation or not (lines 356–360).

During a sermon, Curtis indicated how he felt his church should be responding to LGBT people. Curtis said to his congregation,

> There is no person who's wrestling with the issue of homosexuality in North America that does not know what the Evangelical Church believes about this, you don't need to tell them again. You don't need to tell them six ways from Sunday, you don't need to lecture them. You need to love them. You need to just love them. You need

to be the guy that they go out and they say wow, that's completely different from what I encountered from the Baptists down the street because we as Wesleyans, it's all about love (lines 92–101).

Curtis added, "It' about loving people. It's really just about loving people whatever they're like and wherever they're at" (lines 586–587). Harold echoed a similar sentiment when he said,

I think that love is the ethic that I use and so, as a result, because love is the ethic, it really has less to do with biology, compatible body parts and more to do with what's the most loving way of responding to each other (lines 217–220).

Harold also commented,

I think that human sexuality is such an important part of what it means to be human that to deny that to another person is not very loving. The issue for me isn't even orientation or practice, but how do we practice, how do we love? (lines 956–959).

Matt had a two-fold purpose to his ministry. Because of his ministry to the LGBT community, the Nazarene church has invited him to consult with other Nazarene churches about how to be more open and welcoming to LGBT people. Matt said, "Our purpose is to help churches become more welcome and open to LGBT individuals" (lines 180–181). About his church's ministry to the LGBT community, Matt said, "Our job, we believe, is to be a nonjudgmental, loving presence in the community" (lines 217–218). "Our goal here is to build a community that people can come in and feel loved" (lines 222–223). Matt added, "That's the type of place that we're trying to put together, a place where anybody can feel welcome" (lines 271–272).

Keith's church focuses on extending a gracious invitation to worship to everyone (lines 76–77). Of this Keith said it is,

An invitation that we try to extend as a community here to persons no matter where you are in life's journey, no matter what brokenness you're dealing with—and we all are dealing with our brokenness—that this community can be a place where healing can happen and that that gracious invitation is the first thing that that's what we lead with, that that's what we lead with as a people (lines 78–82).

Keith added,

One of the things we do often with that is try to create a very hospitable setting where there's room at the table for everyone. We try to make that very clear; there's this invitation for all, there's a place set for you today at this table (lines 87–90).

Kendall remembered a comment made by someone at a Nazarene General Assembly that influenced his think about the vision for his church and the purpose of its ministry. Kendall said,

I've always remembered that comment of whoever it was at the General Assembly who said if somebody's driving by a church and would see our name, a homosexual who's need of spiritual help and saw our church's name, would they feel welcome to come in church for that spiritual help? I've always hoped to pastor a church and be the kind of person who would be seen in that way (lines 1017–1022).

Kendall admitted however, "As a pastor, I wrestle with that as to how we best provide hospitality and warmth and love to someone who is so closely identified with what we call sin" (lines 1036–1038).

Bradley felt that "the church just needs to try to do what it can to minister to everyone, whoever God happens to send your way and not push anyone back because of something" (lines 836–838). Bradley commented, "I think we need to be more loving and accepting. We probably err on the side of judging; we're pretty good at that. Not as good on the other side" (lines 846–848),

In planning for how to respond when LGBT individuals come to his church, Blake said, Part of planning and goal setting is creating scenarios of which you're not yet in. Well, one of the scenarios we need to be prepared for is this very thing. What if…? Are we ready? What would it look like to be ready? What does part of our discipleship need to include? That would help us, I think, as practitioners, as pastors to prepare ourselves as well as our people (lines 1179–1187).

Outreach to LGBT people and bridge building with the LGBT community. Here, participants discussed their efforts to connect with the LGBT community. Many of the participants admitted that they had not made an intentional effort to reach out LGBT people. Harrison said, "As a local church pastor, I don't know that I've ever intentionally gone after the homosexual community" (lines 906–907). Harrison also commented,

I fear that a suburban congregation like mine, which is still __% white, suburban, upper- middle-class, or at least middle-class, is going to have a much more difficult time with that picture. But I've also not given up on trying to make sure that we minister (lines 915–918).

Several other participants expressed similar responses about outreach efforts to the LGBT community. Derek said, "We don't have any ministry that to reach out to [LGBT people] or whatever to reach out to them in anyway. We haven't had that. Yeah, we haven't" (lines 787–788). Travis confessed a similar position: "We haven't created endeavors, you know programming to, 'Let's reach out to the homosexual population'" (lines 1640–1641). Curtis commented, "I haven't done any real, deliberate reaching out, intentional reaching out to that community. I've dealt with it as it's come into my church" (lines 753–754). Curtis added,

So I don't know that I've ever done any real particularly reaching out that to community. And probably wouldn't be my style necessarily, I tend to work with individuals and work with people more so than getting involved in the larger political agendas and all that kind of piece of it (liens 761–764).

Regarding reaching out to the LGBT community in his area, Blake said, "I don't know how to reach out to [LGBT people]. Part of it may be because I'm not where they are. My responses have been because they've come to me either because of my family or it's because of counseling" (lines 947–949).

Commenting on his efforts to reach the LGBT community, Bradley admitted, "I don't do a very good job with that. I mean I don't—I'm not proactive in that sense" (lines 644–645).

Bradley continued, "I'm not currently trying to discover people who are gay or trying to help them, you know, not at all" (lines 650–651). However, Bradley said,

> I would hope that if I lived in a community where there were significant numbers of homosexuals that we would be willing to minister to them and try to help them any way we could, accept them for who they are (lines 669–672).

Darrell felt that people who might attend his church would feel welcome, but he did not think that an LGBT person would attend a conservative church. Darrell said it thusly,

> I don't know that anybody would come to our church and feel unwelcome, but I would anticipate maybe somebody who is in a homosexual lifestyle wouldn't necessarily come to more a conservative church. I don't know. That's all part of my curiosity with that is how do we reach out? (lines 493–496).

Regarding outreach efforts to LGBT people Darrell pondered, "If this is a group that has needs, how do we meet that need? We haven't asked that question" (lines 841–842).

Although many of the participants expressed no outreach to LGBT people, Matt and his church were immersed in the LGBT community. Matt said of his church, "A majority of our time is spent…at the bars, gay bars, our local gay bars. So I mean we're pretty immersed in the community" (lines 157–159). Commenting further on the church's ministry, Matt said, "What we do as a group here, is we immerse ourselves into the

[LGBT] community. We obviously don't participate in anything that goes against our morals, but we're there when life happens" (lines 212–214). Matt continued, "My job is to build a bridge (lines 313–314)…our job is not to ask anybody's sexual orientation, our job is to love people, and because of the radical love that we show, they respond with, "Why are you different?" (lines 316–318).

Harold had a conversation with an LGBT woman who attended his church. During their conversation, the woman told Harold what he needed to do to reach the LGBT community. She told Harold,

> If you want to be a welcoming community then just say, "We welcome you no matter what your orientation is." She said put a rainbow flag on your website and you get 50 people the next week. She said you would not believe how many people [LGBT people] are hungry, just starving for spiritual connection, but don't know if [the church] is a safe place or not (lines 1003–1007).

Multi/cross-cultural experience with LGBT people. Several of the participants talked about the cross-cultural or multi-cultural experience of ministering to LGBT individuals. Allen encountered a transgender individual at a store. When he became aware that the woman was a man, Allen said it stirred self-reflection about the current cultural climate:

> I would say one of the things that I have to think about, particularly as culture is evolving, is what is normal? Analogous, if someone from another culture, Indian or African, Oriental, were to be in front of me, dressed in their cultural garb that wouldn't faze me. In fact, I'd probably be kind of appreciative of it. But with this particular issue, it unsettles me either because of the longtime societal stigma that this is deviant or because—I don't know. I've had to come to consider if a person is a person of value, if they're a person who is uniquely made and loved by God, why does their public appearance or persona cause just that gut negative reaction? Or how can I appropriately redirect that, so that my reaction isn't the barrier to a relationship (lines 458–469).

Keith said he had noticed cultural differences in the LGBT community when he was invited to a Christmas party where LGBT people were present. Keith described it thusly,

> If I'm in a context where the majority of people are gay, and I've been in those situations, especially [at] _____ and _____'s Christmas party where at least half of the group is gay, I noticed anthropologically as person who's had theological training, the cultural aspects. I started to see a glimpse of a world there that I know very little about. The way gay men greet one another, I just noticed that there is—I don't know how to articulate what it is, but from just looking at things anthropologically, I'm like, "Wow, there's a whole culture here that I just have no access to" (lines 477–485).

Curtis had pastored a church that had become multi-racial. Curtis said that in a multi-cultural church one must work harder to keep open lines of communication. Curtis shared the following about his experience:

> The church I pastored in _____ _____ went from all-white to multicultural, five languages in addition to English and lots of people of color. So I know whenever you're working across culture, you have to work harder because it's easier for miscommunication to happen. So with those folks that are gay that come to this church, same sort of thing applies for me: I think of that as a cross-cultural experience and it's easier for my not shaking hands with them or not talking to them to be understood in the larger context of our religious subculture [as], "Oh, he doesn't like me" or "He thinks there's something wrong with me." So I work harder at it with them, but it's not different (lines 326–336).

Curtis continued,

> I'm not aware of anything I do differently, other than going out of my way to make sure that I connect with them and affirm them not because they're gay as much as I know I'm doing a cross-cultural kind of thing (lines 353–356).

Harrison used his church as an example to provide insight about the cross-cultural nature of ministering to LGBT people. Harrison provided a snapshot of the cultural make up of his congregation:

> This church is now __% Chinese…we have broken into a sizeable Chinese community here.…For several years, I can remember in my mind I had seen my Anglo congregation and I [had seen] the Chinese.…I remember distinctly two years ago coming back from vacation as I was sitting on platform scanning across the crowd I no longer saw Chinese faces and Anglo faces. I remember distinctly thinking, "I see my people." That analogy is how I would feel about [LGBT people] in pastoral care and counseling or in relationships or in any other aspect of life (lines 669–687).

Harold compared the cross-cultural intersection between LGBT people and the church reminiscent of racism in the 1950s. Talking with the LGBT individuals who attend his church, Harold described his feelings saying,

> I feel oftentimes like I'm pastoring an Anglo church in Mississippi in 1954 that's not integrated and there's tons of racism everywhere. I said, if I were to walk into that congregation in 1954 in Mississippi and say, "You bunch of sorry bigots. You're all going to rot in hell for how bigoted you are and the way you're treating African-Americans around here. You better knock it off or God's going to smack you upside the head." I'd be lynched up before noon in the nearest oak tree and my prophetic voice would disappear with that. I think I would have made more progress as a pastor in that situation. I see a lot of parallels to that to sort of where we're at today (lines 425–442).

Kendall said he recognized the need to spend more time with other people groups, including LGBT people. Kendall confessed,

> I frequently tell myself I need to spend more time with African-American people and spend more time with homosexual people

because I just, there's ways of thinking that those folks have because of cultural experiences that for me to talk about, or think
about even, how they're really experiencing life is just, I don't
know (lines 834–80).

Allen shared his feeling that diversity should characterize the church.
Allen observed, "I think there is a strength to diversity" (line 897). Allen
queried, "Our God is a God of diversity, so why would he eschew diversity in his church?" (lines 902–903). Continuing Allen said,

I think the church would do much better if we could accept one
another and say, you know what? That's not our thing but that's
okay that it's your thing. Rather than polarize, we're right, you're
wrong. We're going to heaven; you're going to hell. Nothing good
comes out of that discussion (lines 905–909).

COMPOSITE ESSENCE: NAZARENE CLERGY'S RESPONSES TO HOMOSEXUALITY AND INTERACTIONS WITH LGBT PEOPLE

The salience of phenomenological research is the reduction of data to arrive
at the essential essence of the phenomenon for the individual participants
that characterizes the experience of all participants in the study (Creswell,
2007; Moustakas, 1994). In this manuscript, the individual essences for
each participant are presented at the end of each participant's case display,
which can be found in the Appendix (see Appendix H). The following is a
statement of the composite or essential essence of experience of Nazarene
clergy responses to homosexuality and their interactions with LGBT people.

Homosexuality is complex and controversial topic in the Church of
the Nazarene. Although most Nazarene clergy express agreement with the
church's position on homosexuality, opinions about the *Manual* statement differ dramatically ranging from balanced and gracious to harsh
and incendiary. Many Nazarene clergy want the denomination to revise
the *Manual* statement to include a more nuanced, gracious response to
homosexuality. Nazarene pastors subscribe to a biblical sexuality agreeing
that God designed intimate sexual relationships and marriage for man
and woman.

The Church of the Nazarene and its educational institutions strongly influence clergy beliefs about homosexuality. Nazarene clergy are nearly unanimous in their belief that scripture condemns same-sex practice. Although they maintain that same-sex orientation or attraction is *not* sinful, they believe that same-sex practice *is* sinful. Nazarene clergy are quick to point out however, that same-sex practice is no worse than any other sin outlined in the scripture. Nazarene clergy feel strongly than same-sex practice and Christian life are incompatible—a same-sex oriented person can be either practicing *or* Christian, but one cannot do/be both.

Nazarene clergy experience a variety of affective responses to LGBT people running along a continuum of revulsion and discomfort to compassion and love. Nazarene clergy also admit that knowing an LGBT person increases their sensitivity to homosexuality and their compassion for LGBT people. Conversely, Nazarene pastors feel the tension of responding lovingly and graciously to LGBT people without implicitly condoning same-sex practice or relationships. While some Nazarene clergy are cautious about LGBT people attending their church, other Nazarene pastors are receptive and desire to create an atmosphere in which all people are welcome to worship. Most Nazarene clergy admit that they do not reach out to the LGBT community; rather, they minister to LGBT people as they come into the church.

Most Nazarene clergy are adamant that opportunities for full membership, leadership, and ordination are denied to LGBT people who actively engage in same-sex practice. On the other hand, clergy stress that a non-practicing, celibate LGBT person is not precluded from church membership, leadership, or even ordination. Nazarene clergy face challenges regarding homosexuality and LGBT concerns, for example, adhering to the denominational position on homosexuality while ministering to LGBT people and, the legalization of gay marriage with the unique pastoral concerns that accompany it. Nazarene clergy clearly recognize the divisive nature of homosexuality and same-sex relationships and exhibit extreme caution in approaching the topic. Nazarene clergy express the need for forums and opportunities for dialog in a safe, confidential environment.

Nazarene clergy confess that homosexuality, ministry to LGBT people, and the accompanying concerns is an exceedingly complex issue with no clear or easy answers. Nazarene clergy want the denomination to provide clearer instruction, education, and training about how to minister effectively to LGBT people.

SUMMARY

In this chapter I described the focus of my study and reviewed the research question that guided it. I presented the demographic data and participant profiles. I described the use of interview questions to collect the data as well as how and where the interviews were conducted. I provided an overview of the procedures I used for data analysis. I included a description of the development of the codebook that was used to code participant transcripts. I discussed the use of a research team to establish accuracy in the data analysis. I also highlighted the coding procedures utilized to identify the salient themes of the participants' experience, after which participants were contacted to verify the accuracy of data interpretation. Following the identification of themes and their verification, I constructed an essence of the phenomenon for each participant. From these individual essences emerged the essential or composite essence of the phenomenon revealing Nazarene clergy responses to homosexuality and their responses to LGBT people.

Prior to this study, no research existed that documented the experience of Nazarene clergy's responses to homosexuality or LGBT individuals. The purpose of this study, therefore, was to discover the lived experiences of Nazarene clergy's feelings and thoughts about homosexuality as well as their interactions with LGBT people. From the data collection and analysis I identified seven dominant themes that illustrated Nazarene clergy's lived experience.

The first theme identified by this study was titled, *The Church of the Nazarene: Denominational and Individual Responses to Homosexuality*. This theme referred to the Nazarene church's position on homosexuality and included Nazarene clergy's thoughts and feelings about the church's position. The second theme identified by this study was labeled *Homosexuality in Light of Biblical Sexuality*. This theme illustrated the clergyperson's understanding of human sexuality grounded scripture and theology as well as beliefs about temptation, sin, and human frailty. The third theme,

Ministerial Journey, described the clergyperson's affiliation with the Nazarene church, length of time in ministry, and academic and theological training. The fourth theme entitled *Beliefs about Homosexuality* referred to beliefs about the origins of homosexuality and delineated the differences between same-sex attraction, orientation, and practice. Issues surrounding gay marriage were also included. The fifth theme *Clergy Response and Disposition toward LGBT People* described the pastor's interactions with and personal knowledge of LGBT persons and illustrated the clergyperson's affective, attitudinal, and behavioral responses to LGBT people. The sixth theme labeled *LGBT Presence in the Local Church and Community*. This theme highlighted the presence of LGBT people attending the Nazarene pastor's church and/or the presence of LGBT people in the larger community. This theme also indicated LGBT individuals' response to the Nazarene position on homosexuality and LGBT people's response to Nazarene clergy. The seventh theme titled, *Challenges Facing Nazarene Clergy* referred to the complex nature of dealing with homosexuality and LGBT persons in the context of pastoral ministry. It also addressed the possibilities, or lack thereof, for membership, leadership, and ordination in the Church of the Nazarene for LGBT individuals. This theme also described the resistance to dialog about LGBT concerns by both the Nazarene church and LGBT people. Outreach efforts to the LGBT community limited were also addressed. In the next chapter, I discuss the findings of my research in light of the current extant professional literature on the Church's response to homosexuality. I will also present the limitations of this study, implications for the Nazarene church and pastors, and suggestions for future research.

CHAPTER IV

Discussion

In this chapter, I compare the findings of my research (Chapter III) to the professional, scholarly literature (Chapter I) that informs the current landscape of Nazarene clergy responses to homosexuality and interactions with LGBT individuals. This chapter consists of six principle sections: (a) a comparison of the results to the professional/scholarly literature and the emergent themes that correspond to the literature, (b) new findings/information, (c) limitations of this research, (d) implications of this study, (e) recommendations for future research and, (f) the conclusion. As I compare the results of this study to the professional literature, the reader will notice references from current scholarship related to homosexuality and excerpts from participants' comments that concur with the findings in professional literature. I also reference the corresponding theme(s) discussed in Chapter III. I chose this approach in order to demonstrate the relationship between the results of this study, i.e., themes, and the extant scholarship related to homosexuality and LGBT issues.

There is a dearth of scholarly research and professional literature specifically related to Nazarene clergy responses to homosexuality and their interactions with LGBT individuals. As such, some of the comparisons discussed in this chapter are indirect rather than direct associations with the literature as it relates to homosexuality and LGBT concerns. Since there is no current scholarship addressing Nazarene clergy and homosexuality, I also discuss the "new findings" of this research, which may contribute to current scholarly research and the professional literature.

I now turn to a review of the existing literature related to attitudes about homosexuality and compare it to Nazarene clergy responses to homosexuality and their interactions with LGBT people. I link the primary sections of Chapter I with the seven dominant themes outlined in Chapter III. I draw on brief statements from participant interviews to illustrate their relationship to the literature and the individual themes.

ETIOLOGY OF HOMOSEXUALITY

Current results of Nazarene clergy interviews did not reveal an explicit understanding of the essentialist or social constructionist paradigms of the etiology homosexuality as reviewed in Chapter I. Although participants differed in their understanding of how a same-sex orientation develops, participants demonstrated a cursory knowledge of the three basic etiological factors that contribute to developing a same-sex orientation: biology, environment, and personal choice (Drescher, 2006, 2008; Engle et al., 2006; Hughes, 2006; Sheldon et al., 2007). As represented in the literature, Nazarene clergy understanding of these etiological factors suggest an overlap of nature, nurture, and/or personal choice as factors that contribute to a homosexual orientation. *Theme Four: Nazarene Clergy Beliefs about Homosexuality* illustrated participants' understanding of the etiological factors contributing to a same-sex orientation.

While some Nazarene clergy were conversant about etiology, others admitted their lack of understanding. For example, Bradley, and others, believed that "Some people are just born that way" (line 747). Derek implied that a homosexual orientation might arise from childhood sexual abuse. Conversely, Travis argued that a same-sex orientation may have "been a reality in [one's] self-awareness since their earliest memories… with no trauma attached to it" (lines 658–660). One participant confessed a lack of understanding about how a same-sex orientation develops saying, "The whole nature/nurture kind of conversation in terms of homosexual lifestyle is one that I have to humbly say, 'I don't know'" (Kendall: lines 978–980).

The literature revealed that people are generally more accepting of LGBT individuals who are biologically predisposed toward a same-sex orientation, and that they demonstrate negative attitudes toward same-sex oriented individuals who choose a homosexual way of life (Drescher, 2008; Hewitt & Moore, 2009; Sheldon et al., 2007; Trail et al., 2008).

In fact, individuals who believe that LGBT people choose their sexual orientation demonstrate less tolerance toward same-sex individuals than do advocates of the genetic theory (Marmor, 1998).

Participants expressed sensitivity to the sexual orientation concerns of LGBT individuals yet, Nazarene clergy were steadfast in their belief that gay and lesbian individuals must refrain from the practice of same-sex relationships and "live lives of purity" (Preston: line 592). Despite these etiological factors, however, most participants argued that celibacy/abstinence was the only God-honoring choice for LGBT people. Demanding celibacy creates a paradox for LGBT individuals that may be both unfair and unrealistic. Although a few participants acknowledged the dilemma, it did not alter their conviction that celibacy was the only option for LGBT people.

One interesting result was the frequency participants used the phrase "homosexual lifestyle" or its equivalent (n=67). Participants' use of this term may imply that choice is a key factor in same-sex relationships and that LGBT people consciously choose to engage in a "homosexual lifestyle." If true, this may contribute to participants' belief that same-sex relationships are prohibited and sinful.

Nazarene clergy would benefit from more education about the etiology of homosexuality and the development of sexual orientation. It would also behoove them to consider the implications of requiring celibacy for LGBT people and the impact this may have on the LGBT person's life and relationships. It may also be important for Nazarene clergy to reframe their language when talking about same-sex relationships so as not to implicitly convey the message that a "homosexual lifestyle" is a simply a choice LGBT people make. Viewing LGBT relationships as a choice contributes to the belief that same-sex relationships are sinful.

CULTURAL AND DEMOGRAPHIC INFLUENCES

Current results did not reveal an association between race or ethnicity related to Nazarene clergy responses to homosexuality or interactions with LGBT individuals. One explanation for this may be that all research participants were Caucasian. Data analysis, however, did show association between other variables (e.g., gender, heterosexuality, geographical location, educational level, age, personal contact/knowledge, and political affiliation) and Nazarene clergy responses to homosexuality and their interactions with same-sex oriented individuals. The emergent themes represented in this section are *Theme One: The Church of the Nazarene: Denominational and Individual Responses to Homosexuality*, *Theme Three: Ministerial Journey* and, *Theme Five: Clergy Response and Disposition toward LGBT People*.

All of the research participants were heterosexual males, and as revealed in the literature, gender (Stoever & Morera, 2007; Walch et al., 2010) and heterosexuality correlate with negative attitudes toward homosexuality (Herek, 2002; Steffens, 2005). In general, Nazarene clergy responses to homosexuality are consistent with these findings. Allen said, "At the base level, being a heterosexual male, there is still a gut-revulsion when I think about the practice. I mean to me it's unnatural" (lines 188– 189). After observing a gay couple's interaction, Keith said, "I watched their interaction. It was just like a husband and wife interaction. There was something in me that turned a little bit. I responded slightly viscerally in a negative way to seeing that" (lines 490–493). Darrell stated, "For me to think about a man desiring another man is not a pleasant thought. It's just like, 'Oh, that's…ugh.' It's that creepy feeling" (lines 963–964). These comments illustrate that participant reactions to homosexuality tend to fall along the spectrum of discomfort to "gut revulsion." Participant statements lend support to the professional literature that gender and heterosexuality influence responses to homosexuality.

Geographical location also influences attitudes about homosexuality. People from the Northeast and West coast regions of the United States demonstrate the most favorable attitudes, while those in the middle and southern states are less accepting of homosexuality (Butler, 2005; Glick & Golden, 2010; Sullivan, 2003). Nazarene clergy responses suggested that geographical location has little or no effect on Nazarene clergy feelings about homosexuality. Harold's congregation is located in a western region of the United States densely populated with Nazarenes. Harold declared, "I feel oftentimes like I'm pastoring an Anglo church in Mississippi in 1954 that's not integrated and there's tons of racism everywhere" (lines 426–427). Travis said of a Nazarene church in the Northeast, "If a homosexual left the sanctuary to go the bathroom, the ushers were instructed to follow them to the bathroom to make sure they did not molest any children" (lines 413–416).

Although the literature revealed more accepting attitudes toward homosexuality in the Northeast and Western regions of the United States and more negative attitudes in the Midwest and Southern U.S., Nazarene clergy responses to homosexuality do not appear influenced by their geographical location. Participants demonstrated similar views about homosexuality and their responses to LGBT people were largely consistent with the Church of the Nazarene's denominational statements about homosexuality.

Education has a mitigating effect on negative responses to homosexuality (Hewitt & Moore, 2002; Lewis, 2003; Walch et al., 2010). *Theme Three: Ministerial Journey* briefly describes the influence of the Nazarene church and its academic institution(s) on participant views of homosexuality. Participant comments in this section represent the current professional scholarship and the influence of education on Nazarene clergy thoughts about homosexuality.

Each of the participants in this study possessed a master's degree from Nazarene Theological Seminary; some had earned a doctorate. A few participants' comments supported the literature regarding the mitigating effect of education on attitudes about homosexuality. Curtis observed that more education may make a pastor less likely to respond "viciously" (line 210) to issues related to homosexuality. Curtis stated it thusly, "Probably the more education a pastor has, the less likely he's to be in that spot. It tends to be people who probably have less theological education in general…" (lines 219–221). Although only a few Nazarene clergy commented directly about the effect of education on responses to homosexuality, these responses were in keeping with the current professional literature.

Age of participants in this study ranged from 28–61 years old. Two of the participants (age 28 and 47) demonstrated the most progressive responses to homosexuality and positive interactions with LGBT people. Age is a cultural/demographic factor represented in *Theme One: Denominational and Individual Responses to Homosexuality*. As illustrated in the literature, age has a moderating effect on feelings about homosexuality (Glick & Golden, 2010; Walch et al., 2010). Nazarene clergy did not comment specifically about the influence of age on their own responses to homosexuality. However, participant statements about the age groups represented among their constituency supported the literature indicating that age has moderating effect on attitudes about homosexuality. Matt's comments concurred with the literature, "Our hardest demographic to get [loving LGBT people] across to are the ages between 30 and 50. That's our hardest, toughest crowd…above 50, they tend to be more okay. And under 30? We got them" (lines 460–466). Harrison said, "The majority of young people in the church under the age of 30 do not see an incompatibility between homosexual practice and Christian faith. The opposite is true for people who are approaching 50 and older" (lines 152–154).

Current scholarship maintains that personal contact with LGBT persons decreases negative responses to homosexuality (Herek, 2002; Hewitt & Moore, 2002). Moreover, personal knowledge of an LGBT person or having an LGBT friend or relative increases positive responses to same-sex oriented individuals (Glick & Golden 2010). Clergy responses agreed with the literature and provided salient information for *Theme Five: Clergy Response and Disposition toward LGBT People*. For example, Allen confessed, "…the more experience I have with gay-lesbian people in conversations with them, the more compassion I feel about them" (lines 66–68). Having a gay son increased Blake's sensitivity to LGBT concerns. Blake confessed, "I have become much more compassionate. I think this was easier for me to speak to when it wasn't so personal. Now that it's become personal, I'm more compassionate to the issue" (lines 156–158). As illustrated by these comments, the overall results of this research align with professional literature.

Political affiliation has also been associated with responses to homosexuality (Brown & Henriquez; 2008). Conservative political views have been associated with homonegative responses (Morrison & Morrison, 2003) while liberal political views have been associated with more positive responses (Schulte & Battle, 2004). Although participants did not discuss their own political affiliation, participant statements about the influence of conservative politics on the church's response to homosexuality correspond with the literature. Commenting on the official Nazarene stance on homosexuality, Curtis commented, "I think we've adopted way too much from probably conservative politics or something (lines 41–43).

Referring to his congregants, Travis observed, "Even the Democrats in my church you know, largely orient moral issues around typically Republican or conservative political issues" (lines 1727–1728). Citing its alliance with conservative politics and the far right Republican Party, Harrison stated that, "The church does not have the capacity to speak into this subject [i.e., homosexuality]…with any integrity" (lines 266–272).

Of these cultural and demographic factors, only level of education, and personal knowledge of LGBT persons had a mitigating effect on participants' views of homosexuality and LGBT people. One participant argued that clergy with more education might be less "vicious" toward LGBT people and issues related to homosexuality. Several participants stated that knowing an LGBT person increased their sensitivity and compassion. This suggests that educating clergy about LGBT issues and encouraging personal interactions with LGBT persons may enhance awareness and sensitivity to LGBT people and their concerns.

SEXUAL PREJUDICE

Sexual prejudice (e.g., homophobia, heterosexism, homonegativity, disgust, aversion, hostility, revulsion) is the demonstration of negative responses and attitudes toward another person because of one's sexual orientation (Adolfson et al., 2010; Herek, 2000a, 2000b; Herek, 2004). The literature reveals that religious involvement is positively associated with homonegative attitudes and sexual prejudice toward LGBT people (Olatunji, 2008; Mak & Tsang, 2008). Although Nazarene clergy in this study did not demonstrate explicit sexual prejudice, there were indications of implicit sexual prejudice among some of the participants. Allen said, "At the base level being a heterosexual male there is still a gut-revulsion when I think about the practice. I mean to me it's unnatural (lines 187–189). Travis commented, "Unless the guy is coming on to me you know, I'm not repulsed by being around them gay folk, which I think is uncommon with evangelicalism (lines 738–741). Continuing, Travis observed, "I would be leaning towards revulsion especially if the guy is coming on to me" (lines 1204–1205).

Some participant comments revealed a subtle, covert homophobia. Homophobia can issue from a fear of being labeled gay by one's peers

(Herek, 2000a, 2000b). Preston received an invitation to lunch from an LGBT person. Preston admitted, "I had to work through the fear that others might presume that the meeting was something that it wasn't (lines 163–164). Participants also acknowledged homophobic responses from their congregants. When asked about how his congregation might respond to the presence of an LGBT person in the church, Bradley said of his congregation, "We might not want to have that influence around [our] teenagers. I'm not sure I agree with that, but I have to understand the fear" (lines 489–491).

While homonegativity is associated with conservative religious beliefs, cultural ideologies, and institutional oppression perpetuate heterosexism and opposition to same-sex oriented people (Herek; 2004; Marsh & Brown, 2009). Descriptively, homonegativity and heterosexism are present within the Nazarene church. Participants' comments about the denomination's position on homosexuality revealed an underlying institutional heterosexism. Keith stated it thusly, "We can find ourselves in trouble always, especially institutionally and in communities like ourselves, if what we're doing is really responding out of fear" (108–110). Clergy comments citing "gut-revulsion," experiencing a "visceral response," having a "creepy, ugh" feeling or "fear of what others would think" likely betray underlying homophobia and homonegative attitudes.

Many participants appeared unaware of their latent sexual prejudice. It may be important, therefore, to raise Nazarene clergy awareness about the meaning and implications of sexual prejudice and the subtle, perhaps unintentional ways they express homophobia and homonegative attitudes. The findings of this study support the current professional literature regarding sexual prejudice. Participants' comments supporting the literature were illustrated in *Theme Five: Clergy Response and Disposition toward LGBT People.*

RELIGIOUS INFLUENCES

Religion and religious beliefs are also associated with negative views about homosexuality (Ford et al., 2009; Zahniser & Boyd, 2008). Factors embedded in religion and religious beliefs include conservative religious views, extrinsic and intrinsic orientation of religious beliefs, right-wing authoritarianism, fundamentalism, Christian orthodoxy, and the Protestant Work Ethic (Ford et al., 2009; Herek, 2000a, 2000b; Jonathan, 2008; Morrison & Morrison, 2011; Whitley, 2009). Of these factors conservative religious views, right-wing authoritarianism and fundamentalism were indicated in participant statements. Factors not addressed by participants included extrinsic or intrinsic religious beliefs, Christian orthodoxy, and Protest Work Ethic. *Theme One: The Church of the Nazarene: Denominational and Individual Responses to Homosexuality* amply illustrates Nazarene clergy thoughts and feelings about the church and its position on homosexuality. Describing the denomination, Derek said, "The Nazarene Church is very conservative" (line 125). Bradley said he pastors a theologically conservative congregation that wanted him to preach "more forcefully" against relevant social concerns including homosexuality (lines 199–200). As a conservative, evangelical denomination, the Church of the Nazarene's position on homosexuality supports the literature that indicates conservative religious beliefs correlate with negative responses about homosexuality.

The literature shows an association between right-wing authoritarianism, political conservatism and negative attitudes and responses to LGBT people (Ford et al., 2009: Morrison & Morrison, 2008). Although Nazarene clergy did not directly cite right-wing authoritarianism as a factor, two participants implicated the influence of right-wing conservative politics on Nazarene church's response to homosexuality and LGBT individuals. Participant statements supplied data for *Theme One: Denominational and Individual Responses to Homosexuality* and supported the corresponding extant scholarship. Harrison talked about a pastoral guide published by the denomination that addressed homosexuality. Harrison said the guide "was just a piece of garbage and no more than a right-wing, hard line, 'This is the worst sin in the world' kind of approach which is not helpful at all in any way" (lines 226–234). About the church Curtis commented, "I think we've adopted way too much from probably conservative politics or something. I see a lot of Nazarenes who are functionally anti-gay and that's a real problem for us theologically" (lines 41–44). Nazarene clergy comments supported the literature that right-wing authoritarianism coupled with political conservatism produce negative attitudes and responses to homosexuality.

Fundamentalism is also associated with negative attitudes about homosexuality. Some participant's comments about fundamentalism were consistent with the findings in the professional literature. One Nazarene clergy person suggested that people with a fundamentalist theology would not be comfortable worshiping at his church: "If they're raging homophobes and fundamentalists, they're not going to like it here" (Keith: lines 679–680). Travis argued that the Nazarene church is divided between the Wesleyan-Anglican Nazarene and the 19th Century Holiness stripe Nazarene (lines 452–469). Travis observed that those of the holiness ilk tend to be more fundamentalist and legalistic in their adherence to scripture and theology.

Definitions of fundamentalism in the literature vary. Within some Christian denominations, including the Nazarene church, fundamentalism typically denotes a negative connotation. Based on definitions in the professional literature, the Nazarene church exhibits some fundamentalist characteristics. Nazarene clergy responses to homosexuality fit the fundamentalist view: homosexuality is immoral and explicitly forbidden by scripture (Jonathan, 2008). Although Nazarene clergy expressly stated that homosexuality was no worse than other sins, they felt homosexual practice was an abomination before the Lord and that practicing LGBT people were sinners (Hendershot, 2001). Participant statements supported the professional literature and from their comments emerged *Theme Two; Homosexuality in Light of Biblical Sexuality* and *Theme Four: Beliefs about Homosexuality.*

Analysis of participant interviews did not reveal data related to extrinsic or intrinsic orientations of religious beliefs, insight into the influence of Christian orthodoxy, or references to the Protestant Work Ethic. There may be at least two reasons for this. First, participants may lack knowledge or understanding of extrinsic and intrinsic orientations of religious belief and their influence on attitudes and responses to homosexuality. Second, the interview questions developed to collect the data did not elicit responses about these specific factors.

Participants' responses indicated that the Church of the Nazarene is a conservative denomination aligned with a conservative political affiliation. Two participants suggested conservative politics influences denominational policy. This means the church may need to evaluate the influence of conservative politics on the denominational statements about homosexuality and its responses to LGBT people. Several participants indicated that their congregants were conservative and wanted the participant to preach against homosexuality. Participants seemed convinced that attempts to increase awareness and sensitivity to LGBT concerns among one's constituency would likely result in opposition and division. This may be one of the reasons participants expressed reservation about addressing the topic with their congregants.

TRADITIONAL CHRISTIAN AND BIBLICAL WORLD VIEWS

For many Christians, homosexuality is sinful, contrary to scripture, and undermines the traditional Christian values of heterosexual marriage and family (Burdette et al., 2005; Trevino et al., 2012). Likewise, many Christian churches oppose homosexual relationships and have developed denominational statements forbidding them (Ford et al., 2009; Zerilli, 2010). Nazarene clergy statements aligned with these findings, and provided some of the supporting information for the development of *Theme 2: Homosexuality in Light of Biblical Sexuality.*

The Church of the Nazarene is a traditional, conservative Protestant Christian organization. Drawing from scripture and Christian tradition, the Church of the Nazarene deems homosexual practice sinful and opposes homosexuality and same-sex relationships. Most Nazarene clergy agree with and support the denomination's position regarding same-sex practices. Harrison summarized it thusly, "…as I understand church history, church tradition, [and] biblical teaching, homosexual practice is considered sinful in the scriptures at a point in which the Church of the Nazarene identifies homosexual practice as sinful. I'm in agreement with that" (lines 76–79). Travis also referred to tradition and scripture saying, "…it seems like the historic stance of Christianity has always been to interpret the scriptures to say [homosexuality] is not God's intent for human life and flourishing" (lines 223–226). As illustrated in the literature, the Church of the Nazarene, as well as many of its clergy, draw from Christian tradition and scripture to support their belief that homosexual practices are sinful and to validate their opposition to same-sex relationships.

Based on their interpretation of the Bible, Nazarene clergy agreed that scripture proscribes homosexuality. Allen stated, "As I understand scripture, the practice of homosexuality is condemned" (line 90). Curtis acknowledged, "I can't get to a place where I can say scripture says the practice of homosexuality is okay" (line 624). These, and other statements like these, reveal that Nazarene clergy believe the Bible prohibits same-sex relationships.

Barton (2010) posited that traditional Christian views of homosexuality explicitly and implicitly convey the message that LGBT people are perverse and sinful. Nazarene clergy statements supported the literature and provided salient information for *Theme One: The Church of the Nazarene: Denominational and Individual Responses to Homosexuality* and, *Theme Four: Beliefs about Homosexuality.*

The *Manual* statement of the Church of the Nazarene expressly states that homosexuality is a perversion of human sexuality (Blevins et al., p. 56). One Nazarene clergy stated, "I do think homosexuality is a perversion of what God had intended and said was good" (Darrell: lines 1185–1186). Of the word "perversion," Travis commented, "There's no sin in the *Manual* that describes it with the words depth and perversion, right? Nothing else. So we do special treatment for that one [i.e., homosexuality]" (lines 54–56).

In a survey, the Barna Group (2007) found that the Church often communicates homosexuality is a greater sin than other sins. Corresponding to these findings, participants affirmed that the Church of the Nazarene views homosexuality as a greater sin than other sins. Harrison said, "I'm conflicted with the way the church generally has dealt with people who express this orientation or who are founded in this lifestyle. It's treated, in my opinion, as a sin greater than other sins. It's treated quite negatively" (lines 89–91). Keith stated, "...the Church of the Nazarene calls homosexuality a sin. Not only do we call it a sin, but we also tend to like to point it out as being the big one, bigger than others (lines 882–885).

Although participants did not discuss it, there is a sentence in the *Manual* of the Church of the Nazarene stating that, "homosexual acts... are subject to the *wrath* of God" (p. 56, *italics mine*). A word search of the *Manual* revealed that word "wrath" is used only once, and it is used in association with homosexual acts. This may add credibility to participants' assessment that the Nazarene church views homosexual as a sin greater than other sins. Interestingly however, participants were nearly unanimous in their personal assertions that homosexuality is neither worse, nor greater, than any other sin. Nearly all participants felt the church should revise its *Manual* statement to communicate a more gracious response to homosexuality and same-sex oriented individuals.

Christians typically believe homosexuality undermines heterosexual marriage (Burdette et al., 2005). Although Nazarene clergy did not specifically address this issue, several expressly supported the biblical concept of marriage between one man and one woman. *Theme Two: Homosexuality in Light of Biblical Sexuality* and *Theme Four: Beliefs about Homosexuality* illustrated participants' beliefs about marital relationships and clergy's opposition to same-sex relationships—including gay marriage. Allen said, "The Christian ethic is one man and one woman married" (lines 840–841). Bradley confessed, "I have a hard time dealing with the word marriage attached to those who are not men and women. To me, I want to keep that word for a man and woman" (lines 697–699). Harrison affirmed his conviction that, "Marriage from the Christian perspective is the coming together of a man and a woman before God and witnesses (lines 256–258). Blake said of the Nazarene church, "We stand for marriage as being between a man and a woman" (lines 568–569). These statements indicate that Nazarene clergy support the idea of heterosexual marriage.

Two fundamental assertions of traditional Christian belief are the sin and perverse nature of homosexuality and the sanctity of heterosexual marriage. Most participants expressed the belief homosexual acts are sinful and perverse. Most participants also argued for the traditional understanding of marriage between a man and a woman and stated they struggled with "marriage" to describe a same-sex union. Moreover, participants agreed that they could not endorse or perform a marriage for same-sex couples.

A few participants in this study acknowledged that some LGBT people do not choose their orientation; yet many participants felt the practice of homosexuality is a personal choice. They argued that same-sex oriented individuals have the same responsibility to remain celibate, as do unmarried heterosexual Christians who choose to remain celibate until they are married. Admittedly, choice may be a consideration in the debate, but most Nazarene clergy in this study understood choice from a single perspective: single heterosexual individuals and same-sex oriented people can, and should, abstain from sexual relationships. What most participants did not address was when a heterosexual individual chooses celibacy the option for an intimate marital relationship remains open. Requiring a same-sex oriented person to choose celibacy, removes the possibility of intimate relational connection with another person.

OTHER RELIGIOUS VARIABLES

Biblical literalism, church attendance, and religiosity are positively correlated with negative attitudes and responses to homosexuality and LGBT persons (Deeb-Sossa & Kane, 2007; Marsh & Brown, 2011; Schulte & Battle, 2008; Whitley, 2009). Although the literature demonstrates these variables contribute to homonegative attitudes, none of these factors was explicitly represented among Nazarene clergy as affecting their responses to homosexuality or LGBT persons. Despite believing that same-sex relationships are sinful and do not align with a biblical sexuality, Nazarene clergy expressed concern and compassion for LGBT people. This may be due in part because the Nazarene church does not subscribe to biblical literalism, at least as defined by the literature (Burdette et al., 2005). Rather, the Church of the Nazarene affirms that the Bible is divinely inspired and authoritative in matters related to faith and salvation. Neither church attendance nor religiosity was indicated among Nazarene clergy.

DENOMINATIONAL AFFILIATION AND DENOMINATIONAL RESPONSES

Denominational affiliation influences responses to homosexuality and LGBT individuals (Olsen et al., 2006). Liberal and mainline denominations demonstrate the most accepting attitudes, while evangelical and conservative denominations are the least accepting (Lewis, 2003). Nazarene clergy statements supported the current professional scholarship and provided support for *Theme One: The Church of the Nazarene: Denominational and Individual Responses to Homosexuality.*

The Church of the Nazarene is an evangelical denomination. As with many evangelical denominations, Nazarene opposition to homosexual relationships finds its grounding in scripture. Nazarenes argue that homosexuality is a perversion of human sexuality and that homosexual acts are "subject to the wrath of God" (Blevins et al., 2013, p. 56). Nazarene clergy readily admitted that because of its position on homosexuality, the Church of the Nazarene is not a denomination where most LGBT people would feel welcome or comfortable. Keith said, "It's going to be an ill-fitting suit in the Church of the Nazarene for gay people. It's going to be a difficult place for them to be" (lines 864–866). Several other Nazarene clergy made similar observations indicating the barriers and challenges LGBT people would face attending a Nazarene church.

However, participants were also aware of denominations that demonstrated tolerance regarding homosexuality and churches that welcomed and affirmed LGBT individuals. Keith stated, "There are enough welcoming and affirming churches which have made the issue of homosexuality very central to their identity where persons who want to be Christian and are gay [can] go to these churches" (lines 709–712). Darrell referred to an Episcopal church "where homosexuality is not an issue" (line 835–836). Harold said he knew an LGBT couple who "ended up landing at a Methodist Church that was a little bit more open" (lines 760–761). Harold expressed surprised at how well informed LGBT people were about other denominational positions on homosexuality. He said, "I've always been amazed at how much they know in terms of the different denomination stances on stuff...they're all very aware of what places are safe and what places are not"(lines 991–994).

Nazarene clergy were aware that views about homosexuality and acceptance of LGBT people vary widely by denomination. While most participants agreed with the Church of the Nazarene's position on homosexuality, they knew there were options for LGBT people to attend more welcoming, affirming churches. Conversely, participants also said some people in their church purposively chose to attend their church because of the Nazarene position on homosexuality. These individuals made a decision to leave their mainline denomination because they felt their church had "given in" or "caved in" to the issue of same-sex relationships (Blake: line 560). Similarly, Preston said he had families who left their mainline church because it was accepting LGBT people; these families were now attending a Nazarene church (lines 79–84).

Interestingly, two Nazarene clergy articulated opposing responses to the denomination's position on homosexuality. One stated that if the Church of the Nazarene softened its position on homosexuality he would leave the denomination to join one that maintained a firm stance against homosexuality. The other Nazarene clergy explicitly stated that if the Nazarene church remained unwilling to have a conversation about the issue, he might choose to find a denomination that is willing to engage the dialog.

Nazarene clergy were aware that the church's position on homosexuality created a barrier for LGBT people and that it was unlikely that LGBT people would feel comfortable attending a Nazarene church, especially with more welcoming denominations available to them. This notwithstanding, some LGBT people may seek a denomination that emphasizes entire sanctification and personal holiness. Consequently, the church may need to revisit, reevaluate, and/or rewrite its denominational position on homosexuality to include a more gracious response or, at the very least, convey a more welcoming response to LGBT persons. One participant said, LGBT people are "hungry just starving for spiritual connection but don't know if the [church] is a safe place to go or not" (Harold: 1006–1007). About this one may ask, "Is the Nazarene church a safe place for LGBT people?" and, "Is it ready/willing to meet LGBT peoples' spiritual needs?

DEVELOPING A COMPASSIONATE RESPONSE

Scholars recommend that the Church respond with greater compassion to LGBT persons (Yarhouse & Carr, 2011). Likewise, some Protestant denominations have recognized that LGBT people deserve a more compassionate response from the Church (Kapinus et al., 2010; McGinniss, 2010; Merritt, 2009). Nazarene clergy comments agreed with this literature and provided the supporting data for *Theme One: The Church of the Nazarene: Denominational and Individual Responses to Homosexuality; Theme Five: Clergy Response and Disposition toward LGBT People* and, *Theme Six: LGBT Presence in the Local Church and Community.*

While the literature calls for the Church to develop a more compassionate response to homosexuality and LGBT individuals, participants were divided as to how well the Nazarene church is achieving this goal. Harrison stated, "I consider the church's response in practice to be anything but godly" (line 118). Similarly, Keith said, "I don't really feel like where we are right now is commensurate with a gracious attitude toward them [LGBT people], institutionally speaking" (lines 69–72). Conversely, Kendall felt, "There's been within the [Nazarene] position some room for both a gracious and loving response and movement toward this portion of our population as well as a strong support of biblical material and biblical world view" (lines 37–40).

Although Nazarene clergy opinions differed dramatically regarding the Nazarene church's response to homosexuality and LGBT persons, all participants affirmed their personal efforts to respond to LGBT people with love and compassion. Harrison reflected, "I have ministered to the best of my ability in a loving, compassionate and as helpful as I can way to those…who've I've encountered and become aware that that's who they are" (lines 907–910). Travis said, "I feel that gay folk are human beings like everybody else and that we're called to minister to them and that they deserve no less love than anybody else (lines 641–643). About his church Matt stressed, "Our goal here is to build a community that people can come in and feel loved" (line 222).

Some clergy were careful to indicate that a loving, compassionate response did not equate to agreement that same-sex relationships are an acceptable lifestyle. However, participants affirmed that love should be the guiding ethical principle that influences interactions with LGBT people. During one of his sermons, Curtis said to his congregation, "You need to love them [i.e., LGBT people] because as Wesleyans, it's all about love" (lines 98–100). Likewise, Harold commented, "I view it different theologically than the Nazarene statement…love is the ethic that I use" (lines 217–218).

Although participants verbally stated their desire to respond lovingly and compassionately to LGBT people, some participants' nonverbal communication indicated hesitancy regarding an LGBT presence in the church. It seemed that many participants demonstrated a "quasi-acceptance" of LGBT people but not complete acceptance of their presence, role, or function in the church. This suggests that participants provided the expected answer, but their reservation and hesitancy was evident.

Nazarene clergy's belief that homosexuality is a sin coupled with the call to love regardless of sexual orientation is paradoxical. This creates a dilemma for Nazarene pastors as they attempt to minister to LGBT people while upholding the Church of the Nazarene's denominational position on homosexuality. Participants discussed the tension of balancing these paradoxical concepts in *Theme Seven: Challenge Facing Nazarene Clergy.*

THE CHURCH OF THE NAZARENE

The *Manual of the Church of the Nazarene 2013–2017* describes homosexuality as a perversion of human sexuality and states that same-sex relationships are sinful and punishable by God. Furthermore, the Church of the Nazarene "deplores" any action or statement implying "compatibility between Christian morality and the practice of homosexuality" (Blevins et al., 2013, pp. 56–57). The *Manual* cites six scripture references to support its position on homosexuality.

Many, but not all, participants expressed agreement with the Nazarene position on homosexuality believing it to be in keeping with scripture, church history, and tradition. Despite their overall agreement, participants articulated a wide range of opinion regarding how the church addresses homosexuality in the *Manual* and the *Pastoral Perspectives.* Some clergy said the Nazarene position was "balanced," "biblical," "gracious," "helpful," "loving," and "solid."

Others said the position was "aggressive," "antagonistic," "antiquated," "harsh," "incendiary," "incomplete," "lacking instruction," "theologically confused," "troubling," "unhelpful," "ungracious" and, needing "revision." Although participants were divided regarding the sensitivity of the *Manual* statement on homosexuality, most participants agreed with the church's position that homosexual acts are sinful. More than half the participants felt the positional statement in the *Manual* needs to be rewritten to encompass a more gracious statement about homosexuality and a more compassionate response toward LGBT people.

The Church of the Nazarene makes a distinction between same-sex orientation and same-sex practice: orientation is not a choice; it is amoral and therefore, not sinful. Same-sex practice, on the other hand, is a choice, and is considered immoral and sinful (Porter et al., 2011). Participants were largely in agreement with the church's written statements differentiating same-sex orientation and same-sex practice. For most participants, LGBT involvement in the church, i.e., membership and/or leadership was determined by whether the individual had a same-sex orientation or was practicing a "homosexual lifestyle." Some participants discussed spiritual maturity as a consideration, but this was tangential to orientation verses practice; orientation and practice were central to clergy statements. Most participants said that same-sex practice precluded LGBT people from full church membership and positions of leadership. Many of the participants disclosed that same-sex practice precluded LGBT people from serving in leadership positions, e.g., usher, Sunday school teacher, church board member, etc. One participant stated that same-sex practice disqualified a person from ordained ministry. On the other hand, participants affirmed that non-practicing same-sex oriented individuals could participate in full membership and serve in leadership positions in the local church. Four participants said they would support a non-practicing, same-sex oriented person for ordination. It seemed apparent, however, that despite these affirmations, many participants were implicitly cautious.

The Church of the Nazarene states the same-sex oriented individual must be single and celibate or experience sexual reorientation to be "invited into full participation in the church" (Diehl et al., n.d.). Although most participants agreed with the church's position, some understood the dilemma created for same-sex oriented individuals by requiring that s/he remain celibate. Keith observed, "I think that the 'you have to be celibate' is a tough sell because sexuality isn't just something you do in bed, it is your identity, it's a part of who you are" (lines 1016–1017). Bradley said, "The church tends to think [sexual orientation] can be solved rather than dealing with the ambivalence or the reality that some people are wired that way and there is no changing them (lines 131–134).

As suggested by these statements, some participants have considered the dilemma a same-sex oriented person faces when celibacy is the only option to be "invited into full participation" in the Church of the Nazarene. One participant said—off off-the-record—that celibacy is a "calling" and to insist that a person—heterosexual or homosexual—choose celibacy is an institutional directive, not a divine one.

The *Manual* of the Church of the Nazarene states, "We deplore any action or statement that would seem to imply compatibility between Christian morality and the practice of homosexuality" (Blevins et al., 2013, p. 57). When asked about Christianity and homosexuality, most participants agreed that a person can have a same-sex orientation and be a Christian; however, same-sex practice is contradictory to Christian life. Some participants felt that the idea of a "homosexual Christian" was and "oxymoron," implying that "gay and Christian" are mutually exclusive terms, especially if the LGBT person is "practicing." One participant said he had never met a gay Christian; he believed gay Christians exist, but he had not met one. Some Nazarene clergy believed that a person can be both homosexual and Christian, but hoped the LGBT person would eventually recognize the incompatibility of these two identities and make a choice in keeping with traditional Christian beliefs.

It was evident among the participants that idea of LGBT Christians is a multifaceted issue. Some argued that a person cannot be both homosexual and Christian. Others maintained that the possibility exists, but believed God would eventually reveal the incongruence of a homosexual identity and Christian faith. Some participants stated that they accept people where they are because it is not their place to judge a person's sexual orientation or their relationship with God. These participants were, however, quick to add that God will judge. Three participants maintained that being homosexual and Christian was neither incompatible, nor mutually exclusive. In some cases, participant responses revealed uncertainty about the compatibility of homosexuality and Christianity. This was most evident in Matt's response when he observed, "Do I think when we get to the other side there will be those who are in same-sex relationships? Probably" (lines 656–657).

Participants also acknowledged that the church and its educational institutions influenced their views about homosexuality. Most Nazarene clergy views about homosexuality and their responses to LGBT people continue to be influenced by the church's official (*Manual*) and unofficial statements (e.g., *Pastoral Perspectives*) on homosexuality. A few participants demonstrated independent and/or critical thought on these issues but ultimately adhered to the denominational position in ministerial practice stating the church's position provided safety. With the impact of denominational influence on participants' thought, this may suggest that if or when the denomination reframes its position on homosexuality, Nazarene clergy are likely to follow. In fact, it may reduce the paradoxical tension Nazarene clergy feel when attempting to minister to LGBT people—with one caveat: Nazarene clergy will need to overcome their own overt and covert fears and concerns about homosexuality in order to minister in a truly non-prejudicial manner.

The degree of discomfort among participants regarding same-sex relationships demonstrates the need for further education and training for Nazarene clergy. Participants felt the tension, challenge, and complexity of balancing the denominational statement about homosexuality with the real world practice of ministering to LGBT people. Many Nazarene clergy felt underprepared to engage or interact with LGBT individuals and wished the denomination provided instruction and training about how to minister to this population.

Not surprisingly, participants expressed a desire for better and more denominational preparation to help them deal with issues related to homosexuality and ministry to LGBT people. One participant observed that the Church of the Nazarene has said homosexuality is wrong but has done little else to help its clergy minister to LGBT individuals. If the Church of the Nazarene is not educating or training its clergy, pastors may need to educate themselves about how to effectively minister to LGBT individuals and couples. Some clergy admitted that with all of their other administrative and pastoral responsibilities they simply had not taken the time to inform themselves. The literature reviewed for this research revealed numerous journal articles and books addressing homosexuality and LGBT issues. Resources such as these may help Nazarene clergy to feel more equipped to minister to LGBT people.

NEW FINDINGS

In this section, I discuss findings for which there was no supporting extant professional literature. These findings demonstrate that new data has emerged which may help to bridge a gap in the literature. Most of the new findings discussed below were the basis for *Theme Seven: Challenges Facing Nazarene Clergy*. I briefly described this theme as the challenges of adhering to the Church of the Nazarene's denominational position on homosexuality and the tension of pastoral ministry in the local church, especially to LGBT people.

Based on participant reports, Nazarene clergy may devote minimal energy to critical thought or reflection about the Nazarene position on homosexuality and its implications for LGBT persons. Several participants acknowledged that prior to the interview they had not given much thought to the issue. Three participants however, stated that they had engaged in conversations with other Nazarene clergy on the topic. Eight participants were mostly comfortable with the denomination's stance and expressed support of the church's position, although five participants acknowledged the tension they felt as they wrestled with the issue in light of the denomination's position. Nazarene clergy in this study demonstrated little knowledge regarding the differences between same-sex attraction, same-sex orientation, and same-sex identity (Yarhouse, 2010). It may be, therefore, important for the denomination to take more initiative to educate its clergy about homosexuality, LGBT concerns, and the differences between attraction, orientation, and identity. This may help Nazarene clergy experience greater sensitivity and understanding of LGBT persons.

A second new finding revealed that the denominational position on homosexuality provided a sense of safety for Nazarene clergy. Two participants explicitly stated that the denominational position provided a sense of safety in pastoral ministry. Several other participants implicitly expressed this same idea. Participants admitted that when difficult questions about same-sex issues arose (e.g., orientation, relationships, marriage) they were grateful to have the denominational position to rely on. One participant summarized it well, "There is safety in the fact that if I'm fairly comfortable with their position, and I'm in the Church of the Nazarene and people maybe give me grief for my position I can say well, that's what the Church of the Nazarene says" (Bradley: lines 77–80). Other participants echoed similar feelings.

This may suggest that some Nazarene clergy do not want to have to think too deeply about the practical implications of ministering to LGBT people and the accompanying issues. However, relying too heavily on the denominational position without critical reflection and discernment may result in spiritual discrimination toward LGBT individuals. For example, one participant indicated that an LGBT person attending his church asked to be baptized. The clergyman, as he understood his ordination vows, could not baptize the woman because she had a same-sex partner. The participant also expressed concern that the denomination might revoke his ordination if he baptized an LGBT person. In addition to the participant's concerns about denominational policy, he acknowledged that he was uncomfortable administering the sacraments to individuals participating in a same-sex relationship.

By virtue of their ordination vows and loyalty to the church, Nazarene clergy may believe they are gatekeepers of the "means of grace" (i.e., the sacraments). When homosexuality and sin equate, some Nazarene clergy may feel an obligation to withhold the sacraments from LGBT worshippers. If or when this occurs, it further marginalizes LGBT persons. This in turn, may confirm LGBT feelings that they are not welcome in the Church of the Nazarene and, more tragic, that they are unacceptable to God.

Despite the aforementioned concerns, participants interviewed for this research appeared to be kind individuals who genuinely cared about people—straight and LGBT alike. It was apparent, however, that they struggled with how to best minister to LGBT people. It was evident that Nazarene clergy in this study wrestled with how to navigate the challenges and manage the tension between pastoral ministry, homosexuality, and LGBT people.

This led to a third novel finding: Nazarene clergy feel the tension of attempting to balance the denominational position on homosexuality with the practice of pastoral ministry to LGBT individuals. One participant posed, "When everything about our denominational stand on this says this practice is sinful, there's a huge tension that I have. How do I respond to that?" (Allen: lines 782–784). Denominational literature addressing homosexuality creates a dilemma for Nazarene clergy when it asserts that every person be treated with "dignity, grace, and holy love" regardless of sexual orientation while, at the same time, condemning homosexual lifestyle as sin and contrary to scripture (Porter et al., 2011).

Denominational declarations such as this create tension for Nazarene clergy as they try to balance the denominational position with actual pastoral ministry. Implicit questions for many participants were, How does one lovingly affirm LGBT persons without condoning same-sex relationships? How does one live in the tension of Jesus' words, "Neither do I condemn you. Go and sin no more" (John 8:11; KJV)? One participant admitted that only his tacit disagreement with the church's position and his differing views about homosexuality and responses to LGBT people allowed him to navigate the tension. This, in turn, helped the LGBT individuals attending his church feel safe and loved.

Nazarene clergy in this study were mindful that language stressing "hate the sin, love the sinner" creates its own set of challenges. Participants acknowledged that when same-sex orientation is deemed sinful, the church communicates that the LGBT person is sinful—and LGBT people often feel that way. One participant summarized LGBT feelings well, "If you think I'm a sinner condemned to hell, if you think I'm that awful, then you don't love me, and you can't really care for me because you look at me as a condemned person" (Kendall: lines 818–820). Blake recalled what his LGBT son said to him: "Don't tell me that God loves me…and hates the sin because I identify with my homosexuality and if you say that God hates the sin, then you're in effect saying that God hates me" (lines 310–312).

To associate one's sexual orientation with sin equates the person with the sin. If a person's sexual orientation is fixed, as some participants believed, how does the church address homosexuality? The Nazarene church has put forth two options: limit the LGBT person's options for intimate sexual relationship i.e., singleness and celibacy, or hope and pray for a change of sexual orientation (reorientation).

Participants in this study highlighted several additional challenges they face related to pastoral ministry and LGBT concerns: (a) ministering to LGBT people without implying that the Church of the Nazarene condones same-sex relationships, (b) relating to LGBT individuals when their lifestyle does not align with Christian beliefs, (c) communicating to LGBT people that "lifestyle" is the issue, not the LGBT person him or herself, (d) helping LGBT individuals move forward in their relationship with Christ and, (e) navigating the complexities of the legalization of same-sex marriages.

A fourth novel finding of this research was that issues related to homosexuality and LGBT concerns touched the lives of all the participants in this study. Participants acknowledged that they knew at least one LGBT person. Nazarene clergy connections to LGBT people included immediate and extended family members, friends who expressed a same-sex orientation and LGBT individuals or couples attending the participant's church. All participants knew of LGBT people residing in their local community. For most participants knowing an LGBT individual produced more sensitivity and greater compassion for LGBT people in general. Personal knowledge of LGBT people did not however appear to influence participants' beliefs about homosexuality or motivate them to reach out to the LGBT community. From this study, it became apparent that for Nazarene clergy LGBT people are no longer in the "closet." LGBT people live in the neighborhood; they are on the doorstep and, in some cases, the pews of Nazarene churches. As such, it may be that many Nazarene clergy throughout the denomination are dealing with pastoral concerns about homosexuality and balancing the denominational position while attempting to minister to LGBT people.

The fifth new finding to emerge from this research was that even though all participants were personally and professionally aware of the LGBT community, only one had made an intentional effort to reach the LGBT population. The other participants admitted that they waited for LGBT people to attend their church and that their interactions with same-sex oriented individuals were limited to these instances. Some participants provided reasons for their hesitation to reach out to the LGBT community. One participant was concerned about how his congregation would respond if LGBT people started attending his church. Another participant admitted that his church created a mailer inviting people by binary distinction, e.g., Democrats, Republicans, cat people, dog people, etc. to attend. The pastor elected not to include gay/straight on the invitation because the participant was concerned about creating disunity among his constituency. Another participant admitted that he had thought about reaching out to LGBT people but said he did not know how they would respond to him, and he did not want to be misperceived. One clergyman shared that an LGBT person in his church had said if he wanted to reach the LGBT community, he could put out a rainbow flag. The LGBT person said, "If you do you'll have 50 in attendance the next week." The clergyman admitted that his church was not ready to take that step.

The denominational position on homosexuality may make some Nazarene clergy hesitant to reach out to the LGBT community. Clergy might be reluctant to conduct outreach to LGBT people because they know that the Church of the Nazarene does not respond to or receive LGBT individuals well. One participant stated his reluctance was because he knew that the Church of the Nazarene was not a good fit for LGBT people. If Nazarene clergy want to minister to LGBT people, waiting for them to come to the Nazarene church is unlikely; a few may attend as indicated by participant statements; however, developing a thriving ministry that includes LGBT people is improbable. As one participant indicated, Nazarene institutional barriers to LGBT individuals are already in place. One participant queried, Why would LGBT people want to be part of a denomination where they already feel unwelcome?

The sixth new finding suggested by this research is the imminent challenges Nazarene clergy face with the legalization of gay marriage. Some participants lived in states that had legalized or were in the process of legalizing same-sex marriage. Consequently, several Participants were already considering the implications of same-sex marriage and its effect on their ministry and the church. One participant expressed a concern that in states sanctioning gay marriage, the State may attempt to mandate clergy to perform both straight and gay marriages.

Some participants were anticipating the potential complexities of ministering to married LGBT couples coming into or attending their church. One participant expressed concern saying he felt unprepared to provide pastoral care and counseling to same-sex couples. He provided examples of the questions he had considered but for which he had no answers: (a) How to counsel same-sex couples experiencing marital difficulties, (b) How to provide pastoral direction to a same-sex couple requesting parenting advice, (c) How to counsel gay couples considering adoption or divorce. Another participant wrestled with whether "legal marriage is equivalent to spiritual marriage." Although opposed to gay marriage, one participant said he understood why same-sex couples want state sanctioned protections of legal marriage—parental rights, spousal rights, insurance and pension benefits, will, etc.

Participants said they felt unprepared to answer these questions and face these challenges. They also struggled with how to respond to LGBT couples in a way that maintains the denominational position on homo-sexuality and marriage while at the same time demonstrating love and compassion to LGBT identified people. Perhaps echoing a question—and concern—for many Nazarene pastors, one participant pondered, "How do we stay in a compassionate relationship with a person who is in [same-sex] relationship who now by law has been made legal? If we start allowing that in our church, are we going to lose our identity…as follow-ers of Christ?" (Blake: lines 571–574).

It appears that even denominational leaders (e.g., General Superin-tendents) are considering the implications of gay marriage for the church and its pastors. During a conversation with a General Superintendent, one clergyperson said the G.S. instructed him on what he could and could not do as an ordained clergyman regarding LGBT people. The G.S. told the participant he was not to officiate at a gay marriage; however, he could attend a same-sex wedding, and he could pray at a gay wedding cer-emony if he wanted too. (As an aside, the G.S. stated that the clergyman was not to refuse the sacraments, i.e., communion or baptism, to LGBT individuals and stressed that if the participant received any criticism, he could contact the G.S. directly.)

The Church of the Nazarene is facing similar challenges around same-sex marriage in Europe. One participant reported that nearly 20% of the church in Sweden is LGBT and LGBT people there want the church to recognize gay unions. According to the participant, the Board of General Superintendents faces a quandary because the church could lose a signifi-cant portion of its constituency if the denomination maintains its current position on marriage. Another participant summarized the dilemma with the following question: "Are same-sex monogamous relationships gen-uinely Christian and can the church approve of that?" (Harrison: lines 1019–1020).

Nazarene clergy in this study were quick to assert their agreement with the Church of the Nazarene's position that Christian marriage is between a man and a woman; however, one participant emphasized that the church has provided no clear instruction about how to minister to LGBT people, or married same-sex couples. The participant stated, there is "no language" to help clergy address these issues—and some Nazarene clergy are already dealing with them. Participants felt the church needs to do more theological reflection on this subject, and provide clearer direction about navigating the perplexing yet imminent legalization of gay marriage.

The results of this research indicate that Nazarene clergy are aware of the impending challenges they will face regarding same-sex marriage. Participants readily admit that same-sex marriage is a complicated issue and creates unique questions in ministry for which they felt largely unprepared to answer. It may soon be that all states will legalize gay marriage and/or recognize same-sex marriages. The church will benefit its clergy by educating and training them how to manage the inherent complexities of gay marriage and pastoral care.

LIMITATIONS OF THE STUDY

In spite of my best efforts to ensure a rigorous study, several limitations exist. The first limitation is my relative inexperience as a qualitative researcher. Although a novice qualitative researcher, I attempted to ensure rigor by maintaining regular contact with, and input from, my dissertation chair who served as the auditor, two research team members, and a peer-debriefer; all of whom are experienced in qualitative research. I conducted regular member checks to verify that the participants' voices were accurately interpreted and represented throughout the data analysis. Even with these checks and balances in place, inexperience may factor as a limitation to this study. If I had previous qualitative research experience, my perceptions about codes and themes may have been different.

Another limitation to this research was selection bias. Participation in this study required that participants were ordained in the Church of the Nazarene, a graduate of Nazarene Theological Seminary, and the lead/senior pastor of their local church. Ordination in the Nazarene church insured that all participants were recognized by the denomination as one whose gifts, calling, and training accurately represented the values and core beliefs of the Church of the Nazarene and were authorized to administrate the church and dispense the sacraments. Being a graduate of Nazarene Theological Seminary was necessary to establish academic consistency. It was also necessary to ascertain the similarities and differences of clergy feelings about homosexuality and responses to LGBT individuals related to the denominational position on homosexuality. I elected to interview only senior/lead pastors because they were most likely to experience the intersection between the overall ministry of the local church and homosexuality and LGBT people. While these three criteria were established for this study, they also served as limitations to it. Interviewing a different group of Nazarene clergy may have produced different results.

Another limitation of this study was its lack of diversity. All participants were married Caucasian males. Twelve of the thirteen participants were heterosexual in orientation; one participant affirmed a bisexual orientation. Including a more diverse sample with female Nazarene clergy and/or Nazarene clergy of various ethnic origins and racial backgrounds would have enhanced the richness of this study and perhaps yielded additional important data.

Another limiting factor was that all participants served in churches within the continental United States. One participant intimated that Nazarene clergy in other world areas may respond differently to homosexuality and LGBT issues than U.S. Nazarene pastors. This suggests that culture and worldview may have an impact on Nazarene clergy responses to homosexuality. The only way to determine the validity of this, however, would be to conduct research with Nazarene clergy outside North America.

One other limitation emerged following the finalization of the codebook and the data analysis. It may have been instructive to make "gay marriage" one of the dominant themes rather than simply one of the 47 codes used to analyze the data. Numerous participant comments were related to same-sex marriage, traditional Christian views of marriage, and the anticipated challenges clergy will face dealing with same-sex couples. In retrospect, I do not think gay marriage as a code did justice to participants' concerns about the inherent complexities of same-sex marriage for Nazarene clergy in pastoral ministry.

IMPLICATIONS OF STUDY

Participants in this study were nearly unanimous that homosexuality is a complicated and complex issue for which there are no easy answers. Although homosexuality and ministry to LGBT people may be complex, the findings of this research offer implications for Nazarene clergy, the Church of the Nazarene, LGBT people, counselor educators, and clinical practice.

Nazarene Clergy

Participants felt uncertain about how to effectively minister to LGBT people, especially how to demonstrate a loving and gracious response without communicating acceptance of same-sex practice or relationships. Nazarene clergy may consider educating themselves about homosexuality and LGBT concerns; several insightful books are available on the subject (Brownson, 2013; Marin, 2009; Vines, 2014; Yarhouse, 2010). Nazarene clergy may also choose to attend workshops or training events to learn about the LGBT community and to equip them for ministering to LGBT people. Nazarene clergy may also ask their district leadership to provide education and training opportunities to address clergy concerns and LGBT issues. Nazarene clergy can be more proactive in their outreach efforts to the LGBT population.

The Church of the Nazarene

Participants in this study expressed an interest in more scholarly, theological reflection about homosexuality. Participants strongly supported revising the *Manual* statement to move away from pejorative language for a softer statement with a more compassionate response. Participants also requested that the denomination provide more than theoretical or theological statements about homosexuality. Participants wanted practical education and training about ministering to LGBT people.

The denomination may consider inviting its biblical and theological scholars to develop a more nuanced *Manual* statement about homosexuality that includes a compassionate and welcoming response to LGBT people. The denomination might develop a strategic plan and instruction to assist clergy in ministering to LGBT people and encourage outreach efforts to the LGBT community. Denominational leaders should consider creating safe, confidential forums and opportunities for its clergy to discuss their feelings, concerns, and the challenges they face in ministry regarding LGBT issues. Additionally, Nazarene universities and seminaries can add curriculum that increases awareness and teaches students about LGBT issues and concerns.

It is important to demystify LGBT concerns through education and training. Some potential training modules can include (a) intersecting and reaching out to the LGBT community, (b) educating clergy on the differences of attraction, orientation, behavior, and identity, (c) cultivating understanding the multifaceted issues related to gay marriage and, (d) teaching pastoral counseling skills to clergy working with married same-sex couples.

LGBT People

The results of this study may offer hope to LGBT identified people. Although the Church of the Nazarene's position on homosexuality is condemning, not all Nazarene clergy respond to LGBT people the way the *Manual* statement may indicate they would. This research revealed that there are Nazarene clergy who make an effort to demonstrate sensitivity to LGBT concerns and compassion to LGBT people. Some Nazarene clergy may even welcome LGBT people into their church. Despite being uncharted territory for many Nazarene clergy, there are those who attempt to understand the intricacies of homosexuality and the complexities of ministering to LGBT persons.

Counselor Educators

According to the American Counseling Association's (2014) *Code of Ethics*, section F.7.c. reads as follows: "Counselor educators infuse material related to multiculturalism/ diversity into all courses and workshops for the development of professional counselors" (p. 14). Additionally, section F.11.c. of the ACA code (2014) states that counselor educators are to, "actively infuse multicultural/diversity competency in their training and supervision practices. They actively train students to gain awareness, knowledge, and skills in the competencies of multicultural practice" (p. 15). Counselor educators at Christian academic institutions may be called upon to hold in tension their personal beliefs and values while advocating for and infusing into their curriculum core concepts of multicultural diversity competencies that promote LGBT sensitivity and awareness.

Counselor educators recognize LGBT concerns are multicultural issues that extend beyond theoretical constructs or academic enterprise. LGBT people are advocating for basic human rights: dignity, worth, value, and protections of the law—these are social justice issues. The struggle for LGBT equality and civil rights is underway. Counselor educators are privileged to watch history unfold and to be actively engaged in preparing future counselors and educators in ways that preserve the dignity and worth of every human being.

CLINICAL PRACTICE

Also suggested by this research are implications for clinical practice. Practitioners may see LGBT people wounded by the church, doubting God's love, and seeking answers to questions about faith and spirituality come for counseling services. Professional counselors also may have LGBT individuals and couples coming to therapy to address relationship issues such as marriage, divorce, children, adoption, etc. Practitioners may also have clergy seek therapy to address their own spiritual needs or sexual identity concerns. Professional counselors can model grace and compassion to LGBT people and clergy alike in an effort to help each recognize that sexual orientation and spiritual identity are valuable aspects of one's humanity.

Counselors working within the context of the Church, or the Nazarene church, may need additional education and training to ensure that personal beliefs, religious influences, and/or denominational positions on homosexuality do not impinge on their work with LGBT clients. Section C.5. of the ACA *Code of Ethics* (2014) states,

> Counselors do not condone or engage in discrimination against prospective or current clients, students, employees, supervisees, or research participants based on age, culture, disability, ethnicity, race, religion/spirituality, gender, gender identity, sexual orientation, marital/partnership status, language preference, socioeconomic status, immigration status, or any basis proscribed by law (p. 9).

Clinical practitioners do well to educate themselves about same-sex issues and concerns and respond with unconditional positive regard, practicing beneficence and nonmalfeasance, encouraging client autonomy, and utilizing best practices in their work with LGBT people.

SUGGESTIONS FOR FUTURE RESEARCH

Having scoured the professional literature, it became apparent that this study is the first of its kind. I found no other scholarly research about Nazarene clergy or Nazarenes related to homosexuality and LGBT individuals. As a result, and during the course of this research, I became aware that this area is ripe with future research possibilities.

One such possibility is to conduct a qualitative study that seeks to discover the lived experience of LGBT people who are currently part of the Nazarene church and/or LGBT people who were part of the Nazarene church and chose to leave. This would provide a rich description of LGBT people's experience of the Nazarene church and its response to homosexuality and LGBT people.

If a study such as this was conducted, other research might compare and contrast those findings with the results of the current study. This would allow the researcher to discover the similarities and differences of experience for both Nazarene clergy and LGBT people related to the Church of the Nazarene. The results may provide valuable information to LGBT people and to the Church of the Nazarene. This information may inform the church about how it is perceived among the LGBT population. This in turn may help the church as it considers its denominational position on homosexuality and its response to LGBT people.

The current study utilized only Nazarene clergy who were graduates of the denomination's seminary. Future research may include expanding the participant selection process to include Nazarene clergy of various academic backgrounds including, Nazarene Bible College, graduates of one of the Nazarene four year liberal arts colleges, and/or Nazarene clergy who received their education at an academic institution other than Nazarene.

One participant indicated that administrators at a nearby Nazarene University are concerned because they fear younger generation, college-age students may choose not to attend a school with such strict policies against homosexuality, which could result in lower student enrollment and loss of revenue. At the same time, the university recognizes that if it softens its position on homosexuality, it may lose financial support from the denomination. If true, Nazarene colleges and universities find themselves in a difficult position. Therefore, another area of future research may include Nazarene University/College administrators and faculty members to discover the effects of this controversial topic at the institutional level. Additional research might include interviewing Nazarene Headquarter department heads and/or district superintendents.

The literature demonstrated that females tend to be more accepting of same-sex relationships than are their male counterparts. Unfortunately, none of the participants in the current study was female. A qualitative study of female Nazarene clergy may yield important insights regarding their responses to homosexuality and interactions with LGBT people.

Since all of the participants for this study were located within the continental United States, future research might also include Nazarene clergy in other world areas. It might be interesting to discover whether culture and worldview affect Nazarene clergy responses to homosexuality and LGBT persons around the world.

Another suggestion for future research are the implications of gay marriage and the inherent challenges faced by Nazarene clergy as they minister to and provide pastoral care to same-sex married couples. For example, gay couples seeking premarital or marital counseling, renewal of marriage vows, issues surrounding divorce or infidelity, children, adoption, blended families, wills, benefits, and/or end of life issues. The list is as varied for same-sex couples as it is for heterosexual couples and, perhaps more complex for clergy working with gay couples.

When the idea to research the topic of Nazarenes and homosexuality first entered my awareness, the original intent was to conduct a quantitative study to determine Nazarenes' attitudes about homosexuality. I intended to develop a survey/questionnaire for distribution to Nazarenes—clergy and layperson alike—to elicit responses determining their attitudes about homosexuality. To date, no quantitative research to ascertain Nazarene attitudes about homosexuality has been conducted. A quantitative study to determine the general Nazarene constituencies' responses to homosexuality is another possibility for future research. With more than two million members, raw data is plentiful.

Several participants spoke of their internal discomfort and visceral response to homosexuality and same-sex relationships. Participants used words such as "disgust," "creepy," "ugh," and statements like, "turned in me," and "responded slightly viscerally." From these comments, it appears that some individuals do experience an internal reaction and visceral response to homosexuality and the idea of same-sex encounters. This suggests another possibility for future research: investigating the aesthetic quality of homosexuality and same-sex relationships. Research on this topic may yield interesting data.

CONCLUSION

This study was a phenomenological inquiry to ascertain the essential essence of Nazarene clergy responses to homosexuality and their interactions with lesbian, gay, bisexual, and transgender individuals. My interest in this research occurred organically and is threefold in its development. I was raised in the Nazarene church and during the 1980s God called me to prepare for ministry. As a long time Nazarene, I naturally gravitated toward Nazarene schools for academic preparation and ministerial training.

While I was in college, my youngest sister told me she was a lesbian. She shared her concerns about revealing this information with our family and her fears about the church's response. She had heard pastors decry homosexuality and listened to sermons stating that a homosexual lifestyle resulted in eternal damnation. In the church where she once felt the unconditional love of Christ, she now sensed judgment and recrimination. For the church, her same-sex orientation betrayed a spurning of scripture and rebellion against God. Despite her belief in and love for God, well-meaning believers questioned the trajectory of her spiritual life. This issued in self-doubt and uncertainty. She eventually left the Church of the Nazarene. Now, as a member of the LGBT community, she struggles to discern the difference between how the church responds to homosexuality and how God feels about her sexual orientation. She describes herself as "confused." Still grappling with her spiritual identity, she has not returned to the church.

Years later, I was privileged to provide pastoral counseling to an LGBT person. He arrived at my office feeling "lost and suicidal" because of the way his denomination had responded to him and the accompanying beliefs that God was angry with him, hated him, and had rejected him. Unfortunately, the Church infused in him a grossly distorted image of God that took years to reframe. Following more than two years of weekly therapy, he embraced the truth about the God who loved him unconditionally and longed for relationship with him. Still identifying as an LGBT person, he dedicated his life to Christ and became an involved and invested member in a Nazarene community of faith. The church was blessed by his testimony, his spirit, and his contribution to its ministry.

These experiences—plus many others—supplied the soil and the seed from which grew my interest in how the Church—and its constituency—respond to homosexuality and LGBT people. Familiarity and relationship with the Church of the Nazarene, my family member's experience with the same, and counseling experiences with LGBT individuals were the genesis for this study. Currently, there is no extant scholarly research in the professional literature that has investigated this topic. My intent for this study was to bridge the gap in the professional literature regarding Nazarene clergy's responses to homosexuality and their interactions with LGBT people. I hope the results of this research will facilitate a dialog between Nazarene clergy and LGBT people. In addition, I hope this research encourages the Nazarene church to evaluate is language regarding homosexuality and assist its clergy in ministering to LGBT people and the LGBT community. In the concluding paragraphs, I summarize my research.

Chapter I provided a comprehensive review of the current professional, scholarly literature that focused on the numerous factors that contribute to attitudes about homosexuality and responses to same-sex oriented individuals. The information in Chapter I began broadly as I described the paradigmatic or worldviews of sexual orientation. I followed this with an overview of the etiology, i.e., origins/causes of homosexuality. I then addressed the social, cultural, demographic, and religious factors that influence attitudes about same-sex orientation. Next, I examined the impact of sexual prejudice on attitudes about homosexuality. Sexual prejudice included homophobia, heterosexism, and homonegativity. I then discussed various Christian denominational positions related to homosexuality. Narrowing the scope, I focused on the Church of the Nazarene's *Manual* statement about homosexuality, additional denominational literature addressing homosexuality, and the church's disposition toward and response to LGBT people. I concluded the literature review with a rationale for investigating Nazarene clergy responses to homosexuality and their interactions with LGBT persons.

Chapter II outlined the research methods and procedures I used to conduct the study. The purpose of this research was to discover the lived experiences of Nazarene clergy responses to homosexuality and their interactions with LGBT individuals. The research question I wanted to answer was, "What are the lived experiences of Nazarene clergy responses to homosexuality and their interactions with LGBT people?" I provided the rationale for selecting a qualitative research design using the phenomenological tradition to arrive at the essential essence of the participants' experience of the phenomenon. Under the larger heading of my rationale for utilizing a qualitative methodology, I described the historical development of the phenomenological tradition. I also discussed the philosophical underpinnings and worldviews of qualitative research. Following this, I outlined the core concepts of phenomenological data analysis including bracketing, horizontalization and construction of the structural and textural descriptions from which derive the essential essence of experience. From here I provided an explanation of my role as the researcher for this study including potential researcher assumptions and biases, bracketing to eliminate these, and researcher objectivity and subjectivity. Next, I delineated the strategies I utilized to maintain objectivity and subjectivity. These included leading from a position of curiosity, verification of accuracy via participant checks, use of a research team, auditor, and peer-debriefer; all of whom were utilized during the data analysis process. I also provided a list of key terms and their definitions used in this study. Procedural steps followed with a description of the participant selection process and sampling criteria. From here, I outlined the data collection methods and included the semi-structured interview questions developed for participants. I elected to use Moustakas (1994) adaptation of van Kaam's phenomenological data analysis (1959, 1966) to analyze the data. I described Moustakas' seven step protocol I used to analyze the data.

Next, I outlined the strategies I employed to optimize the trustworthiness of this study. These strategies included credibility, dependability, confirmability, and transferability. Lastly, I addressed the ethical considerations utilized to ensure confidentiality and best practices during and after this research.

Chapter III demonstrated the results of a thorough analysis of the data from which emerged 47 individual codes with seven overarching themes. All 47 codes were subsumed within the seven larger themes. In the chapter, I listed each theme, provided definitions of the themes, and illustrated each theme with participant statements from the data. Theme One: *The Church of the Nazarene: Denominational and Individual Responses to Homosexuality* highlighted the participant's understanding of the Nazarene church's position on homosexuality. Within this theme, participants described their feelings about the church's position. As part of this theme, participants discussed the cultural climate of the church, the counter-cultural nature of the denominational position, shifts in understanding, demographic influences, and mainline and other denominational positions on homosexuality.

Theme Two: *Homosexuality in Light of Biblical Sexuality* described participants' beliefs about human sexuality grounded in their understanding of scripture and theology. Also encompassed in this theme were participants' feelings, thoughts, and beliefs about the compatibility of homosexuality and Christianity.

Theme Three: *Ministerial Journey* provided insight into each participant's ministerial development and its influence on their responses to homosexuality and their interactions with LGBT people. These developmental influences included theological education, time affiliated with the Nazarene church and, for some, their call to ministry.

Theme Four: *Beliefs about Homosexuality* highlighted the participants' beliefs about homosexuality, including etiology. Participants described differences between same-sex attraction, same-sex orientation, and same-sex practice. Participants also shared their thoughts—and beliefs—about same-sex relationships and gay marriage.

Theme Five: *Clergy Response and Disposition toward LGBT People* revealed the participants' affective, attitudinal, and behavioral responses to LGBT individuals. Participants indicated that knowing an LGBT person influenced their views about homosexuality and their understanding of LGBT people. Several participants discussed their attempts to help LGBT individuals feel welcomed and included in their church.

Theme Six: *LGBT Presence in the Local Church and Community* illustrated participants' awareness of LGBT individuals attending their church and presence in the local community. Some participants talked about how they think LGBT people respond to the church, the Nazarene position on homosexuality, and in some cases, how LGBT people have responded to them. Brokenness among LGBT people and in the LGBT community was also considered.

Theme Seven: *Challenges Facing Nazarene Clergy* disclosed the complexity for clergy of adhering to the Nazarene church's position and providing ministry to LGBT people. Participants described communication challenges as well as the resistance of both Nazarenes and LGBT people to discuss same-sex relationships. Clergy considered the opportunities—or the lack thereof—for membership, leadership, and/or ordination for LGBT persons. Also addressed were participants' attempts to minister to LGBT people and clergy outreach efforts to the LGBT community. These seven themes and participants' statements supporting them comprised the essential elements of Chapter III.

In Chapter IV I compared the findings of my research to the current professional literature related to the church and clergy responses to homosexuality and LGBT individuals. Since there is no extant literature specifically addressing Nazarene clergy responses to homosexuality and interactions with LGBT individuals, I elected to conduct this research in order to bridge that gap in the literature. Within the discussion section of Chapter IV, I compared my findings to the literature to understand how my results were supported or were not supported by professional scholarship. I noted when my findings supported the literature, indicated when my findings were not supported by the literature, and indicated when the literature addressed issues that were not addressed in my data. In this process I demonstrated how one or more of the themes tied to the current professional scholarship. Following this, I presented "new findings" that contribute new knowledge to the current scholarship and literature. I also presented the limitations of this study as well as the implications of this research applicable to Nazarene clergy, the Nazarene church, LGBT people, counselor educators, and professional clinicians. Finally, I provided suggestions for future research endeavors.

Denominational leaders in the Church of the Nazarene state, "Homosexuality is real and sooner or later we may be asked to respond to the serious questions regarding the attitude of the Church regarding this important topic" (Porter et al., 2011, p. 6). The time to address these questions has arrived. Fortunately, it appears the church may now be considering these "serious questions." A recent conversation with one Nazarene scholar, who knows the Nazarene community well, revealed that the consensus among the denomination's biblical and theological scholars is that homosexuality and genuine Christian faith are compatible. These same scholars, however, hesitate to state this explicitly among the denomination's constituency because of current Nazarenes' views about homosexuality and the *Manual* statement that addresses it. What is not known at this time is whether these scholars believe or agree that intimate same-sex relationships are compatible with Christian faith. It may be some time before the answer to this question is known. It is my hope that the results of this research will help to facilitate dialog, stimulate reflection, encourage compassion, foster acceptance, and most importantly, be a small part of God's work to give all people—regardless of sexual orientation or relationship—greater access to God and the church.

References

Adamczyk, A., & Pitt, Cassidy. (2009). Shaping attitudes about homosexuality: The role of religion and cultural context. *Social Science Research, 38,* 338–351.

Adolfsen, A., Iedema, J., & Keuzenkamp, S. (2010). Multiple dimensions of attitudes about homosexuality: Development of a multifaceted scale measuring attitudes toward homosexuality. *Journal of Homosexuality, 57,* 1237–1257.

Allport, G.W. (1954). *The nature of prejudice.* Cambridge, MA: Addison-Wesley.

Allport, G. W., & Ross, J. M. (1967). Personal religious orientation and prejudice. *Personality and Social Psychology, 5,* 432–443.

Altemeyer, B. (2002). Changes in attitudes toward homosexuals. *Journal of Homosexuality, 42,* 63–75.

Altemeyer, B. (2003). Why do religious fundamentalists tend to be prejudiced? *The International Journal for the Psychology of Religion, 13,* 17–28.

Altemeyer, B., & Hunsberger, B. (1992). Authoritarianism, religious fundamentalism, quest, and prejudice. *The International Journal for the Psychology of Religion, 2,* 113–133.

American Counseling Association. (2014). *American Counseling Association code of ethics.* Alexandria, VA: Author. Retrieved from http://www.counseling.org/docs/ethics/2014-aca-code-of-ethics.pdf?sfvrsn=4

Ashley, K. B. (2013). The science on sexual orientation: A review of the recent literature. *Journal of Gay & Lesbian Mental Health, 17,* 175–182.

Bakker, J. (2011). *Fall to grace: A revolution of God, self, and society.* New York, NY: FaithWords.

Barna Group, LTD. (2007, September 24). A new generation expresses its skepticism and frustration with Christianity. Retrieved from https://www.

barna.org/barna-update/teens-nextgen/94-a-new-generation-expresses-its-skepticism-and-frustration-with-christianity#.VSEdk_nF_2c.

Barnes, D. M., & Meyer, I. H. (2012). Religious affiliation, internalized homophobia, and mental health in lesbians, gay men, and bisexuals. *American Journal of Orthopsychiatry, 82*, 505–515.

Barringer, M. N., Gay, D. A., &; Lynxwiler, J. P. (2013). Gender, religiosity, spirituality, and attitudes toward homosexuality. *Sociological Spectrum, 33*, 240–257.

Barton, B. (2010). "Abomination" - Life as a bible belt gay. *Journal of Homosexuality, 57*, 465–484.

Bean, L., & Martinez, B. C. (2014). Evangelical ambivalence toward gays and lesbians. *Sociology of Religion, 75*, 395–417.

Beck, J. R. (1997). Evangelicals, homosexuality, and social science. *JETS, 40*, 83–91.

Bent-Goodley, T. B. & Fowler, D. N. (2006). Spiritual and religious abuse. *Journal of Women & Social Work, 21*, 282–295.

Bieber, I. (1965). Clinical aspects of male homosexuality. *Sexual inversion: The multiple roots of homosexuality*, 248–267.

Blevins, D. G., Rodes, S. J., Seaman, J. E., Sowden, T. S., & Wilson, D. P. (Eds.). (2013). *MANUAL/2013–2017 Church of the Nazarene*. Kansas City, MO: Nazarene Publishing House.

Bloomberg, L. D., & Volpe, M. (2012). *Completing your qualitative dissertation: A road map from beginning to end*. Thousand Oaks, CA: Sage.

Board of General Superintendents: Church of the Nazarene. (2011, October 3). *"Further clarification concerning the document 'A pastoral perspective on homosexuality'"*. Retrieved from http://nazarene.org/files/docs/ClarificationonHomosexualitybooklet.pdf

Bogdan, R. C., & Biklen, S. K. (2003). *Qualitative research for education: An introduction to theories and methods*. (4th ed.). Boston: Allyn & Bacon.

Brown, M. J. & Henriquez, E. (2008). Socio-demographic predictors of attitudes towards gays and lesbians. *Individual Differences Research, 6*, 193–202.

Brownson, J. V. (2013). *Bible, gender, sexuality: Reframing the church's debate on same-sex relationships*. Grand Rapids, MI: William B. Eerdmans.

Burdette, A. M., Ellison, C. G., & Hill., T. D. (2005). Conservative protestantism and tolerance toward homosexuals: An examination of potential mechanisms. *Sociological Inquiry, 75*, 177–196.

Butler, A. C. (2005). Gender differences in the prevalence of same-sex partnering: 1988–2002. *Social Forces, 84*, 417–446.

Cadge, W., Olson, L. R., & Wildeman, C. (2008). How denominational resources influence debate about homosexuality in mainline protestant congregations. *Sociology of Religion, 69*, 187–207.

Cadge, W., & Wildeman, C. (2008). Facilitators and advocates: How mainline protestant clergy respond to homosexuality. *Sociological Perspectives, 51*, 587–603.

Cassidy, R. (2004). The clear teaching of the bible on homosexual practice. *Expository Times, 115*, 298–301.

Childs, J. M. (2009). Transsexualism: Some theological and ethical perspectives. *Dialog: A Journal of Theology, 48*, 30–41.

Cowie, S. E. (2009). The meanings and manifestations of religion and spirituality among lesbian, gay, bisexual, and transgender adults. *Journal of Adult Development, 16*, 250–262.

Creswell, J. W. (2007). *Qualitative inquiry & research design: Choosing among five approaches.* (2nd ed.). Thousand Oaks, CA: Sage.

Creswell, J. W. (2012). *Qualitative inquiry and research design: Choosing among five approaches.* (3rd ed.). Thousand Oaks, CA: Sage.

Creswell, J. W., & Miller, D. L. (2000). Determining validity in qualitative inquiry. *Theory into practice, 39*, 124–130.

Croy, N. C. (2008). Rules of engagement: Civility and clarity in the church's debate about homosexuality. *Trinity Seminary Review, 29*, 17–26.

Davis, E. F. (2008). Reasoning with scripture. *Anglican Theological Review, 90*, 513–519.

Deeb-Sossa, N., & Kane, H. (2007). "It's the word of God": Students' resistance to questioning and overcoming heterosexism. *Feminist Teacher, 17*, 151–169.

Denzin, N. K., & Lincoln, Y.S. (Eds.). (2000). *Handbook of qualitative research.* Thousand Oaks, CA: Sage.

Diehl, J. H., Cunningham, P. G., Porter, J. D., Middendorf, J. C., Gunter, N. G., & Warrick, J. K. (n.d.). *Pastoral perspectives on homosexuality: From your general superintendents.* Kansas City, MO: Nazarene Publishing House.

Djupe, P. A., & Gilbert, C. P. (2002). The political voice of clergy. *Journal of Politics, 64*, 596–609.

Drescher, J. (2002). Causes and becauses: On etiological theories of homosexuality. *Annual of Psychoanalysis, 30*, 57–68.

Drescher, J. (2008). A history of homosexuality and organized psychoanalysis. *Journal of the American Academy of Psychoanalysis and Dynamic Psychiatry, 36*, 443–460.

Duffield, I. K. (2004). The clear teaching of the bible? A contribution to the debate about homosexuality and the church of england. *Expository Times, 115*, 109–115.

Dukes, S. (1984). Phenomenological methodology in the human sciences. *Journal of religion and health, 23*, 197–203.

Duncan, M. L., & Kemmelmeier, M. (2012). Attitudes toward same-sex marriage: An essentialist approach. *Analyses of Social Issues& Public Policy, 1*, 377–399.

Eisner, E. W. (1997). *The enlightened eye: Qualitative inquiry and the enhancement of educational practices.* New York: Macmillan.

Engle, M. J., McFalls, J. A., Gallagher, B. J., & Curtis, K. (2006). The attitudes of american sociologists toward causal theories of male homosexuality. *The American Sociologist, 37*, 68–76.

Finlay, B., & Walther, C. S. (2003). The relation of religious affiliation, service attendance, and other factors to homophobic attitudes among university students. *Review of Religious Research, 44*, 370–393.

Ford, T. E., Brignall, T., VanValey, T. L., & Macaluso, M. J. (2009). The unmaking of prejudice: How christian beliefs relate to attitudes toward homosexuals. *Journal for the Scientific Study of Religion, 48*, 146–160.

Fullerton, J. T., & Hunsberger, B. (1982). A unidimensional measure of christian orthodoxy. *Journal for the Scientific Study of Religion, 21*, 317–326.

Furnham, A. (1990). *The protestant work ethic: The psychology of work-related beliefs and behaviours.* London: Routledge.

Further clarification concerning the document 'A pastoral perspective on homosexuality.' (Unknown author, n.d.). Retrieved from http://nazarene.org/files/docs/ClarificationonHomosexualitybooklet.pdf-2011–10–03.

Gagnon, R. A. (2005). Scriptural perspectives on homosexuality and sexual identity. *Journal of Psychology and Christianity, 24*, 293–303.

Ganzevoort, R. R., van der Laan, M., & Olsman, E. (2011). Growing up gay and religious.

Conflict, dialogue, and religious identity strategies. *Mental Health, Religion & Culture, 14*, 209–222.

Gentry, C. S. (1987). Social distance regarding male and female homosexuals. *Journal of Social Psychology, 127*, 199–208.

Giorgi, A. (1985). *Phenomenology and psychological research.* Pittsburgh, PA: Duquesne University Press.

Giorgi, A. (1994). A phenomenological perspective on certain qualitative research methods. *Journal of Phenomenological Psychology, 25*, 190–220.

Giorgi, A. (1997). The theory, practice, and evaluation of the phenomenological method as a qualitative research procedure. *Journal of phenomenological psychology, 28*, 235–260.

Glick, S. N., & Golden, M. R. (2010). Persistent racial differences in attitudes toward homosexuality in the united states. *Journal of Acquired Immune Deficiency Syndromes, 55*, 516–523.

Groenewald, T. (2004). A phenomenological research design illustrated. *International Journal of Qualitative Methods, 3*, 1–26.

Haidt, J., & Hersh, M. A. (2001). Sexual morality: The cultures and emotions of conservatives and liberals. *Journal of Applied Social Psychology, 31*, 191–221.

Haider-Markel, D. P., & Joslyn, M. R. (2008). Beliefs about the origins of homosexuality and support for gay rights: An empirical test of attribution theory. *Public Opinion Quarterly, 72*, 291–310.

Halkitis, P. N., Mattis, J. S., Sahadath, J. K., Massie, D., Ladyzhenskaya, L., Pitrelli, K.,…

Halwani, R. (1998). Essentialism, social constructionism, and the history of homosexuality. *Journal of Homosexuality, 35*, 25–51.

Halwani, R., Jaeger, G., Stramel, J. S., Nunan, R., Wilkerson, W. S., & Murphy, T. F. (2008). What is gay and lesbian philosophy? *Metaphilosophy, 39*, 433–471.

Haslam, N., & Levy, S. R. (2006). Essentialist beliefs about homosexuality: Structure and implications for prejudice. *Personality and Social Psychology Bulletin, 32*, 471–485.

Hays, D. G., & Singh, A. A. (2012). *Qualitative inquiry in clinical and educational settings.* New York: The Guilford Press.

Helminiak, D. A. (2008). Homosexuality in world religions: A case study in the psychology of spirituality. *The Journal of Individual Psychology, 64,* 139–160.

Hendershot, H. (2001). Holiness codes and holy homosexuals: Interpreting gay and lesbian christian subculture. *Camera Obscura, 45,* 150–193.

Herek, G. M. (1992). Psychological heterosexism and anti-gay violence: The social psychology of bigotry and bashing. In G. M. Herek & K. T. Berrill (Eds.), *Hate crimes: Confronting violence against lesbians and gay men* (pp. 149–169). Thousand Oaks, CA: Sage.

Herek, G. M. (1994). Assessing heterosexuals' attitudes toward lesbians and gay men: A review of empirical research with the ATLG scale. In B. Greene & G. M. Herek (Eds.). *Lesbian and gay psychology: Theory, research, and clinical applications* (pp. 206–228). Thousand Oaks, CA: Sage.

Herek, G. M. (2000a). The psychology of sexual prejudice. *Current Directions in Psychological Science, 9,* 19–22.

Herek, G. M. (2000b). Sexual prejudice and gender: Do heterosexuals' attitudes toward lesbians and gay men differ? *Journal of Social Issues, 56,* 251–266.

Herek, G. M. (2002). Gender gaps in public opinion about lesbians and gay men. *Public Opinion Quarterly,* 40–66.

Herek, G. M. (2004). Beyond "homophobia": Thinking about sexual prejudice and stigma in the twenty-first century. *Journal of National Sexuality Resource Center: Sexuality Research & Social Policy, 1,* 6–24.

Herek, G. M., & Capitanio, J. P. (1996). "Some of my best friends": Intergroup contact, concealable stigma, and heterosexual's attitudes toward gay men and lesbians. *Personality and Social Psychology Bulletin, 22,* 412–424.

Hewitt, E. C., & Moore, L. D. (2002). The role of lay theories of the etiologies of homosexuality in attitudes towards lesbians and gay men. *Journal of Lesbian Studies, 6,* 58–72.

Hodge, D. R. (2005). Epistemological frameworks, homosexuality, and religion: How people of faith understand the intersection between homosexuality and religion. *Social Work, 50,* 207–218.

Hughes, J. R. (2006). A general review of recent reports on homosexuality and lesbianism. *Sexuality & Disability, 24*, 195–205.

Hunsberger, B. (1996). Religious fundamentalism, right-wing authoritarianism, and hostility toward homosexuals in non-christian religious groups. *International Journal for the Psychology of Religion, 6*, 39–49.

Jennings, J. L. (1986). Husserl revisited: The forgotten distinction between psychology and phenomenology. *American Psychologist, 41*, 1231–1240.

Johnson, L. T. (2007, June 15). Homosexuality and the church: Scripture & experience. *Commonweal*, pp. 14–17.

Jonathan, E. (2008). The influence of religious fundamentalism, right-wing authoritarianism, and christian orthodoxy on explicit and implicit measures of attitudes toward homosexuals. *The International Journal for the Psychology of Religion, 18*, 316–329.

Jones. L. E. (1996). Should CSWE allow social work programs in religious institutions an exemption from the accreditation nondiscrimination standard related to sexual orientation? No? *Journal of Social Work Education, 32*, 302–310.

Jones, S. L., & Kwee, A. W. (2005). Scientific research, homosexuality, and the church's moral debate: An update. *Journal of Psychology and Christianity, 24*, 304–316.

Kapinus, C. A., Kraus, R., & Flowers, D. R. (2010). Excluding inclusivity: Protestant framing of homosexuality. *Interdisciplinary Journal of Research on Religion, 6*, Special section, 1–22.

Kahn, K. B., & Fingerhut, A. W. (2011). Essentialist beliefs and sexual prejudice against gay men: Divergence at the levels of categories versus traits. *Psychology & Sexuality, 2*, 137–146.

Kailla, E. (2012). Evangelicalism, sexual morality, and sexual addiction: Opposing views and continued conflicts. *Journal of Religion & Health, 51*, 162–178.

Keefe, J. (2011). Outreach to homosexual persons: The understanding heart - part 1. *The Priest, 67*, 45–49.

Kelstedt, L. & Smidt, C. (1991). Measuring fundamentalism: An analysis of different operational strategies. *Journal for the Scientific Study of Religion, 30*, 259–278.

Kinnaman, D., & Lyons, G. (2007). *unChristian: What a new generation really thinks about christianity…and why it matters.* Grand Rapids, MI: Baker Books.

Kitchener, K. S. (1984). Intuition, critical evaluation and ethical principles: The foundation for ethical decisions in counseling psychology. *Counseling Psychologist, 12,* 43–55.

Kinsey, A. C., Pomeroy, W. B., & Martin, C. E. (1948). *Sexual behavior in the human male.* Philadelphia, PA: W.B. Saunders.

Kite, M. E. (1984). Sex differences in attitudes toward homosexuals: A meta-analytic review. *Journal of Homosexuality, 10,* 69–81.

LaFave, A.D., Helm, H. W., &; Gomez, O. (2014). The relationship between gender and heterosexual attitudes toward homosexuality at a conservative christian university. *Journal of Research on Christian Education, 23,* 283–293.

Lalich, J., & McLaren, K. (2010). Inside and outcast: Multifaceted stigma and redemption in the lives of gay and lesbian jehovah's witnesses. *Journal of Homosexuality, 57,* 1303–1333.

LaMar, L. & Kite, M. (1998). Sex differences in attitudes toward gay men and lesbians: A multidimensional perspective. *The Journal of Sex Research, 35,* 189–196.

Larsen, K. S., Reed, M., & Hoffman, S. (1980). Attitudes of heterosexuals toward homosexuality: A likert-type scale and construct validity. *The Journal of Sex Research, 16,* 245–257.

Laythe, B., Finkel, D. G., Bringle, R. G., & Kirkpatrick, L. A. (2002). Religious fundamentalism as a predictor of prejudice: A two-component model. *Journal for the Scientific Study of Religion, 41,* 623–635.

Laythe, B., Finkel, D., & Kirkpatrick, L. A. (2001). Predicting prejudice from religious fundamentalism and right-wing authoritarianism: A multiple-regression approach. *Journal for the Scientific Study of Religion, 40,* 1–10.

Lease, S. H., Horne, S. G., & Noffsinger-Frazier, N. (2005). Affirming faith experiences and psychological health for caucasian lesbian, gay, and bisexual individuals. *Journal of Counseling Psychology, 52,* 378–388.

Lee, J. (2012). *Torn: Rescuing the gospel from the gays-vs.-Christians debate.* New York: Jericho Books.

LeVasseur, J. J. (2003). The problem of bracketing in phenomenology. *Qualitative Health Research, 13,* 408–420.

Lewis, G. B. (2003). Black-white differences in attitudes toward homosexuality and gay rights. *Public Opinion Quarterly, 67,* 59–78.

Lincoln, Y. S., & Guba, E. G. (1985). *Naturalistic inquiry.* Beverly Hills, CA: Sage.

Lincoln, Y. S., & Guba, E. G. (2000). Paradigmatic controversies, contradictions, and emerging confluences. In N. K. Denzin & Y. S. Lincoln (Eds.), *Handbook of qualitative research* (2nd ed.). 163–188. Thousand Oaks, CA: Sage.

Locke, K. A. (2005). The bible on homosexuality. *Journal of Homosexuality, 48,* 125–156.

Loftus, J. (2001). America's liberalization in attitudes toward homosexuality, 1973 to 1998. *American Sociological Review, 66,* 762–782.

Mak, H. K., & Tsang, J. (2008). Separating the "sinner" from the "sin": Religious orientation and prejudiced behavior toward sexual orientation and promiscuous sex. *Journal for the Scientific Study of Religion, 47,* 379–392.

Malcomnson, K. M., Christopher, A. N., Franzen, T., & Keyes, B. J. (2006). The protestant work ethic, religious beliefs, and homonegative attitudes. *Mental Health, Religion & Culture, 9,* 435–447.

Marin, Andrew (2009). *Love is an orientation: Elevating the conversation with the gay community.* Downers Grove, IL: Inter Varsity Press.

Marmor, J. (1998). Homosexuality: Is etiology really important? *Journal of Gay and Lesbian Psychotherapy, 2,* 19–28.

Marsh, T., & Brown, J. (2011). Homonegativity and its relationship to religiosity, nationalism and attachment style. *Journal of Religion & Health, 50,* 575–591.

Martin, D. B. (2008). Beyond: A response to Richard Norris. *Anglican Theological Review, 90,* 521–526.

McFarland, S. G. (1989). Religious orientations and the targets of discrimination. *Journal for the Scientific Study of Religion, 28,* 324–336.

McGinniss, M. (2010). The church's response to the homosexual. *The Journal of Ministry and Theology, 14,* 129–163.

McMinn, L. G. (2005). Sexual identity concerns for christian young adults: Practical considerations for being a supportive presence and compassionate companion. *Journal of Psychology and Christianity, 24,* 368–377.

McQueeney, K. (2009). "We are God's children, y'all:" Race, gender, and sexuality in lesbian- and gay-affirming congregations. *Social Problems, 56*, 151–173.

Meaney, G. L., & Rye, B. J. (2010). Gendered egos: Attitude functions and gender as predictors of homonegativity. *Journal of Homosexuality, 57*, 1274–1302.

Merriam, S. G., & Associates. (2002). *Qualitative research in practice.* San Francisco: Jossey-Bass.

Merritt, J. (2009, April 20). An evangelical's plea: 'Love the sinner.' *USA Today*, p. A11. Mitchell, R., & Dezarn, L. (2014). Does knowing why someone is gay influence tolerance? Genetic, environmental, choice, and 'reparative' explanations. *Sexuality & Culture, 18*, 994–1009.

Mitchell, S. A. (2002). Psychodynamics, homosexuality, and the question of pathology. *Studies in Gender and Sexuality, 3*, 3–21.

Montoya, A. D. (2008). The church's response to homosexuality. *The Master's Seminary Journal, 19*, 233–248.

Morgan, A. R. (2008, May 1). *Attitudes toward premarital sex and homosexuality and the church's response.* Retrieved from http://nazarene.org/files/docs/morgan_paper.pdf

Morrison, M. A., & Morrison, T. G. (2003). Development and validation of a scale measuring modern prejudice toward gay men and lesbian women. *Journal of Homosexuality, 43*, 15–37.

Morrison, M. A., & Morrison, T. G. (2011). Sexual orientation bias toward gay men and lesbian women: Modern homonegative attitudes and their association with discriminatory behavioral interventions. *Journal of Applied Psychology, 41*, 2573–2599.

Morrison, M. A., and Morrison, T. G. (2002). Development and validation of a scale measuring modern prejudice toward gay men and lesbian women. *Journal of Homosexuality, 43*, 15–37.

Morrow, S. L. (2005). Quality and trustworthiness in qualitative research in counseling psychology. *Journal of Counseling Psychology, 52*, 250–260.

Moustakas, C. (1994). *Phenomenological research methods.* Thousand Oaks: CA: Sage. Neisen, J. H. (1990). Heterosexism: Redefining homophobia for the 1990s. *Journal of Gay and Lesbian Psychotherapy, 1*, 21–35.

Neisen, J. H. (1993). Healing from cultural victimization: Recovery from shame due to heterosexism. *Journal of Gay and Lesbian Psychotherapy, 2*, 49–63.

Newman, B. S. (2002). Lesbians, gays, and religion: Strategies for challenging belief systems. *Journal of Lesbian Studies, 6,* 87–99.

Nissinen, M. (1998). *Homoeroticism in the biblical world: A historical perspective.* Minneapolis: Fortress Press.

Norris, R. A. (2008). Some notes on the current debate regarding homosexuality and the place of homosexuals in the church. *Anglican Theological Review, 90,* 437–511.

Oates, W. E. (1971). *Confessions of a workaholic: The facts about work addiction.* New York: World Publishing Company.

Olatunji, B. O. (2008). Disgust, scrupulosity and conservative attitudes about sex: Evidence for a meditational model of homophobia. *Journal of Research in Personality, 42,* 1364–1369.

Olson, L. R., & Cadge, W. (2002). Talking about homosexuality: The views of mainline protestant clergy. *Journal for the Scientific Study of Religion, 41,* 153–167.

Olson, L. R., Cadge, W., & Harrison, J. T. (2006). Religion and public opinion about same-sex marriage. *Social Science Quarterly, 87,* 340–360.

Padgett, D. K. (2004). Finding a middle ground in qualitative research. *The Qualitative Research Experience.* Belmont, CA: Wadsworth.

Patton, M. Q. (2002). *Qualitative research and evaluation methods.* (3rd ed.). Thousand Oaks, CA: Sage.

Petersen, L. R., & Donnenwerth, G. V. (1998). Religion and declining support for traditional beliefs about gender roles and homosexual rights. *Sociology of Religion, 59,* 353–365.

Pew Research Center. (2013, June 6). In gay marriage debate, both supporters and opponents see legal recognition as 'inevitable.' Washington, D. C.: Pew Research Center. Retrieved from http://www.people-press. org/files/legacy-pdf/06-06-13%20LGBT%20General%20Public%20 Release.pdf.

Polkinghorne, D. E. (1989). Changing conversations about human science. In S. E. Kvale (Ed.), *Issues of validity in qualitative research* (pp. 13–46). Lund, Sweden: Studentlitteratur.

Ponterotto, J. G. (2005). Qualitative research in counseling psychology: A primer on research paradigms and philosophies of science. *Journal of Counseling Psychology, 52,* 126–136.

Porter, J. D., Middendorf, J. C., Warrick, J. K., Duarte, E. R., Graves, D. W., & Toler, S. A. (2011). *A pastoral perspective on homosexuality.* Kansas City, MO: Nazarene Publishing House.

Rand, D. (2004, October/November). The strange universe of the homosexual christian. *Free Inquiry-Buffalo Then Amherst, 24,* 49–51.

Reimer, S., & Park, J. Z. (2001). Tolerance (in)civility? A longitudinal analysis of white conservative protestants' willingness to grant civil liberties. *Journal for the Scientific Study of Religion, 40,* 735–745.

Richards, P., & Bergin, A. E. (2000). *Handbook of psychotherapy and religious diversity.* American Psychological Association.

Robinson, D. C. (2000). Metaphors of love, love as a metaphor: Language, ritual and moral agency in the theological politics of identity. *Theology & Sexuality, 12,* 72–87.

Rodriguez, E. M. (2010). At the intersection of church and gay: A review of the psychological research on gay and lesbian christians. *Journal of Homosexuality, 57,* 5–38.

Rogers, J. (2007). Presbyterian guidelines for biblical interpretation: Their origin and application to homosexuality. *Biblical Theological Bulletin, 37,* 174–183.

Rosik, C. H. (2003). Motivational, ethical, and epistemological foundations in the treatment of unwanted homoerotic attraction. *Journal of Marital and Family Therapy, 29,* 13–28.

Rosik, C. H. (2007a). Ideological concerns in the operationalization of homophobia, part I: An analysis of Herek's ATLG-R scale. *Journal of Psychology and Theology, 35,* 132–144.

Rosik, C. H. (2007b). Ideological concerns in the operationalization of homophobia, part II: The need for interpretive sensitivity with conservatively religious persons. *Journal of Psychology and Theology, 35,* 145–152.

Rosik, C. H., Griffith, L. K., & Cruz, Z. (2007). Homophobia and conservative religion: Toward a more nuanced understanding. *American Journal of Orthopsychiatry, 77,* 10–19.

Rossman, G. B., & Rallis, S. F. (2011). *Learning in the field: An introduction to qualitative research* (3rd ed.). Thousand Oaks: CA: Sage.

Rowatt, W. C., & Franklin, L. M. (2004). Christian orthodoxy, religious fundamentalism, and right-wing authoritarianism as predictors of implicit racial prejudice. *The International Journal for the Psychology of Religion, 14,* 125–138.

Rowatt, W. C., Tsang, J., Kelly, J., LaMartina, B., McCullers, M., & McKinley, A. (2006).

Associations between religious personality dimensions and implicit homosexual prejudice. *Journal for the Scientific Study of Religion, 45*, 397–406.

Sandage, S. J., Cook, K. V., Hill, P. C., Strawn, B. D., & Reimer, K. S. (2008). Hermeneutics and psychology: A review and dialectical method. *Journal of General Psychology, 12*, 344–364.

Satcher, J., & Schumacker, R. (2009). Predictors of modern homonegativity among professional counselors. *Journal of LGBT Issues in Counseling, 1*, 21–36.

Sayer, A. (1997). Essentialism, social constructionism, and beyond. *The Sociological Review, 45*, 453–487.

Schope, R. D., & Eliason, M. J. (2000). Thinking verses acting: Assessing the relationship between heterosexual attitudes and behaviors toward homosexuals. *Journal of Gay & Lesbian Social Services, 11*, 69–92.

Schuck, K. D., & Liddle, B. J. (2001). Religious conflicts experienced by lesbian, gay, and bisexual individuals. *Journal of Gay & Lesbian Psychotherapy, 5*, 63–82.

Schulte, L. J., & Battle, J. (2004). The relative importance of ethnicity and religion in predicting attitudes toward gays and lesbians. *Journal of Homosexuality, 47*, 127–142.

Schwartz, J. P., & Lindley, L. D. (2005). Religious fundamentalism and attachment: Prediction of homophobia. *The International Journal for the Psychology of Religion, 15*, 145–157.

Seidman, F. (2006). *Interviewing as qualitative research* (3rd ed.). New York, NY: Teachers College Press.

Shackelford, T. K., & Besser, A. (2007). Predicting attitudes toward homosexuality: Insights from personality psychology. *Individual Differences Research, 5*, 106–114.

Sheldon, J. P., Pfeffer, C. A., Jayaratne, T. E., Feldbaum, & M., Petty, E. M. (2007). Beliefs about the etiology of homosexuality and about the ramifications of discovering its possible genetic origin. *Journal of Homosexuality, 52*, 111–150.

Sheler, J. L. (2000, May 15). Christian doctrine and gays. *U.S. News and World Report, 128*, 50. Retrieved from http://www.usnews.com/usnews/issue/000515/religion.b.htm

Sherkat, D. E., & Ellison, C. G. (1997). The cognitive structure of a moral crusade: Conservative protestantism and opposition to pornography. *Social Forces, 75*, 957–982.

Siegelman, M. (1974). Parental background of male homosexuals and heterosexuals. *Archives of Sexual Behavior, 3*, 3–18.

Sokolowski, R. (2000). *Introduction to phenomenology.* New York: Cambridge University Press. Steensland, B., Park, J. Z., Regnerus, M. D., Robinson, L. D., Wilcox, W. B., & Woodberry, R. D. (2000). The measure of american religion: Toward improving the state of the art. *Social Forces, 79*, 291–318.

Steffens, M. C. (2005). Implicit and explicit attitudes towards lesbians and gay men. *Journal of Homosexuality, 49*, 39–66.

Steffens, M. C., & Wagner, C. (2004). Attitudes toward lesbians, gay men, bisexual women, and bisexual men in germany. *The Journal of Sex Research, 41*, 137–149.

Stein, T. S. (1998). Social constructionism and essentialism. *Journal of Gay & Lesbian Psychotherapy, 2*, 29–49.

Stenschke, C. (2009). Faithful conversation: Christian perspectives on homosexuality. *Evangelical Quarterly, 81*, 373–377.

Stoever, C. J., & Morera, O. F. (2007). A confirmatory factor analysis of the attitudes toward lesbians and gay men (ATLG) measure. *Journal of Homosexuality, 52*, 189–209.

Subhi, N., & Geelan, D. (2012). When christianity and homosexuality collide: Understanding the potential intrapersonal conflict. *Journal of Homosexuality, 59*, 1382–1402.

Sullivan, M. K. (2003). Homophobia, history, and homosexuality: Trends for sexual minorities. *Journal of Human Behavior, 8*, 1–13.

Sullivan, M., & Wodarski, J. S. (2002). Social alienation in gay youth. *Journal of Human Behavior in the Social Environment, 5*, 1–17.

Super, J. T., & Jacobson, L. (2011). Religious abuse: Implications for counseling lesbian, gay, bisexual, and transgender individuals. *Journal of LGBT Issues in Counseling, 5*, 180–196.

Tate, R. (2003). Towards an evaluation of pro-gay theological perspectives. *Evangel, 21*, 77–89.

Trail, S. M., McCreary, M. J., Gray, J., Burt, J., Saibil, J., & Leung W. (2008). Lesbian, gay, bisexual, and transgender issues in the student forum. *The Journal of Individual Psychology, 64*, 224–245.

Trevino, K. M., Desai, K., Lauricella, S., Pargament, K. I., Mahoney, A. & Farber, D. (2012).

Perceptions of lesbian and gay (lg) individuals as desecrators of christianity as predictors of anti-lg attitudes. *Journal of Homosexuality, 54,* 535–563.

Tsang, J., & Rowatt, W. C. (2007). The relationship between religious orientation, right-wing authoritarianism, and implicit sexual prejudice. *The International Journal for the Psychology of Religion, 17,* 99–120.

Tushnet, E. (2007, June 15). Homosexuality & the church: Experience & tradition. *Commonweal- New York, 134,* 18–21.

Valera, P., & Taylor, T. (2011). Hating the sin but not the sinner: A study about heterosexism and religious experiences among black men. *Journal of black studies, 42,* 106–122.

Van Geest, F. (2007a). Research note: Christian denominational political action on the subject of homosexuality. *Review of Religious Research, 48,* 401–419.

Van Geest, F. (2007b). Changing patterns of denominational political activity in north america: The case of homosexuality. *Review of Religious Research, 49,* 199–221.

Van Geest, F. (2008). Christian denominational and special interest political action on public policy issues related to sexual orientation. *Sociology of Religion, 69,* 335–354.

van Kaam, A. (1959). Phenomenological analysis: Exemplified by a study of the experience of really feeling understood. *Journal of Individual Psychology, 15,* 66–72.

van Kaam, A. (1966). *Existential foundations of psychology.* Pittsburgh, PA: Duquesne University Press.

van Manen, M. (1990). *Researching lived experience: Human science for an action sensitive pedagogy.* New York: State University of New York Press.

van Manen, M. (2006). Writing qualitatively, or the demands of writing. *Qualitative Health Research, 16,* 713–722.

Vicario, B. A., Liddle, B. J., & Luzzo, D. A. (2005). The role of values in understanding attitudes toward lesbians and gay men. *Journal of Homosexuality, 49,* 145–149.

Vidich, A. J., & Lyman, S. M. (2003). Qualitative methods: Their history in sociology and anthropology. *The Landscape of Qualitative Research. Theories and Issues.* Thousand Oaks, CA: Sage.

Vines, Matthew (2014). *God and the gay christian: The biblical case in support of same-sex relationships*. New York: Convergent Books.

Walch, S. E., Orlosky, P. M., Sinkkanen, K. A., & Stevens, H. R. (2010). Demographic and social factors associated with homophobia and fear of aids in a community sample. *Journal of Homosexuality, 57,* 310–324.

Weiss, E. M., Morehouse, J., Yeager, T., & Berry, T. (2010). A qualitative study of ex-gay and ex-ex-gay experiences. *Journal of Gay & Lesbian Mental Health, 14,* 291–319.

White, S. M., & Franzini, L. R. (1999). Heteronegativism. *Journal of Homosexuality, 37,* 65–79.

Whitehead, A. L. (2010). Sacred rites and civil rights: Religion's effect on attitudes toward same-sex unions and the perceived cause of homosexuality. *Social Science Quarterly, 91,* 63–79.

Whitehead, A. L., & Baker, J. O. (2012). Homosexuality, religion, and science: Moral authority and the persistence of negative attitudes. *Sociological Inquiry, 82,* 487–509.

Whitley, B. E. (1988). Sex differences in heterosexuals' attitudes toward homosexuals: It depends on what you ask. *The Journal of Sex Research, 24,* 287–291.

Whitley, B. E. (2009). Religiosity and attitudes toward lesbians and gay men: A meta-analysis. *The International Journal for the Psychology of Religion, 19,* 21–38.

Whitley, B. E., & Lee, S. E. (2000). The relationship of authoritarianism and related constructs to attitudes toward homosexuality. *Journal of Applied Social Psychology, 30,* 144–170.

Wilcox, C., & Jelen, T. (1990). Evangelicals and political tolerance. *American Politics Research, 18,* 25–46.

Wilcox, M. M. (2002). When sheila's a lesbian: Religious individualism among lesbian, gay, bisexual, and transgender christians. *Sociology of Religion, 63,* 497–513.

Wilkinson, W. W. (2004). Religiosity, authoritarianism, and homophobia: A multidimensional approach. *The International Journal for the Psychology of Religion, 14,* 55–67.

Wilson, N. (1995). *Our tribe: Queer folks, God, Jesus, and the bible*. San Francisco: HarperCollins.

Wood, P. B., & Bartkowski, J. P. (2004). Attribution style and public policy attitudes toward gay rights. *Social Science Quarterly, 85*, 59–74.

Yakushko, O. (2005). Influence of social support, existential well-being, and stress over sexual orientation on self esteem of gay, lesbian, and bisexual individuals. *International Journal for the Advancement of Counseling, 27*, 131–143.

Yarhouse, M. A. (2004). Homosexuality, ethics and identity synthesis. *Christian Bioethics, 10*, 239–257.

Yarhouse, M. A. (2010). *Homosexuality and the christian: A guide for parents, pastors, and friends.* Bloomington, MN: Bethany House Publishers.

Yarhouse, M. A. (2011). Round peg, square hole: Being an evangelical christian in glb studies. *Edification: The Transdisciplinary Journal of Christian Psychology, 4*, 5–12.

Yarhouse, M. A. (2012). Integration in the study of homosexuality, glbt issues, and sexual identity. *Journal of Psychology & Theology, 40*, 107–111.

Yarhouse, M. A., & Burkett, L. A. (2002). An inclusive response to lgb and conservative religious persons: The case of same-sex attraction and behavior. *Professional Psychology: Research and Practice, 33*, 235–241.

Yarhouse, M. A., & Carr, T. L. (2011). The exemplar project: Finding what makes a church exemplary in its ministry to persons who experience same-sex attraction or who struggle with sexual identity concerns. *Edification: The Transdisciplinary Journal of Christian Psychology, 4*, 32–40.

Yarhouse, M. A., & Tan, E. S. N. (2005). Sexual identity and being a christian. *Journal of Psychology and Christianity, 24*, 60–64.

Yarhouse, M. A., Tan, E. S. N., & Pawlowski, L. M. (2005). Sexual identity development and synthesis among lgb-identified and lgb dis-identified persons. *Journal of Psychology and Theology, 33*, 3–16.

Zahniser, J. H., & Boyd, C. A. (2008). The work of love, the practice of compassion and the homosexual neighbor. *Journal of Psychology and Christianity, 27*, 215–226.

Zahniser, J. H., & Cagle, L. (2007). Homosexuality: Toward and informed, compassionate response. *Christian Scholar's Review, 36*, 323–348.

www.ingramcontent.com/pod-product-compliance
Lightning Source LLC
Chambersburg PA
CBHW031545260326
41914CB00002B/270